Douglas Brooke Wheelton Sladen

Australian Ballads and other Poems

Douglas Brooke Wheelton Sladen

Australian Ballads and other Poems

ISBN/EAN: 9783743307988

Manufactured in Europe, USA, Canada, Australia, Japa

Cover: Foto ©Thomas Meinert / pixelio.de

Manufactured and distributed by brebook publishing software (www.brebook.com)

Douglas Brooke Wheelton Sladen

Australian Ballads and other Poems

The Canterbury Poets.

Edited by William Sharp.

AUSTRALIAN BALLADS.

AUSTRALIAN BALLADS AND OTHER POEMS. SELECTED AND EDITED BY DOUGLAS B. W. SLADEN, B.A. OXON.; B.A., LL.B., MELBOURNE.

SECOND EDITION.

LONDON:
WALTER SCOTT, LIMITED,
24 WARWICK LANE.
NEW YORK: 3 EAST FOURTEENTH STREET.

This Little Volume,

INSPIRED BY LIFE IN THE GREATER BRITAIN

UNDER THE SOUTHERN CROSS,

Is Dedicated

TO THE ENGLISH OF THREE CONTINENTS.

We all are sprung from men who fought at Crecy;
   We all were Englishmen when Shakspeare wrote;
And we are still compatriots *in esse*,
   Though called Australians, Yankees, and what not.

Yes, we are English: centuries will find us
   Living in homes with old familiar names
Of England's towns and battles, to remind us
   That we, who now are pilgrims, have our claims

To those whom Westminster entombs in glory,
   To Devonshire's sea kings and Chaucer's Tales,
To Wiclif and the proud Armada Story,
   Alfred the Great, and him who conquered Wales.

DEDICATION.

We all are English, one in our devotion,
   Whether the York we boast be old or New,
And whether Boston face the German Ocean,
   Or have the broad Atlantic in her view.

We all are English, though new Melbourne poses
   Upon Port Philip as a southern queen,
And old in dales of Derbyshire still dozes,
   A fit handmaiden for a rustic scene.

We all are English, born in one great union
   Of blood and language, history and song,
All English, and to cherish our communion
   We will present a common front to wrong.

                        Douglas B. W. Sladen.

CONTENTS.

THE DEDICATION.
                                                                PAGE
To the English of Three Continents . . . v
    DOUGLAS B. W. SLADEN in *Australian Lyrics*.

ANONYMOUS.
    A Voice from the Bush. *Temple Bar* . . 1

AUSTRAL.
    Fairyland. *The Australasian* . . . 5
    A Spring Afternoon, New Zealand. *The Australasian* 6

AUSTRALIE.
    From the Clyde to Braidwood. *The Balance of Pain* 8
    The Explorer's Message. *The Balance of Pain* 13

ALEX. W. BATHGATE.
    Our Heritage. *N.Z. Papers* . . . 20
    The Moko-Moko (Bell Bird). *N.Z. Papers* . 22

H. H. BLACKHAM.
    Forsaken Homes and Graves . . . 19

JOHN BRIGHT.
    When I am Dead. *Wattle Blossoms and Wild Flowers* 263

CONTENTS.

	PAGE
JENNINGS CARMICHAEL.	
Tomboy Madge. *Weekly Times, Melbourne* .	24
ALFRED T. CHANDLER.	
Bess. *A Bush Idyll*	28
Catching the Coach. *A Bush Idyll* . .	31
A Bush Idyll. *A Bush Idyll* . . .	34
MARCUS CLARKE.	
Lines in a Lady's Album	26
J. F. DANIELL.	
The Jubilee of Melbourne. *Rhymes for the*	
Times	38
ALFRED DOMETT.	
The Prelude. *Ranolf and Amohia* . .	40
The Legend of Tawháki. *Ranolf and Amohia*	42
The Haunted Mountain. *Ranolf and Amohia*	48
The Pink Terraces. *Ranolf and Amohia* .	50
LINDSAY DUNCAN.	
Christmas Guests. *Adelaide Paper* . .	55
WILLIAM FORSTER.	
Then are there Gods indeed? etc. *Midas* .	58
FRANCES TYRRELL GILL.	
The Wind in the She-oak. *The Australasian*	62
Beneath the Wattle Boughs. *The Australasian*	64
Love's Loyalty. *The Australasian* . .	65
KEIGHLEY GOODCHILD.	
While the Billy Boils. *Who are You* .	67

CONTENTS.

	PAGE
ADAM LINDSEY GORDON.	
The Sick Stock-Rider. *Volume published by Massina & Co.*	69
The Exile's Farewell. *Temple Bar*	73
HENRY HALLORAN.	
Vide Introduction	
CHARLES HARPUR.	
The Cloud. *Volume published by Geo. Robertson & Co.*	75
The Creek of the Four Graves. *Volume published by Geo. Robertson & Co.*	78
A Storm on the Mountains. *Volume published by Geo. Robertson & Co.*	86
The Aboriginal Mother's Lament. *Volume published by Geo. Robertson & Co.*	91
E. S. HAY.	
Ideal Beauty. *N.Z. Papers*	93
THOMAS HENEY.	
The Hut on the Flat. *Fortunate Days*	94
PHILIP J. HOLDSWORTH.	
My Queen of Dreams. *Station-Hunting on the Warrego*	104
Station-Hunting on the Warrego. *Station Hunting on the Warrego*	105
R. H. HORNE.	
Vide Introduction.	

CONTENTS.

JOHN HOWELL.
    Selections from the Cantata. *Rose-leaves from an Australian Garden* . . . 120

JOHN LIDDELL KELLY.
    The Arrival at Tahiti. *Tahiti, the Land of Love and Beauty* 121

HENRY KENDALL.
    Vide Introduction

FRANCES SESCA LEWIN.
    The Story of Abel Tasman. *Songs of the South* 122

GEORGE GORDON MCCRAE.
    Balladeādro. *Balladeādro* . . . 125

ARTHUR PATCHETT MARTIN.
    The Cynic of the Woods. *Fernshawe* . . 143
    A Romance in the Rough. *Fernshawe* . 145
    A Bush Study, à la Watteau. *Fernshawe* . 147
    The Storm. *Fernshawe* 150
    My Cousin from Pall Mall. *Fernshawe* . 151

E. G. MILLARD.
    The Black Warrigal Horse. *Sydney Mail* . 155

AGNES NEALE.
    Australia. *Adelaide Papers* . . . 159
    The Blue Lake—Mt. Gambier. *Adelaide Papers* 161

SIR HENRY PARKES.
    Solitude. *The Beauteous Terrorist* . . 164

ROBERT RICHARDSON.
    On the River. *Sydney Echo* . . . 165

CONTENTS.

J. STEELE ROBERTSON.
    Musk Gully, Dromona. *Melbourne University Review* 168
J. HOWELL ROSS.
    In Memoriam : Henry Kendall. *Melbourne University Review* 169
PERCY RUSSELL.
    The Birth of Australia. *Tasmanian Paper* . 171
J. SADLER.
    The Proclamation Tree. *Adelaide Paper* . 172
WILLIAM SHARP.
    Bell Birds. *Earth's Voices* 174
    The Stock Driver's Ride. *Earth's Voices* . 175
    In the Ranges. *Earth's Voices* . . . 178
    Australian Transcripts. *Earth's Voices* . 179
CHARLES ALLAN SHERARD.
    Solaced. *The Australasian* . . . 184
    Lost in the Mallee. *The Australasian* . 186
    Satan's Ganymede. *The Australasian* . 190
DOUGLAS BROOKE WHEELTON SLADEN.
    The Squire's Brother. *Frithjof and Ingebjorg, and Australian Lyrics* . . . 194
    Out West in Queensland. *Australian Lyrics* . 201
    To Australia. *Australian Lyrics* (2nd Ed.) . 205
    Mrs Watson, a Queensland Heroine. *Australian Lyrics* 210
    A Christmas Letter. *A Poetry of Exiles* (2nd Edition) 213

CONTENTS.

A. C. SMITH.
    The Bushman. *Australian Paper* . . 216

WALTER SMITH.
    The Drought. *The Death of Oswald* . . 261

J. BRUNTON STEPHENS.
    The Midnight Axe. *The Queenslander* . 218
    The Black Gin. *Convict Once and other Poems* 231
    My other Chinee Cook. *Convict Once and other Poems* 235
    Drought and Doctrine. *Convict Once and other Poems* 238

JAMES THOMAS.
    To a Water Wagtail. *Australian Paper* . 242

GARNET WALCH.
    The Little Tin Plate. *The Little Tin Plate*. 245
    Wool is up. *The Little Tin Plate* . . 252
    Wool is Down. *The Little Tin Plate* . . 254

WILLIAM CHARLES WENTWORTH.
    Australasia. *Briton's Poets and Prose Writers of N.S.W.* 256

ENVOI.

THOMAS L. WORK.
    To Caxton. *Printer's Keepsake* . . . 261

NOTES 265

A STUDY OF HENRY KENDALL AS A BUSH POET . 277

INTRODUCTION.

AUSTRALIA is the country of the future. Separated by oceans from every considerable land except impenetrable and equatorial New Guinea, blessed with an unmalarious climate more brilliant and equable than that of Italy, and peopled from the most adventurous of the colonising Anglo-Saxon stock, this round world in the far South-eastern seas gives race-development its amplest scope.

The vigorous man must be strangely constituted who does not love Australia, with its glittering air, its vast space, its infinite possibilities; and strangely constituted the light-hearted girl who does not revel in its pleasure-days unspoiled by rain, its lustrous nights secure from chill.

Those who have contributed to this volume are for the most part people who love the free air of the mountain-top, and the mysteriousness of the forest, the fierce excitement of race and chase, the honest thrill of manly sports, and the glory of nature—from the magnificent Australian sky down to the fringed violet or the azure wren. Not a few of them have, in what Gordon calls the "old colonial days," had their lives hanging on a thread in the perilous march of exploration or guerilla warfare with bushrangers and aborigines. This volume is essentially the work of people who have meditated in the open air, and not under the lamp; and if its contents oftentimes want the polish that comes only with much midnight oil, they are mostly a transcript from earth and sea and sky, and not from books.

Not that Australia has lacked poets like her own child Kendall, as smooth as a pebble polished with the tireless patience of the waves. But these are the exceptions, and we confess that for the most part we hope to please the reader with what our poets have to say, rather than the way in which they say it.

What is the *raison d'être* of this book? A Scotch paper, well known for the soundness of its criticisms, in referring to it, laid down that to be of any value it must be confined to the productions of Australian natives. This, then, would be an anthology of Australian verse into which admission

INTRODUCTION. xv

was denied to Adam Lindsey* Gordon, the poet *par excellence* of "the old colonial days," to Alfred Domett, the immortaliser of the lost Pink Terraces of New Zealand, to Brunton Stephens, to Marcus Clarke, to William Wentworth (born in Norfolk Island), and half a dozen others whose names are household words in Australia. Indeed, the only two poets popular beyond the borders of their own particular colony, who were born in Australia, are Charles Harpur and Henry Kendall.

What, then, is its *raison d'être?* To lay before the English public A SELECTION OF POEMS INSPIRED BY LIFE AND SCENERY IN AUSTRALIA.

Such being the case, no further answer is necessary to the clever New Zealand writer in *The Weekly Press*, who urged that by this limitation much of the best work of many colonial writers would be excluded, and indeed, by implication, that all local poetry is a mistake. This volume is a collection of local poetry. Poems by Australasian colonists on non-Australasian subjects will find their fitting place in the larger anthology of Australasian poems which the editor is preparing for Messrs. Griffith, Farran, & Co., in which the

---

* It has been customary to spell Gordon's name Lindsay; but in the Register of Cheltenham College, presumably filled in by his father, who was a master, his name is given as Adam Lindsey Gordon.

only limitation is that the poems should be by Australian or New Zealand colonists.

There are, however, a very few poems in the volume in which our limitation has not been enforced: they have only been admitted where some one who was a pillar of literature in Australia yet wrote nothing at once Australian in colouring and sufficiently poetical. Such a man was William Forster, one of the most distinguished of Australian writers. His "Devil and the Governor," almost his only Australian piece, is of historical success, but not as a poem, and he therefore had to be represented from "Midas"—his posthumous work, finished in the rough only, but a great poem, rivalling in parts the facility and felicity of the "Ranolf and Amohia" of the New Zealand Lucretius.

The next questions that may occur to the reader will perhaps be, Why have we so little of Gordon? Why does Kendall only appear in the introduction? Where is Horne? Surely these are the poets of whom we hear most from Australians.

To answer in inverse order: the author of "Orion" (the poem which its author thought so unacceptable to the public that he published the first three editions at one farthing, and which proved so acceptable that ten editions of it have been sold already) wrote very little inspired by Australia, and that little not conspicuously good, but he would have been represented in the volume, as would Kendall, if their representatives had vouchsafed their consent; but the editor was wholly unsuccessful in eliciting any proof of their existence, and the publisher of this series is serving the cause of international copyright by ordering that the author's consent shall be obtained in every case—an order that has been observed with only three exceptions, noticed in their places. As no permission had been sent for Kendall to be represented in the text, an essay, with numerous illustrations, has been devoted to his work as a Bush poet.

With Gordon the case was different. The real author of a poem which has brought Gordon much popularity, ' A Voice from the Bush," not only freely gave his permission for it to be used, but has given the correct version of the poem, which has suffered much at the hands of printers. His name is an open secret to all students of Australian poetry, but he desires that it should not be given in this volume. Messrs. Bentley, the well-known publishers, also freely gave their permission to reprint "The Exile's Farewell," sent to them by Mr. A. Patchett Martin. But Messrs. Massina of Melbourne, who have acquired the copyright of the bulk of Gordon's poems, thought it would be prejudicial to their interests to give leave for more than one of these poems to be used. For this permission the publisher and editor of this volume tender their best thanks. The public must judge if Messrs. Massina acted in their own and Gordon's interest in sending him forth equipped with only one poem to contest the place of honour with poets like Domett and Stephens, who had given *carte blanche*. Everyone who knows anything of the man would like to pay Gordon his tribute in full, and the editor is more than most men bound to Gordon by coming from the same great school, Cheltenham College, and the same great colony, Victoria, and having a special love for all verse breathing the spirit of Anglo-Saxon manfulness. But he cannot gainsay the wishes of the owners of copyrights, and, therefore, he must content himself with giving as good an estimate of Gordon as he can without quotations. Gordon has one supreme merit, he is interesting to everybody—as much to the stable-boy and stockman as to the scholar, as much to the schoolboy as to the sentimentalist; his poems are "ringing"; he carries one away like Lord Macaulay or Professor Aytoun in their stirring battle-pictures. He is generally rhythmical, musical, sonorous. Some of his Swinburnian verses, we feel sure, Swinburne would be proud to father. He is full of homely sayings, that could not be put better if they had been rounded into proverbs in the mouths of millions, in the course of centuries

INTRODUCTION. xix

—to speak of proverbs, he is a very Burns in begetting them—indeed, one can give strangers no better idea of his power in Victoria, than by calling him the Australian Burns; not that his poems bear the least resemblance to those of the immortal ploughman, but because he is essentially the national poet, he who dwells on the tongues of the people. He is a very manful poet—the man ready to fight anyone for two straws, or to jump a horse at anything that mortal horse could jump, is reflected in his poems—but there was one element lacking in his manfulness. Accomplishment did not enter much into his life or writings. Leading a "forlorn hope," selling one's life dearly, succumbing desperately to hopeless odds, were familiar ideas with him, but not "enduring to the end and winning a crown of life" in their plain earthly sense. Gordon could understand a blind King of Bohemia riding forward to be killed at Crecy, but not a Horatius thinking that he might guard the bridge and yet survive the day.

He could write at least four kinds of poems excellently. His ballads, such as "Fauconshawe," are distinguished by unusual ring, and lilt, and go. His Swinburnian poems, besides their metrical merits, are often, as in "Podas Okus," "Doubtful Dreams," etc., full of solemn, dignified manfulness, and, once read, can never be wholly forgotten. His few Bush poems are written as only one who knew the "Bush" so intimately, and had such brilliant poetical gifts, could have written them; and his horse-poems are unequalled in the English language. No other poet of anything like Gordon's gifts has approached him in knowledge of the horse; and it is as a horse-poet that Gordon will principally be remembered. Indeed, riding and swimming are the only branches of sport which his poems show him to have known much about. Shooting, fishing, cricket, etc., receive hardly more than bare mention; but in horse-pieces he stands alone—not, we think, good as they are, for pieces like "How we beat the Favourite," but for pieces like "The Sick Stockrider" and "From the Wreck." "The Sick Stockrider" is a poem that deserves a place in any selection in the English language, a masterpiece, and a masterpiece that no poet whom we know of but Gordon could have written. It was necessary that poetical genius, ringing, spirited, rhythmical writing, manfulness, experience of the "old colonial days," and intimate loving acquaintance with the "Bush," should unite in one man before a poem like "The Sick Stockrider" could be born. Gordon's faults are want of culture and knowledge, narrowness of scope and sympathy, and perhaps a little carelessness, though very likely much that passes for the last is due to faulty printing. But within his scope and sympathies, to find his rival we must look among the great masters of song, as his laurels in Australia and his increasing popularity in England would show. Compared with Australian poets he is not so musical as Kendall, but is very strong in Kendall's weakest point—awaking interest in the semi-cultivated. With Brunton Stephens it is difficult to compare him. Stephens's genius revels in the light and delicate, or light and humorous, while Gordon's strikes strongly and vibratingly; but in their long poems, the exquisitely-finished, highly-cultured, rich, passionate, poetic "Convict Once" is far ahead of "Ashtaroth," as is Harpur's "Witch of Hebron," though Harpur has written very few other poems that could be mentioned with Gordon's. The one man who towers above him is Alfred Domett, a writer whom it is as impossible to represent fairly in selections as it would be to represent the Iliad or the *De rerum Natura*. By far the principal achievement of Australasia in poetry is Domett's great "Ranolf and Amohia." Through six or seven hundred octavo pages it never drags. It is as full of close reasoning as Mr. Browning's masterpieces, while it is written in rhymed, rhythmical, ever-varying metres. The knowledge of books, the knowledge of human nature displayed in it is stupendous. It has embalmed the mythologies, customs, and tribe wars of the Maoris—and with a crowning piece of good fortune has immortalised, in a passage of the most delicate beauty, the famous Pink Terraces, geysers, and mountain marvels, overwhelmed in the recent earthquake. A charming love-story runs through it, and has its surprises to the end of the book; and the language of the poem is a model for describing colloquial subjects in suitable, unstilted, but thoroughly poetical expression. "Waring,"* as Mr. Browning fondly calls him in his poem, has many years ere this been offered his laurels at the hands of Longfellow, Browning, and other great fellow-poets. Marcus Clarke, it must be borne in mind, though he has written a few poems that will always be remembered, made his fame as a novelist (author of the famous *His Natural Life*), a journalist, and a critic.

The first Australian poem of note was Wentworth's "Australasia," published in 1823; but Charles Harpur, who published his first volume a

> * " What's become of Waring
> Since he gave us all the slip,
> Chose land travel or seafaring,
> Boots and chest or staff and scrip,
> Rather than pace up and down
> Any longer London town?'

good many years afterwards, is generally regarded as the grey forefather of Australian poets. The sixties saw the rise of both Gordon and Kendall, the former dying by his own hand in 1870, and the latter just living into the eighties; and it was only on the 3rd of November last that Alfred Domett died, while Brunton Stephens is still alive, and holds a government appointment in Queensland. Alfred Domett's "Christmas Hymn" was published in Longfellow's *Poems of Places*, and Longfellow wrote to him very handsomely about it.

Having mentioned the very best known Australian poets and their chronological order, before proceeding to individualise further, we should wish to discuss some of the characteristics of Australian poetry.

The character of Australian poetry is now determined a good deal by the taste of the editors of the great weekly papers. These in Australia are the substitutes for magazines, and consequently, until pieces are collected into a volume, their columns afford the only medium for publicity, except the capital literary clubs like the Yorick. This must influence authors, and the editors, patriotically, have shewn a desire to encourage an Australian School of Poetry. Most young Colonial poets, therefore, except the few who have an original genius, draw their inspiration from English poets through the medium of either Gordon or Kendall, who are considered the two most standard poets of Australia. They in turn seem to owe most to Swinburne, Bret Harte, and Edgar Allan Poe. But Tennyson, Shelley, Longfellow, and Wordsworth have exercised a large influence, and Kendall and Brunton Stephens have written much in the vein of the late C. S. Calverley, Kendall also writing a good deal that was thoroughly original. Consequently the commonest types of Australian Poems are Bushman's Ballads *à la* Gordon, often very spirited, but often also very rugged; Bush landscape-painting *à la* Kendall, in which much polish is lavished on workmanship; Swinburne Australianised *à la* Gordon, and acclimatised " Bret Harte." And from these types, notably the first and third of them, many beautiful poems have been produced. Gordon himself, for instance, and C. A. Sherard have written in these styles noble pieces that must command appreciation wherever they are read.

Blank verse has found little favour in Australia, which is not surprising, as to a great extent it is the offspring of a classical education. William Morris, quite the founder of a school in Oxford, has exercised hardly any influence in Australia, and Browning has only two prominent disciples, though it is to be owned that one of them, " Waring," wrote the greatest of Antipodean poems, and the other was the author of "Midas." And only one considerable poem has been inspired by Walt Whitman, "The Hut on the Flat." "Australian Lyrics" are lyrics of Australian society, and Arthur Patchett Martin, Garnett Walch, and others among the younger generation of poets whose writings have been inspired by Australia, had previously written several poems of this kind. A. P. Martin and Garnet Walch are busy and successful journalists, which prevents their having more to display in the way of poetry. But both have shewn brilliant capacity, and turned out work so good as, in spite of its small quantity, puts them in the front rank of Australian poets. A. P. Martin may in many respects be called the Australian R. L. Stevenson, and Garnet Walch has the "curiosa felicitas" of Hudibras or Dr. Syntax. George Gordon M'Crae, a poet of first-class reputation and achievements, is difficult to classify; but in his most valuable "Bush" work, his two great lays of the Aborigines, he has followed in the footsteps of Scott, and has gone into his subject with the conscientious care and research of that poet. The poems of Henry Halloran, who has for many years been before the Sydney public; of G. H. Supple, author of "The Dream of Dampier"; of Thomas Bracken, one of the best poets of New Zealand; of F. B. Loughran, the contributor of some of the most delicately beautiful pieces which have appeared in the *Australian;* and those of Farrell and Victor Daley, which have recently been spoken of in the highest terms by the Australian press, we have unfortunately been unable to procure ; and the copy of his poems ordered for us in London by one of the most literary and distinguished of Australian pressmen, Francis Adams, was unfortunately out of stock, sold out. We should have welcomed all of them, and their absence is a distinct gap, which is further increased (we are writing this preface almost a fortnight after the text of the book has gone to press) by the arrival too late for insertion of poems from the well-known sculptor and artist, Margaret Thomas, from Mary Colborne-Veel, Nellie S. Clerk, Mrs. C. Watkins, Mrs. J. A. Bode, the Havilands, and others. James Thomas, of whose pieces we have, to our regret, in our limited space, only been able to quote one, has written many fine poems, reminding one, in their exquisite appreciation of Nature, of Emerson's " Humble Bee," or Bryant's bird-life poems. Of William Sharp, a visitor " out from home," whose photographic " Transcripts from Nature " in Australia we have quoted, it befits us to say nothing, since he is general editor of the series in which this book appears. We have purposely deferred our remarks on

Philip J. Holdsworth and Alfred T. Chandler, the two young native-born Australians whose poems have attracted most notice in England. They are thoroughly Australian, and their volumes are a distinct contribution towards a National literature, a remark which applies equally to a little volume by Keighley Goodchild, and to the poems of Charles Allan Sherard, which, as far as we know, have not yet been collected into a volume. (We believe him also to be an Australian by birth.) Holdsworth has written some poems, notably, " My Queen of Dreams," which most conclusively show where the mantle of Kendall has fallen ; and Chandler's volume proves him to be a genuine poet of the widest sympathies, with (what is sometimes forgotten in philanthropists) a good backbone of manhood in him.

The gravely beautiful poem which has been chosen as an *envoi* to the volume comes from a Printers' Keepsake, the joint effort of some brilliant Victorian compositors, full of good things, but none of the others, except the one quoted, unfortunately within our limits.

Australian poetesses we have not yet mentioned, because one of them is the link between Australia and New Zealand. Judging from the very serious tenor of their poems, few of them can be like the typical Victorian young lady, hit off to the life in this spirited little poem—

INTRODUCTION.

AN AUSTRALIAN GIRL.

> " She's pretty to walk with,
> And witty to talk with ;
> And pleasant, too, to think on."
> —Sir John Suckling.

She has a beauty of her own,
A beauty of a paler tone
    Than English belles.
Yet Southern sun and Southern air
Have kissed her cheeks until they wear
The dainty tints that oft appear
    On rosy shells.

Her frank, clear eyes bespeak a mind
Old-world traditions fail to bind.
    She is not shy
Or bold, but simply self-possessed ;
Her independence adds a zest
Unto her speech, her piquant jest,
    Her quaint reply.

O'er classic volumes she will pore
With joy ; and some scholastic lore
    Will often gain.
In sports she bears away the bell—
Nor, under music's siren spell,
To dance divinely, flirt as well,
    Does she disdain.
    —Ethel Castilla, Melbourne.

Though Miss Nellie S. Clerk, who sends us some poems from the very depths of the Gippsland

Forest, may possibly answer to the description. She writes from an altogether original point of view—the oppressiveness of the forest; to her the forest means ennui—and a prison. She hails with welcome the fall of every tree as opening a new window to sun and sky and air, and writes with considerable grace. Her poems arrived too late for inclusion in the text, otherwise she would certainly be represented. Here are some verses from her poem:—

TO MY FIRST GARDEN FLOWER.

. . . . . .

Short a monarch's life was clipt
    Where you reign, Geranium!
There once a mighty Eucalypt
High plumes in heaven's azure dipped,
And cumbrous bark robes yearly stripped,
    Revealing hidden beauty.

Great the fall that left a throne
    For you, royal Geranium!
The cruel axe cleft through the bone
With rattling crash and thunderous groan,
He fell! a cairn of soft sandstone
    I built to mourn his beauty.

"Twas then you came to glad my eyes,
    A welcome gift, Geranium.
This wilderness of foliaged skies
You brightened with your scarlet dyes;
You were my first flower,—you I prize
    Above all rival beauty.

So slight I thought, three years ago,
    This slip of a Geranium,
Above, around trees restless blow,
Thick tangled bushes crowd below,
Oh! where can it in safety grow
    And best display its beauty?

Tramped the grass-plot on the mound,
    No place for my Geranium,
With long bark hut the summit's crowned,
A lazy packhorse feeds around,
And ringing axes ceaseless sound :—
    No pleasure here but duty.

Ah! that headless trunk will hold
    You safely, sweet Geranium,
On his broad breast some pliant mould
Shall, 'mid the cairn, your roots enfold.
No more I'll mourn his grandeur bold,
    His scars hid by your beauty.

    .   .   .   .

You have watched our homestead rise,
    Shining-eyed Geranium,
Felt the falling forest's sighs,
Blessed each widening glimpse of skies,
Heard the first flock's bleating cries,
    And traced all growth of beauty.

    .   .   .   .

Those who enjoy the greatest reputation in Australia are—"Australie" (Mrs. Hubert Heron), Frances Tyrrett Gill, Agnes Neale (Mrs. Ahcane),

Lindsay Duncan (Mrs. T. C. Cloud), Frances Sesca Lewin, and Philip Dale (Mrs. C. Haviland). Nearly all Antipodean poetesses are native-born. Most of them exhibit the influence of Adelaide Proctor strongly—one of them, Agnes Neale, may fairly be called the Australian Adelaide Proctor. Frances Gill is a beautiful writer of what one may perhaps call the Victorian school—if one may mean thereby C. A. Sherard, E. B. Loughran, Jennings Carmichael, and a few other charming writers who have sprung up in the footsteps of Gordon, and developed that kind of style of their own, modelled originally on Swinburne, to which we referred above in such high terms. To this school in a way also belongs "Austral" (Mrs. J. G. Wilson), a Victorian by birth, but resident in New Zealand, who has written some of the most beautiful things which have appeared in the *Australasian*. New Zealand scenery, the most glorious blending under Heaven of the sub-tropical and the Alpine, a perfect fairyland of palmy foliage and mountain waters, has not, so far, inspired many writers of more than local fame, but besides "Austral," several of them are very high-class. Alfred Domett, as we have expressed an opinion above, towers over Antipodean poets in his achievements, and Thomas Bracken has had a most favourable reception from the English press (we were unfortunately unable to procure a copy of his poems for this volume). Alexander W. Bathgate has written poems of mature excellence—all the poems that he sent us being at an unusually high level in taste and workmanship. Ebenezer Storry Hay is, unhappily, dead. He had all the makings of a New Zealand Shelley, and has left us some of the most exquisite little pieces in Australian literature.

The list of the front rank of New Zealand poets would not be complete without the names of J. L. Kelly, a poet with plenty of imagination, a great command of metre, and an eye for the picturesque, who has made a study of the customs and traditions of the natives, and from whom great things may be expected. Great things may also be expected of Mary Colborne-Veel, whose poems arrived too late for this volume, but will be represented in the other.

The few poems which have reached us from Tasmania have not come within our limitations, but one from Mr. Arthur Green will appear in the anthology.

We have received a good many poems from drovers, stockmen, miners, and others engaged "up the country"—the very men from whom one would have expected the kind of pieces desired for this volume—but, with a very few exceptions, they were

INTRODUCTION. xxxiii

not eligible, most of them because they were not upon the "Bush" subjects on which the writers were so well qualified to write, and others because, though they did relate to the "Bush," they were upon subjects already appropriated in the most famous Australian poems. For it has been the aim of the editor to give as much variety of subject, as many different aspects of Australian life, as he found possible. He could have formed one whole volume of the exploration-poems, another of the wild-horse and other hunts, another of the Bush-landscape-poems, *à la* Kendall, which have been submitted to him; but he has endeavoured to make the volume representative of Bush-life as well as Bush-poems.

It will be noticed that the editor has dispensed with the title of "Mr." In writing of a poet, to drop the "Mr." is to pay him a mark of honour; it, in fact, stamps him as public; and the question was where one was to stop affixing this opprobrious badge of unimportance. To an Australian, "Mr. Gordon," or "Mr. Kendall," would sound as absurd as "Mr. Chaucer," and it would therefore have been invidious to manumit them and yet apply the "Mr." to Stephens, Martin, Walch, and half-a-dozen others.

By the kindness of the editors of the great weekly papers of Australasia, the editor of this volume was able to give his invitation for contributions the widest publicity in the colonies. Those who did not contribute, therefore, he has judged to be unwilling for their poems to appear. With the exception of three little poems, the volume is selected entirely from the contributions sent, every one of which, except those which were in undecipherable manuscript, has been read. The three poems which did not come direct from their authors were the poem by Sir Henry Parkes, which the late Alfred Domett sent as a favourite of his; the Album-verses of the late Marcus Clarke, sent by his friend, Patchett Martin; and the extract from the "Australasia" of the late William Wentworth, inserted as coming from the first well-known Australian poem, and the first great statesman of Australia.

The publisher and editor wish to tender their best thanks to the authors who sent contributions, and the publishers who allowed their copyrights to be used; also to the editors of the great Australian papers, for generously giving in their columns publicity to the scheme; and to Francis Adams, Patchett Martin, and the managers of Griffith, Farran, & Co., in Sydney (Mr. Empson), and George Robertson & Co., in Melbourne (Mr. R. P. Raymond), for procuring by personal application some of the most important contributions to the volume.

AUSTRALIAN BALLADS AND RHYMES.

A VOICE FROM THE BUSH.
"O! mihi præteritos . . ."

High noon, and not a cloud in the sky to break this
    blinding sun !
Well, I've half the day before me still, and most of
    my journey done.
There's little enough of shade to be got, but I'll take
    what I can get,
For I'm not as hearty as once I was, although I'm a
    young man yet.

Young? Well, yes, I suppose so, as far as the seasons go;
Though there's many a man far older than I down
    there in the town below—
Older, but men to whom, in the pride of their man-
    hood strong,
The hardest work is never too hard, nor the longest
    day too long.

But I've cut my cake, so I can't complain ; and I've
    only myself to blame.
Ay ! that was always their tale at home, and here it's
    just the same.

Of the seed I've sown in pleasure, the harvest I'm
    reaping in pain.
Could I put my life a few years back, would I live
    that life again?

Would I? Of course I would! What glorious days
    they were!
It sometimes seems but the dream of a dream that life
    could have been so fair,
So sweet, but a short time back, while now, if one
    can call
This life, I almost doubt at times if it's worth the
    living at all.

One of these poets—which is it? somewhere or another
    sings,
That the crown of a sorrow's sorrow, is remembering
    happier things.
What the crown of a sorrow's sorrow may be I know
    not; but this I know,—
It lightens the years that are now, sometimes to think
    of the years ago.

Where are they now, I wonder, with whom those
    years were passed?
The pace was a little too good, I fear, for many of
    them to last;
And there's always plenty to take their place when
    the leaders begin to decline;
Still I wish them well, wherever they are, for the sake
    of auld lang syne!

Jack Villiers—Galloping Jack—what a beggar he was
    to ride!
Was shot in a gambling row last year on the Cali-
    fornian side;

And Byng, the best of the lot, who was broke in the
    Derby of fifty-eight,
Is keeping sheep with Harry Lepell, somewhere on
    the River Plate.

Do they ever think of me at all, and the fun we used
    to share?
It gives me a pleasant hour or so—and I've none too
    many to spare.
This dull blood runs as it used to run, and the spent
    flame flickers up,
As I think on the cheers that rang in my ears when I
    won the Garrison Cup!

And how the regiment roared to a man, while the
    voice of the fielders shook,
As I swung in my stride, six lengths to the good, hard
    held, over Brixworth Brook:
Instead of the parrot's screech, I seem to hear the
    twang of the horn,
As once again from Barkby Holt I set the pick of the
    Quorn.

Well, those were harmless pleasures enough; for I
    hold him worse than an ass
Who shakes his head at a "neck on the post," or a
    quick thing over the grass.
Go for yourself, and go to win, and you can't very
    well go wrong—
Gad, if I'd only stuck to that, I'd be singing a dif-
    ferent song!

As to the one I'm singing, it's pretty well known to all.
We knew too much, but not quite enough, and so we
    went to the wall;

While those who cared not, if their work was done,
    how dirty their hands might be,
Went up on our shoulders, and kicked us down, when
    they got to the top of the tree.

But though it relieves one's mind at times, there's
    little good in a curse.
One comfort is, though it's not very well, it might be
    a great deal worse.
A roof to my head, and a bite to mouth, and no one
    likely to know
In "Bill the Bushman" the dandy who went to the
    dogs long years ago.

Out there on the station among the lads I get along
    pretty well:
It's only when I come down into town, that I feel this
    life such a hell.
Booted and bearded and burned to a brick, I loaf along
    the street;
And I watch the ladies tripping by, and bless their
    dainty feet.

I watch them here and there with a bitter feeling of
    pain.
Ah! what wouldn't I give to feel a lady's hand again.
They used to be glad to see me once: they might have
    been so to-day;
But we never know the worth of a thing until we have
    thrown it away.

I watch them, but from afar; and I pull my old cap
    over my eyes,
Partly to hide the tears, that, rude and rough as I am,
    will rise,

And partly because I cannot bear that such as they
  should see
The man that I am, when I know, though they don't,
  the man that I ought to be.

   *   *   *   *   *   *

Puff! with the last whiff of my pipe I blow these
  fancies away,
For I must be jogging along if I want to get down into
  town to-day.
As I know I shall reach my journey's end though I
  travel not over fast,
So the end of my longer journey will come in its own
  good time at last.

FAIRYLAND.

Do you remember that careless band,
Riding o'er meadow and wet sea-sand,
  One autumn day, in a mist of sunshine,
Joyously seeking for fairyland?

The wind in the tree-tops was scarcely heard,
The streamlet repeated its one silver word,
  And far away, o'er the depths of woodland,
Floated the bell of the parson-bird.

Pale hoar-frost glittered in shady slips,
Where ferns were dipping their finger-tips,
  From mossy branches a faint perfume
Breathed over honeyed clematis-lips.

At last we climbed to the ridge on high,
Ah, crystal vision! Dreamland nigh!
  Far, far below us, the wide Pacific
Slumbered in azure from sky to sky.

And cloud and shadow, across the deep
Wavered, or paused in enchanted sleep,
   And eastward, the purple-misted islets
Fretted the wave with terrace and steep.

We looked on the tranquil, glassy bay,
On headlands sheeted with dazzling spray,
   And the whitening ribs of a wreck forlorn,
That for twenty years had wasted away.

All was so calm, and pure, and fair,
It seemed the hour of worship there,
   Silent as where the great North Minster
Rises forever, a visible prayer.

Then we turned from the murmurous forest land,
And rode over shingle and silver sand,
   For so fair was the earth in the golden autumn,
We sought no further for Fairyland.
               AUSTRAL (Mrs J. G. Wilson).

A SPRING AFTERNOON, N.Z.

WE rode in the shadowy place of pines,
   The wind went whispering here and there
   Like whispers in a house of prayer.
The sunshine stole in narrow lines,
   And sweet was the resinous atmosphere.
   The shrill cicada, far and near,
Piped on his high exultant third.
   Summer! Summer! He seems to say—
Summer! He knows no other word,
   But trills on it the livelong day;

The little hawker of the green,
Who calls his wares through all the solemn forest
   scene.

A shadowy land of deep repose !
Here where the loud nor'-wester blows,
How sweet, to soothe a trivial care,
The pine trees ever-murmured prayer !
To shake the scented powder down
   From stooping boughs that bar the way
And see the vistas, golden brown,
   Stretch to the sky-line far away.
But on and upward still we ride
   Whither the furze, an outlaw bold,
Scatters along the bare hillside,
   Handfuls of free uncounted gold,
And breaths of nutty, wild perfume,
Salute us from the flowering broom.
I love this narrow sandy road
   That idly gads o'er hill and vale,
Twisting where once a rivulet flowed.
   With as many turns as a gossip's tale.
I love this shaky, creaking bridge,
And the willow leaning from the ridge,
   Shaped like some green fountain playing,
And the twinkling windows of the farm
Just where the woodland throws an arm
   To hear what the merry stream is saying.

Stop the horses for a moment, high upon the breezy
   stair,
Looking over plain and upland, and the depths of
   summer air,
Watch the cloud and shadow sailing o'er the forest's
   sombre breast.

Misty capes and snow-cliffs glimmer on the ranges to
  the west.
Hear the distant thunder rolling, surely 'tis the making
  tide
Swinging all the blue Pacific on the harbour's iron
  side.
Now the day grows grey and chill, but see on yonder
  wooded fold,
Between the clouds, a ray of sunshine slips, and writes
  a word in gold.

AUSTRAL (Mrs J. G. Wilson.)

FROM THE CLYDE TO BRAIDWOOD.

A WINTER morn, the blue Clyde river winds
'Mid sombre slopes, reflecting in clear depths
The tree-clad banks or grassy meadow flats
Now white with hoary frost, each jewell'd blade
With myriad crystals glistening in the sun.

Thus smiles the Vale of Clyde, as through the air
So keen and fresh three travellers upward ride
Toward the Braidwood heights. Quickly they pass
The rustic dwellings on the hamlet's verge,
Winding sometimes beside the glassy depths
Of Nelligen Creek, where with the murmuring bass
Of running water sounds the sighing wail
Of dark swamp-oaks that shiver on each bank;
Then winding through a shady-bower'd lane,
With flickering streaks of sunlight beaming through
The feathery leaves and pendant tassels green
Of bright mimosa, whose wee furry balls
Promise to greet with golden glow of joy
The coming spring-tide.

FROM THE CLYDE TO BRAIDWOOD.

     Now a barren length
Of tall straight eucalyptus, till again
A babbling voice is heard, and through green banks
Of emerald fern, and mossy boulder rocks,
The Currawong dances o'er a pebbly bed,
In rippling clearness, or with cresting foam
Splashes and leaps in snowy cascade steps.
Then every feature changes—up and down,
O'er endless ranges like great waves of earth,
Each weary steed must climb, e'en like a ship
Now rising high upon some billowy ridge,
But to plunge down to mount once more, again
And still again.

     Naught on the road to see
Save sullen trees, white arm'd, with naked trunks,
And hanging bark, like tatter'd clothes thrown off,
An undergrowth of glossy zamia palms
Bearing their winter store of coral fruit,
And here and there some early clematis,
Like starry jasmine, or a purple wreath
Of dark kennedia, blooming o'er their time,
As if in pity they would add one joy
Unto the barren landscape.

     But at last
A clearer point is reached, and all around
The loftier ranges loom in contour blue,
With indigo shadows and light veiling mist
Rising from steaming valleys. Straight in front
Towers the Sugarloaf, pyramidal King
Of Braidwood peaks.

     Impossible it seems
To scale that nature-rampart, but where man

Would go he must and will : so hewn from out
The mountain's side in gradual ascent
Of league and half of engineering skill,
There winds the Weber Pass.

                A glorious ride ?
Fresher and clearer grows the breezy air,
Lighter and freer beats the quickening pulse
As each fair height is gain'd. Stern, strong, above
Rises the wall of mountain ; far beneath,
In sheer precipitancy, gullies deep
Gloom in dark shadow, on their shelter'd breast
Cherishing wealth of leafage richly dight
With tropic hues of green.

                No sound is heard
Save the deep soughing of the wind amid
The swaying leaves and harp-like stems, so like
A mighty breathing of great mother earth,
That half they seem to see her bosom heave
With each pulsation as she living sleeps.
And now and then to cadence of these throbs
There drops the bell-bird's knell, the coach whip's
    crack,
The wonga-pigeon's coo, or echoing notes
Of lyre-tail'd pheasants in their own rich tones,
Mocking the song of every forest bird.
Higher the travellers rise—at every turn
Gaining through avenued vista some new glimpse
Of undulating hills, the Pigeon-house
Standing against the sky like eyrie nest
Of some great dove or eagle. On each side
Of rock-hewn road, the fern trees cluster green,
Now and then lighted by a silver star
Of white immortelle flower, or overhung

By crimson peals of bright epacris bells.
Another bend, a sheltered deepening rift,
And in the mountain's very heart they plunge—
So dark the shade, the sun is lost to view.
Great silver wattles tremble o'er the path,
Which overlooks a glen one varying mass
Of exquisite foliage, full-green sassafras,
The bright-leaf'd myrtle, dark-hued kurrajong
And lavender, musk-plant, scenting all the air,
Entwined with clematis or bignonia vines,
And raspberry tendrils hung with scarlet fruit.
The riders pause some moments, gazing down,
Then upward look. Far as the peeping sky
The dell-like gully yawns into the heights;
A tiny cascade drips o'er mossy rocks,
And through an aisle of over-arching trees,
Whose stems are dight with lichen, creeping vines
A line of sunlight pierces lighting up
A wealth of fern trees; filling every nook
With glorious circles of voluptuous green,
Such as, unview'd, once clothed the silent earth
Long milliards past in Carboniferous Age.
A mighty nature-rockery! Each spot
Of fertile ground is rich with endless joys
Of leaf and fern; now here a velvet moss,
And there a broad asplenium's shining frond
With red-black veinings or a hart's-tongue point,
Contrasting with a pale-hued tender brake
Or creeping lion's foot. See where the hand
Of ruthless man hath cleft the rock, each wound
Is hidden by thick verdure, leaving not
One unclothed spot, save on the yellow road.

Reluctant the travellers leave the luscious shade
To mount once more. But now another joy—

An open view is here! Before them spreads
A waving field of ranges, purple grey,
In haze of distance with black lines of shade
Of ocean-blue o'er whose horizon verge
The morning mist-cloud hangs. The distant bay
Is clear defined. The headland's dark arms stretch
(Each finger-point white-lit with dashing foam)
In azure circlet, studded with rugged isles—
A picturesque trio, whose gold rock sides glow
In noonday sunlight, and round which the surf
Gleams like a silvery girdle.

     The grand Pass
Is traversed now, the inland plateau reach'd,
The last sweet glimpse of violet peaks is lost,
An upland rocky stream is pass'd, and naught
But same same gum trees vex the wearied eye
Till Braidwood plain is reached.

     A township like
All others, with its houses, church, and school—
Bare, bald, prosaic—no quaint wild tower,
Nor ancient hall to add poetic touch,
As in the dear old land—no legend old
Adds softening beauty to the Bunddawong Peak,
Or near-home ranges with too barbarous names.
But everything is cold, new, new too new
To foster poesy; and famish'd thought
Looks back with longing to the mountain dream.
     AUSTRALIE (Mrs Hubert Heron).

THE EXPLORER'S MESSAGE.

Golden, crimson, glows the sunset o'er the wild Australian scene,
Gilding e'en the lonely desert with a glory-tinted sheen,
Purple, purple, gloom the mountains towering in their distant height,
And the blushing air is quivering with the joy of rosy light.
Glorious beauty!—heavenly radiance! beaming o'er the barren earth,
While the weary land is stricken with a life-destroying dearth.
But no joy that glory bringeth—ominous that sunset blaze,
Telling but of rainless sunshine, burning on through cloudless days;
Parch'd, the thirsty ground is gasping for one shower of cooling rain—
Shadeless trees stand gaunt and withering on the grassless arid plain.
Not a sound of living creature, not one blade or leaf of green!
E'en the very birds have vanish'd from the desolated scene!

Hark! what sound of coming footsteps breaks the silence of the air?
Can it be a human being all alone that rideth there?
Jaded, drooping, horse and rider slowly wend their dreary way,
Toiling on as they have toil'd through many, many a weary day.

Wan the rider, wan and fainting—mind and body overwrought;
Worn the steed, and gauntly fleshless, perishing of bitter drought—
"Water, water! oh, for water!" Now the horse sinks to the ground;
And the faithful beast here resting a last halting-place has found;
Now the last, last link is broken! e'en the poor dumb friend is gone,
And the pioneer must turn his eyes unto a heavenly bourn.

But six months a gallant band, the brave explorers had set forth,
Resolute to pierce the mysteries of Australia's unknown north,
Strove they nobly, daring danger, hardships cheerfully endured!
Recking not of death or failure, still by patriot hopes allured.
Onward they had pressed adventurous, till by want and sickness tried,
One by one their ranks had thinn'd, lost, or spear'd, or famish'd, died.
Each day saw a martyr added, each night heard some dying moan,
Till at last *one* man was left in that great wilderness—alone—
Solitary, all untended; none, none left behind to mourn,
Now the last of the explorers lies on dying bed forlorn.
Faint the lonely man is growing, yet before he turns to die,
With one strong expiring effort, with one long-drawn weary sigh,

Draws he from his breast a locket—with onstalking
   death he fights,
While, upon a slip of paper, painfully he trembling
   writes—
"Mary, loved one, in the desert my last thought is
   still of you.
God be with you, guard and bless you. To my
   memory still be true."
His last signature he signeth, gazing lovingly and long
On the face within that locket—tender memories o'er
   him throng
As he folds the tiny letter, mournfully to parch'd lips
   pressed—
Clasps it in the golden casket, lays it to his loving breast;
Then with one deep prayer for mercy—ere the last
   glow leaves the skies,
Resting on his Father's bosom, calm the lone explorer
   dies.
None are near to close the eyelids—none weep o'er that
   bronzed face,
Only night is stealing softly, shrouding him with
   tender grace.

Springs have fled, and summers faded, ten long years
   have come and gone,—
Mary's face still wears its sweetness, though with long,
   long waiting worn;
Many a one has sought to win her—clear her answering words and few—
"I my love long since have plighted—to that love I
   will be true."
Brave men, searching, have gone forth upon the last
   explorer's track,
Unsuccessful, disappointed, they have aye returned
   back ·

Yet, within the maiden's bosom, hope 'gainst hope will quenchless burn,
Still his death is all unproven—still the wanderer may return!
"Let me know his fate," she prayeth, "only one small token send,
Then my heart in resignation to God's holy will shall bend."

Ride two horsemen through the wild lands where man's foot scarce trod before.
"We, the pioneers," they murmur, "we now first this land explore."
Ah! but see what is it then, that on the plain is gleaming there?
Hush'd and lonely is the desert—motionless the silent air,
As with solemn pace the travellers to the hallow'd spot draw nigh,
Where a famish'd lone explorer years agone lay down to die!
By him close his steed is lying—skeleton with harness trapp'd,
While in life's worn mouldering garments still the master is enwrapp'd.

Awe-struck gaze they on the ruins whence a brother's soul has fled;
Then, all loath to leave a comrade nameless on his desert bed,
Search the men for note or journal—some faint clue to name and fate.
Not a trace or record find they—not one letter, word, or date!

THE EXPLORER'S MESSAGE.

Least a grave they will make for him! Gleameth now
   a yellow sheen,
And amid the quiet ashes, where the faithful breast has
   been,
Shining lies a golden locket, with a simple name en-
   graved.
Ah, that name! long mourn'd and honour'd—now from
   cold oblivion saved!
Eagerly they ope the locket—in that dreary desert place
Beams there now upon these rough men, sweetest,
   gentlest woman's face,
Image of some cherished loved one; who, perchance
   these words may tell,
See! here lies a tiny letter, the explorer's last farewell.

Anxiously, yet almost doubting, lest a sacrilege it
   prove,
Strangers now unfold the message from the martyr to
   his love;
Trembling is the pencill'd writing, but the touching
   words are clear,
Mists cloud o'er the eyes now reading, e'en the strong
   men drop a tear
On that tender last love-letter—warm voice from the
   quiet dead;
Reverently they gently lay it on that face he would
   have wed,
And they vow to rest nor linger till that relic they
   have placed
In the keeping of the maiden by such love so deeply
   graced.

Autumn wanes and winter cometh; Mary's hair is
   tinged with grey;
But her eye is beaming softly with calm resignation's ray.

Loving cares have left their traces on the peaceful gentle face,
And youth's beauty now has softened to a sweet diviner grace.
Still her plighted troth she keepeth, bears no ring of circling gold,
But one ornament she weareth, of a fashion quaint and old,
For a golden locket lieth on her bosom evermore.
One alone that true heart loveth—one who long that relic wore,
While his message in its dearness to her soul is ever new—
"God be with you, guard and bless you—to my memory still be true."
Ah! that blessing seems to follow e'en where'er her footsteps go,
While his monument she buildeth in the homes of want and woe.
Dedicated, all unfetter'd, ever sister, never wife—
To God's suffering poor she yieldeth the devotion of a life.
Lonely to the world she seemeth, all unknown her gentle fame,
But in lowly homes soft blessings gather round her well-loved name,
And the lost explorer's lone death, and the maiden's anxious pain,
To full many a sick and sad one have proved yet a deeper gain.
Soon shall come life's golden sunset, and the evening shall close in,
And to heaven's distant mountains Mary then her way may win.

There, perchance, in perfect beauty, **free from earthly
  taint or tie**—
We cannot tell, we know not how—her love may be
  fulfilled on high.

AUSTRALIE (Mrs Hubert Heron).

FORSAKEN HOMES AND GRAVES.

These mountain wilds that rest so still,
  These woods and wastes so vast and deep,
These ravines round each rocky hill,
Where long-lost cattle roam at will
  Beneath the eagle's ken and sweep.

Far from the settlers' haunts are found
  Rude vestiges of life and death,
Forsaken home and burial mound
Of those whose names still cling, around,
  To circling wilderness and heath.

These olden walls, whose ruins low
  Are met in many a lonely ride,
Deserted hearths whose fires did glow
With homelight in the long ago
  By Ti-tree flat or gully side.

Round them the sheen of summer-day
  Falls drearisome and desolate;
Thin shadow lines of branches stray,
O'er waifs of childhood's broken play,
  Untrodden path and fallen gate.

The notes, of wild birds, that elsewhere
  Bring tones of gladness, seem to change
To coronachs of sadness there;
The curlew's cry upon the air
  Sounds like a shriek along the range.

The very dreariness seems rife
  With low and stealthy undertones,
Footfall and voice of former life;
Wraith-presences of sire and wife
  And children cling to wood and stones,

Some woman's hand did plant and train
  That runner by the shattered door,
Which clambered through the splintered pane
And pallid turneth out again,
  As if from spectre on the floor.

Once Life o'er Death hath made its moan;
  There hath been sorrow even here;
In one small grave with weeds o'ergrown
A child sleeps in the wild alone,
  With only silence crooning near.

Here the night-zephyr, passing, wings
  At midnight to that she-oak nigh,
Plays, harplike, on its drooping strings,
And to its dreary cadence sings
  The wildwood's soothing lullaby.

H. H. BLACKHAM.

OUR HERITAGE.

A PERFECT peaceful stillness reigns,
Not e'en a passing playful breeze
The sword-shaped flax blades gently stirs:
The vale and slopes of rising hills
Are thickly clothed with yellow grass,
Whereon the sun, late risen, throws
His rays to linger listlessly.
Naught the expanse of yellow breaks,
Save where a darker spot denotes
Some straggling bush of thorny scrub;
While from a gully down the glen,
The foliage of the dull-leaved trees
Rises to view; and the calm air,
From stillness for a moment waked
By parakeets' harsh chattering,
Swift followed by a tiny thrill
Of bell-like notes, is hushed again.
The tiny orbs of glistening dew,
Still sparkle gem-like 'mid the grass,
While morning mist, their mother moist,
Reluctant loiters on the hill,
Whence presently she'll pass to merge
In the soft depths of the blue heav'ns.

This fertile isle to us is given
Fresh from its Maker's hand; for here
No records of the vanished past
Tell of the times when might was right
And self-denial weakness was,
But all is peaceful, pure, and fair.
Our heritage is hope. We'll rear
A nation worthy of the land;

And when in age we linger late,
Upon the heights above life's vale,
Before we, like the mist, shall merge
In depths of God's eternity,
We'll see, perchance our influence
Left dew-like, working for the good
Of those whose day but dawns below.

ALEXANDER W. BATHGATE.

TO THE MOKO-MOKO, OR BELL-BIRD.*

I.

Merry chimer, merry chimer,
   Oh, sing once more,
   Again outpour,
Like some long-applauded mimer,
   All thy vocal store.

II.

Thy short but oft-repeated song,
   At early dawn,
   Awakes the morn,
Telling that joys to thee belong,
   Greeting day new-born.

III.

Alas! we now but seldom hear
   Thy rich, full note
   Around us float,
For thou seem'st doomed to disappear,
   E'en from woods remote.

* Now rapidly dying out of our land.

IV.

Some say the stranger honey-bee,
  By white men brought,
  This ill hath wrought;
It steals the honey from the tree
  And it leaves thee naught.

V.

The songsters of our Fatherland
  We hither bring,
  And here they sing,
Reminding of that distant strand
  Whence old mem'ries spring.

VI.

But as the old, we love the new;
  Fain we'd retain
  Thy chiming strain,
Thy purple throat and olive hue—
  Yet we wish in vain.

VII.

Thy doom is fixed by nature's law—
  Why? none can tell.
  Therefore, farewell,
We'll miss thy voice from leafy shaw—
  Living silver bell.

VIII.

Why should we ever know new joys,
  If thus they pass?
  Leaving, alas!
Wistful regret, which much alloys
  All that man now has.

ALEXANDER W. BATHGATE.

TOMBOY MADGE.

O ! FOR a swim thro' the reedy river,
   And one long pull with the boys at dawn !
Only a ride on the high-backed Rover,
   And one tennis-round on the grassy lawn !
Once more to see the sun on the wide-waves,
   And feel once more the foam at my feet ;
Give me again the wind in the sea-caves
   Rocking the weeds on the "Tomboy's seat."

Only last week, when the sky was brightest,
   No single cloud in the vaulted blue,
The boys and I, when the sea was calmest,
   Rowed thro' the waves in the *Black-eyed Sue.*
Fred, you remember the great-eyed fishes
   Shining star-like thro' the emerald sea,
How the waves foamed with their gleaming riches ?
   Splendid fun for the boys and me.

Is it a week since we forded the river
   (Low and clear for the time of the year)
And found the wattles and tall red clover,
   Scenting the air from far and near ?
Is it a week since we all went jumping
   From the bent arm of the creeking gum ?
Who would have thought that the half-bent stumpling
   Would lay the Tomboy crippled and dumb ?

Fred, were you frightened when I lay wailing,
   With eyes closed away from the dazzling sun ?
As in a dream I saw your face paling
   Before the sky grew distant and dun.

I can't remember the homeward wending
  Thro' the dark trees and the long spring grass;
Nor how you stopped at the river's bending
  And bathed my face in the stream as we passed.

I woke in this room, where the blinds were darkened,
  And saw the face that was bent o'er mine:
And there was a voice to which I hearkened—
  A voice that rings in my brain like a chime.
"She will linger on for a time," it was telling;
  "Years may pass and ten seasons turn;
But never again will these feet, weak and failing,
  Rise to walk thro' the flowers and fern."

"Ten seasons turn!" One glad month of springtime
  With ferns and flowers I cannot see,
Will make me long for the heavenly sunshine,
  Where you and the boys may come to me.
How can I live under walls and ceiling
  When all my life has been spent in the breeze?
Whenever the bells of the birds are pealing
  I will pine and long for their nests in the leaves.

O! Auntie dear draw the blinds up widely,
  Let stream the sun thro' the bow'ry trees.
O! see the clouds on the deep blue gliding,
  And watch them ride and sport on the breeze.
And, Freddy, boy, I hold your hand gently,
  With its boyish, hard, familiar palm—
The hand I will feel in the far-off country,
  When "Tomboy Madge" will be safe from harm.

May, with the dove eyes gentle and shining,
  Come nearer, darling, and smooth my hair,
And tell me the tale from the deep past chiming
  The saintly mother and infant fair.

Not long ago these same "Good Tidings"
  That brightened the blue of your loving eyes,
Would seem to me but as wearisome chidings
  Heavy as clouds in autumnal skies.

But now I must lie here far from the cool-wave,
  Far from the sounds and the scenes I love,
With nothing before but pain—and a green-grave—
  And nothing to seek but the hope from above.
No grand long walks thro' the dusk at evening,
  Or long-drawn swims in the wind-tossed wave ;
No light to seek but the one that's waning
  Down the dim path to the Tomboy's grave.

" Ten seasons turn " will have seen the grasses
  High and green near the sea-shelled cave,
And the dull stonecrop that Fred pulls as he passes
  Will have twined and hidden my early grave.
The boys, when they swing on the blue-gums bending,
  And hear the hoarse voice of the ocean roar,
Will sometimes think of the Tomboy's ending,
  And wait for her voice on another shore.
                JENNINGS CARMICHAEL.

"IN A LADY'S ALBUM."

(Written in the Album of Mrs H. G. Turner, of Melbourne.)

WHAT can I write in thee, O dainty book,
  About whose daintiness quaint perfume lingers—
Into whose pages dainty ladies look,
  And turn thy dainty leaves with daintier fingers ?

IN A LADY'S ALBUM.

Fitter my ruder muse for ruder song,
  My scrawling quill to coarser paper matches,
My voice, in laughter raised too loud and long,
  Is hoarse and cracked with singing tavern-catches.

No melodies have I for ladies' ear,
  No roundelays for jocund lads and lasses,—
But only brawlings born of bitter beer,
  And chorused with the clink and clash of glasses.

So tell thy mistress, pretty friend, for me,
  I cannot do her 'hest, for all her frowning,
While dust and ink are but polluting thee,
  And vile tobacco smoke thy leaves embrowning.

Thou breathest purity and humble worth—
  The simple jest, the light laugh following after,
I will not jar upon thy modest mirth
  With harsher jest, or with less gentle laughter.

So some poor tavern-hunter steeped in wine,
  With staggering footsteps thro' the streets returning,
Seeing, through gathering glooms, a sweet light shine
  From household lamp in happy window burning,

May pause an instant in the wind and rain,
  To gaze on that sweet scene of love and duty,
But turns into the wild wet night again,
  Lest his sad presence mar its holy beauty.

                        MARCUS CLARKE.

22nd May 1869.

BESS.

Eh? Why am I keeping that old crippled mare?
She ought to be shot? Come now, steady, lad, there!
I keep her because she is crippled—that's why.
Not much of a reason? Well, that I deny.

You see she was true in a test that was rough,
And did what no man could have done—that's enough!
But come down to the paddock, and let me relate
How Bess, through sheer courage, fell down at the gate.

In seventy-one—yes, sir, that was the year,
My Mary and I had selected round here;
Those farms on the flat were then sheep walks I guess,
For we first invaded the lone wilderness.

We'd only been wed for a twelve-month or so,
Were happy and hopeful, like lovers, you know;
And then came a cherub one warm summer morn—
'Twas death or a doctor when "Stranger" was born!

I trembled with fear as I saw my love lie,
For help was away where the earth touched the sky;
Some thirty miles there and some thirty miles back,
Through swamps and through mallee, with scarcely a
    track.

I sprang to the back of that bonny old mare,
And felt, without uttering, a sort of a pray'r:
One look at my Mary, and off then we sped,
Straightway at a gallop—I gave Bess her head.

The sun had just reached yon northern hill's crown,
And we'd to get back before he had gone down :
A life was depending on that, maybe two,
And Bess seemed to know it as forward she flew.

Ten miles of good pacing, without a mishap
Brought Willoughby's Bridge and Victoria Gap,
When right on ahead there I saw to my woe,
The scrub was all smoking, the forest aglow !

'Twas straight through or round it—an hour or a day—
But time was too precious, so fear fled away ;
I spoke to Bess cheerily, called her by name,
Then started to rush through the region of flame.

We soon were amidst it—her strides never broke
Through fierce flying curtains of thick sultry smoke,
Through failing of timber and cracking of boughs,
Through showers of sparks and my mutt'ring of vows !

Bess struggled for love—aye, the noblest of strife—
While I urged her on for love and for life ;
We passed through a miracle—'tis now like a dream,
But God somehow guides when the danger's extreme.

Then two creeks we passed where the bottoms were stiff
And rose on the ranges at Robertson's cliffs ;
Away on the plain where the rivers turned south,
I saw my one hope with my heart in my mouth.

Ere noon we ran into the little bush town,
And Bess was so heated, I watered her down,
Then sought out the doctor, and stammered with pain,
In telling my message—then sped off again.

He rode a stout pony—a deep iron grey,
And made a hand-gallop from first right away,
A long line of dust marked our journey behind,
As eight clattering hoof-strokes sent thuds on the wind.

Some fifteen miles racing, still Bess onward press'd,
Though snow-flakes had whitened her flanks and her
    breast;
I patted and coaxed her, and told her my fears—
She galloped on gamely, and flickered her ears.

But flush as we came to the bush fire with speed,
The grey pony stopped and declined to proceed;
Persuasions both gentle and sterner were vain,
He wouldn't face flames, and he put it quite plain.

And then in the throes of my anxious distress,
I handed the doctor my noble mare Bess;
Away they went flying through danger and heat,
When reckless, though scared, the cob followed as fleet.

We got through that hell looking burnt-up and brown,
And pulled at the gate e'er the sun had gone down;
Well, Mary was saved, but the mare she was done,
And fell at the end of the race she had won!

We nursed her for months, and we watched her with
    care,
For gratitude gets to be purer than prayer;
Though paralyzed then into maimed helplessness,
We'll love her for ever, our bonny mare Bess!

Yon colt is her foal, and that lad on his back
Is "Stranger" or "Cherub"—we now call him Jack.
A beautiful pair? Well, that colt is worth ten—
I'd sooner trust him than my own fellow men.

                        A. T. CHANDLER.

CATCHING THE COACH.

At Kangaroo Gully in "Fifty-two"
   The rush and the scramble was reckless and rough;
"Three ounces a dish and the lead running true!"
   Was whispered around concerning the "stuff."

Next morning a thousand of fellows, or more,
   Appeared for invasion along the brown rise—
Some Yankees, and Cockneys, and Cantabs of yore,
   And B.A.'s from Oxford in blue shirt disguise.

And two mornings later, the "Nugget" saloon,
   With billiards and skittles, was glaring with signs,
A blind fiddler, Jim, worried out a weak tune,
   Beguiling the boys and collecting the fines.

Then tents started up like the freaks of a dream,
   While heaps of white pipeclay dotted the slope,
To "Dern her—a duffer!" or "Creme de la Creme!"
   That settled the verdict of lagging hope.

And bustle and jollity rang 'mong the trees
   In strange combination of humankind traits—
With feverish searchings and gay levities
   The fires of excitement were fully ablaze.

Well, three mornings after, the stringy-bark gums
   All rustled their leaves with further surprise,
They'd seen old stagers and limey new chums,
   But here were galoots in peculiar guise.

With nondescript uniform, booted and spurred,
   A fierce-looking strap on the underneath lip,
An ominous shooter, a dangling sword,
   A grim leather pouch above the right hip !

And maybe a dozen came cantering so,
   All clanking and jaunty—authority vain—
When down through the gully rang out the word "Jo,"
   And "Jo" was sent on with a sneering refrain.

There was hunting for "rights," and producing the same,
   Or passing them on to a paperless mate,
Or hiding in bushes or down in the claim—
   Such various expedients to baffle the State.

Then "Who put him on?"—"Twig his illigant seat !"
   "Cuss me, but its purty !"—"The thing on the horse?"
"His first dacent clothes !"—"What surprise for his feet !"
   Such volleys as these were soon fired at the force.

But duty was duty. Just then through the scrub
   A digger made off—he a culprit no doubt !
"Dismount, you then, Wilson," roared Sergent Hubbub ;
   "Quick ! follow the rascal, and ferret him out."

The sapling cadet with budding moustache,
   Then sprang to the ground in dauntless pursuit,
And, filled with zeal and a soldier-like dash,
   He felt a true hero of saddle and boot.

CATCHING THE COACH.

The gully quick echoed with taunts that were real —
   Keen chaff of defiance allied to revolt—
Such sharp wordy weapons as might have been steel —
   From skirmishers laughing on hillock and holt.

Away went the fugitive, spurred on by haste,
   Escaping the undergrowth, leaping the logs,
Yet ne'er looking back—did he know he was chased ?
   Said Wilson : " He's one of the worst of the dogs !

" Some greater misdeed must have blackened his hand ;
   I'll have him—promotion ! Stop there, or I'll shoot !"
The other ahead didn't hear the command,
   But sprang on unheeding o'er dry branch and root.

The chase settled down to a heavy set to ;
   They ran o'er the hill and across the clear flat ;
And Wilson was chuckling—the villain he knew
   Was making a bee line for gaol—Ballarat !

" I'll follow the rogue safely into the trap —
   Confound him, he's speedy : I can't run him down ;
But there, quite unconscious of any mishap,
   I'll fix him up neatly in gay canvas town ! "

Then over a creek where a line of sage gums
   All flourishing grew, then away to the right ;
Their loud breathings mingled with strange forest hums,
   And Wallabies scampered with terror and fright.

And cockatoos screeched from the loftiest trees,
   The minahs and magpies all fluttered and flew,
The drowsy old 'possums were roused from their ease,
   The locusts and lizards quick stepped out of view.

But on went the pair never noticing this,
  For both had a serious business in hand :
With one there were feelings that prophesied bliss,
  The other saw capture and glory so grand.

O'er hillside and creek, beyond hollow and spur,
  Thro' brief strips of woodland, they hurried on still ;
The trooper lost ground, but he wasn't a cur ;
  Besides, they were nearing on Bakery Hill.

Then suddenly broke on each sweltering sight
  The thousand of tents in the city of gold ;
And straight to the thick of them ran with delight
  The chased and the chaser—what luck for the bold !

The coach was just starting for Melbourne that day
  As Wilson rushed eagerly on to his man.
"I'll put you with care where you won't be so gay,"
  The trooper in triumph already began.

" You've led me a dance in a lively hour's sun ;
  Now trip out your licence, or waltz off to gaol !
What ! got one ? Oh, ho ! Why the —— did you run ? "
  " To post this here letter for Nell by the mail."
A. T. CHANDLER.

A BUSH IDYL.

Why, Ruby, hulloa ! you are pricking your ears !
  Come, what is the matter, old fellow, to-day ?
I thought at your age you had lost all your fears,
  And, like my own youth, they had long passed away.

A BUSH IDYL.

So steady, now steady! Don't ask me to think
  That you're but a colt scarce a year from your dam,
All quiv'ring, and nervous, and frisky, and "pink,"—
  It's only a bell on a little white lamb!

Well, how could you shrink at the melody sweet?
  There's surely no harm in the silvery sound,
Or ribbon of blue knotted carelessly neat,
  Encircling a neck in a delicate round;
Some babe at the station just up on the rise
  Hath decked out her darling in innocent play,
And, while a soft sleep hath come o'er her young eyes,
  Released from caresses her lamb leapt away.

We men often grow just as weak as a child,
  And, Ruby, again you are surely a foal;
For you as a youngster were skittish and wild,
  And trouble enough in those days to control.
Why now dread a bell with a rippling ring?
  'Tis music that murmurs with rhythmical spells,
For you to thus tremble 's a curious thing—
  But somehow you horses don't understand bells.

Well, come, let us go—you are older, you see,
  And I, too, am older.—How memories fly
To those golden days when we two used to be
  By day and by night 'neath the blue southern sky!
How merry we wandered when never as yet
  That shadow of sorrow had saddened our zest—
When all the bright world had no shade of regret,
  Before I fell weary and wishing for rest.

And O! our grand gallops—you bore me so well
  O'er stretches of plain, up the thick-wooded slope,
From rock-covered ridges to never-trod dell,
  With nothing to think of but roseate hope.

You felt a brave pride then in speeding along—
  The pride of a conscious and generous pow'r,—
While I was so happy that many a song
  I trilled in those wild woods from hour to hour.

And what was the theme? Ah, the same olden tale;
  But is it not good it should ever thus be?
You know when we haunted the wattle tree dale
  A glorious girl used to linger with me.
The time was idyllic! what halcyon days
  When we in our joy went to meet her in spring!
Then life seemed to run in most beautiful ways,
  And sorrow was merely a mythical thing.

You know how we kissed 'neath the old lightwood tree,
  That bloom-budding day when the hillsides were green,
And love was there sealed 'tween my darling and me,
  And you became glad in the gay laughing scene.
Ah! such was my theme, and to you I would say,
  That here unto man 'tis the godliest given,
For he who can love from his heart clears away
  Full many a shadow that hides him from heaven.

But all that went by and my song note was changed,
  For sorrow came up like the night on the day,
I know I was 'wildered for reasons estranged,
  Left dark grief to blind me and vanished away
The morning they carried her down to the dell
  To lie near the flowers, the ferns, and the floss:
I prayed to be laid with my heart there as well—
  To sleep or to dream—'neath the delicate moss!

My prayer was in vain, yet the Lord He is good,
  And after a season I bowed to His will;
Though day unto day did I come by the wood,
  To sit and to think at her grave 'neath the hill.

Ah! love shapes our destiny sharper than fate,
  Till evil or good from the issue doth spring;
The fair bud may burst to dark petals of hate,
  Or bright passion blossoms that clamber and cling.

And so, brave old horse, sped our sweet sunny days—
  Our revel of galloping, rollicking prime;
But why should I grieve that it flitted away,
  And left but a dream of that golden-born time?
For tho' I am tired as a weariful bird
  That flutters and longs for a season of rest,
One joy is still left: when the summons is heard,
  To fly to that star where my angel is blest.

Yet Ruby, at times I could covet your lot,
  With no human dread of the leveller death—
You'd stand coolly there to be cruelly shot
  Without the least quiver or bating of breath.
And why should we fear? Ah! no mortal knows,
  Or ever the wonderful mystery can break;
Perhaps 'tis a dreaming that ends with repose,
  Or maybe we slumber and never awake.

. . . .

Away with such thoughts! So you're wanting to roll,
  Well, wait till we camp at the Warrigal Creek,
A bright blazing fire by the old gumtree bole
  Will light up the gloom—let us spell for a week!
You're done by our seven hours' journey to-day
  (That sweet bogie bell is some miles to the west)—
But why am I strangely and mournfully gay,
  And weary yet winged to some dreamland of rest?

. . . .

Come, Ruby, old boy! . . . What! you tremble—
 I see
  Your breathing comes thicker, and following, and
   fast,
Your strong muscles fail you—Oh God! can it be
 That Ruby, brave Ruby—is going at last?
And now I'm alone, for my one faithful friend
 Has left me to battle an innermost pain—
To wander all lonely, awaiting the end
 When death bids me tryst with my darling again.

. . . .

But there 'neath the starlight the tired bushman
   dreamed
  Such beautiful dreams in which mingled a moan,
But ere the pale dawn o'er the dusky hill gleamed
 His spirit had passed to the silent unknown!
And down by the creek the rough station hands found
 Dead rider and horse as they peacefully lay—
A verdict laconic—a lonely bush mound—
 Tell not of the sorrow that bore him away!

                                A. T. CHANDLER.

THE JUBILEE OF MELBOURNE.

FOR ages, wild and restless waves had cast
 Their burden on a low, untrodden shore,
Which never stately, white winged ship had passed,
 Or rugged seamen touched with friendly oar;
  Where never loving comrades flocked to pour
Their boisterous welcomes, or sweet maidens came
To look the language lips were shy to frame.

Here 'neath the scorching heat of summer days
  The shimmering waves stole up to kiss the sands,
And the fair moon with peerless silver rays
  Lent beauty luminous to southern lands
  Whose lonely wild, yet not unlovely strands
Had never echoed to the steps of men,
Who dreamed of unknown worlds beyond their ken.

The waters of this noble bay were fed
  By a pure stream which no pollution knew;
Man's commerce had not stirred its rocky bed,
  But on its banks sweet scented wattles grew
  Amidst whose fragrant boughs soft love birds flew,
And magpies poured from glossy plumaged throats
Their morning song of rich melodious notes.

From out the scrub that fringed the river's bank
  What dusky, strange, and uncouth forms emerge
With matted locks which cling like sedges rank
  Round gaunt old tree trunks on the water's verge,
  Sons of the forest wild whose plaintive dirge—
The mournful wail of hapless destiny—
The sad winds carry to the moaning sea.

There dawned, at last, a day when all was changed,
  The restless overflow of northern lands,
From Old World thoughts and sympathies estranged,
  Winged south their way in bold adventurous bands,
  Bearing courageous hearts and vigorous hands,
To carve their way to wealth with manly toil,
And plant dominion in productive soil.

Here fifty winters since, by Yarra's stream,
  A scattered hamlet found its modest place:
What mind would venture then in wildest dream
  Its wondrous growth and eminence to trace?
  What seer predict a stripling in the race

Would swift, as Atalanta, win the prize
Of progress, 'neath the World's astonished eyes?

. It is no dream, upon those grass-grown streets,
   Has risen up a city vast and fair,
In whose thronged thoroughfares the stranger meets
   With signs of all the world can send most rare
   And costly to her marts. And everywhere
Ascends the hum of nervous, bustling strife—
The splendid evidence of healthy life.

Where stalwart bushmen lounged through sultry hours,
   And large-boned oxen bowed beneath the yoke,
Are parks and gardens, rich with plants and flowers;
   Mansions embowered in ash, and elm, and oak,
   Churches where worshippers heaven's aid invoke,
And towers and steeples, monuments and domes
Rise amidst crowded haunts and peaceful homes.

                              J. F. DANIELL.

THE PRELUDE TO RANOLF AND AMOHIA.

WELL! if truth be all welcomed with hardy reliance,
All the lovely unfoldings of luminous science,
All that logic can prove or disprove be avowed;
Is there room for no faith—though such evil intrude—
In the dominance still of a spirit of good?
Is there room for no hope—such a handbreadth we scan
In the permanence yet of the spirit of man?
May we bless the far seeker, nor blame the fine dreamer?
Leave reason her radiance—doubt her due cloud;
     Nor their rainbows enshroud?

From our life of realities, hard, shallow-hearted,
Has romance, has all glory idyllic departed,
From the work-a-day world all the wonderment flown?
Well, but what if there gleamed, in an age cold as this,
The divinest of poets' ideal of bliss?
Yea, an Eden could lurk in this empire of ours,
With the loneliest love in the loveliest bowers?
In an era so rapid with railway and steamer,
And with Pan and the Dryads, like Raphael, gone—
  What if this could be shown?

O, my friends, never deaf to the charms of denial,
Were its comfortless comforting worth a life-trial,
Discontented content with a chilling despair?
Better ask as we float down a song-flood unchecked,
If our sky with no Iris be glory-bedecked?
Through the gloom of eclipse as we wistfully steal,
If no darkling aureolar rays may reveal
That the future is haply not utterly cheerless:
While the present has joy and adventure as rare,
  As the past when most fair?

And if weary of mists you will roam undisdaining
To a land where the fanciful fountains are raining
Swift brilliants of boiling and beautiful spray
In the violet splendour of skies that illume
Such a wealth of green ferns and rare crimson tree-
 bloom;
Where a people primeval is vanishing fast,
With its faiths, and its fables, and ways of the past;
O, with reason and fancy unfettered and fearless,
Come plunge with us deep into regions of day,
  Come away, and away!

ALFRED DOMETT.

THE LEGEND OF TAWHAKI.

>   Then Amohia, tapping Ranolf's arm,
>   Said, "Listen, *Pakeha!*" and with lifted hand,
>   Rounding—enchantress-wise
>   When double soul she throws into a charm—
>   The solemn archness of her great black eyes
>   Deep lighted like a well,
>   An ancient legend she began to tell
>   Of one God hero of the land,
>   Of which our faithful lay presents
>   Precisely the main incidents,
>   Adorning freely everywhere
>   The better its intents to reach,
>   The language so condensed and bare,
>   Those clotted rudiments of speech.

"Once a race, the Pona-turi, in the oozy depth of ocean,
Fierce, uncouth, in gloomy glory, lived where light is none, nor motion,
More than anything created, Light, their bane, their death, they hated;
So for night they ever waited ere ashore they seal-like clambered;
To their house Manáwa-tanē—their great mansion, lofty-chambered,
Whence, if e'er a windy moon had caught them, you would see them hieing
Homeward, sable shapes beneath the crisping silver floating, flying,
Swift as scattered clouds, on high their snowy courses gaily plying.

"Young Tawháki, well he knew them—did they not his father mangle?

Hang his fleshless bones, a scarecrow, ghastly from
    their roof to dangle?
Keep his mother too, a slave, each day to give them
    timely warning
Ere dark sky from earth uplifting left the first gold gap
    of morning?

"Vengeance with his mother then he plotted. So by
    daylight hiding
In their house-roof thatch he couched, his slimy foes'
    arrival biding.
Darkness comes; they land in swarms; their spacious
    house they crowd and cumber;
Revel through the midnight reckless; drop at last in
    weary slumber.
Like the distant ocean's roaring, sinks and swells the
    mighty snoring.—
Out then steals Tawhaki, chuckling; long ere day be-
    gins to brighten,
Stops up every chink in doorway, window, that could
    let the light in.
And the snoring goes on roaring; or if any sleeper
    yawning
Turned him restless, thinking 'Surely it must now be
    near the dawning,'
Growling, 'Slave, is daylight breaking? are you watch-
    ing? are you waiting?'
Still the mother answered blandly, 'Fear not, I will
    give you warning—
Sleep, O sleep, my Pona-turi, there are yet no streaks
    of morning.'

"So the snoring goes on roaring. Now above the
    mountains dewy,
High the splendour—God careers it—great Te Ra, the
    Tama Nui.

Sudden cries Tawháki's mother, 'Open doors and
    windows quickly ;
Every stop-gap tear out, clear out ! On them pour the
    sunbeams thickly !'
Through the darksome mansion—through and through
    those sons of darkness streaming,
Flash the spear-flights of the Day-God—deadly-silent
    —golden-gleaming !
Down they go, the Pona-turi ! vain their struggles,
    yells and fury !
Like dead heaps of fishes, stranded by the storm's spray,
    gaping, staring—
Stiffened so, astonished, helpless, lay they in the sun-
    beams glaring ;
Fast as shrink upon the shelly beach, those tide-left
    discs of jelly ;
Fast as leathery fungus balls, in yellow dust clouds
    fuming fly off,
So they shrink, they fade, they wither, so those imps of
    darkness die off."

" Now, of heavenly birth to cheer him, beauteous from
    those blue dominions,
Hapae came, divine, a damsel, floating down on steady
    pinions ;
Came, a moving moonbeam, nightly lit with love his
    chamber brightly,
Till that spring-time of her bosom flushed out in a
    baby blossom.
Infant, it had infant failings. Once the dirt-delighted
    bantling,
Scornfully Tawháki jeered at. Straightway all the
    mother mantling
In her heart, her treasure Hapae caught up ; to her
    plumy vesture

Pressed it, nestling; then upspringing with reproachful look and gesture,
Sailed off to her skyey mansion, vanished in the blue expansion,
Like an Albatross that slides into the sunset,—whitely fading
With its fixed rare-winking vans, away into the crimson shading.
Only, ere she parted, while the lagging west wind she invited—
Flapping her broad wings, a tip-toe on the mannikin alighted
(Red—its arms on knees akimbo—squat—the gable apex crowning)
One advice she waved Tawháki, more with grief than anger frowning;
'If you ever feel the child and mother, to your heart grow dearer,
Ever wish to follow and to find us, O unkindly sneerer,
And would climb by tree-dropt trailers, to the sky a little nearer,
O remember, leave the loose ones, only take and trust to surely
Such as hung from loftiest tree-tops, root themselves in earth securely!'

"Many a moon he mourned—Tawháki. Then he started to discover
Where they grew, those happy creepers, that could help a hapless lover.
Many a moon he roamed—Tawháki. And his heart was sore and weary
When he found himself despondent in a forest grand and dreary

(Ah, that wildering wild wood—who can tell how dense
    it was and tangled),
Where in wanton woody ringlets many a rope of trailers
    dangled.
Rapt, absorbed in her pursuit, a blind old crone those
    creepers tended ;
Caught at, groped and felt for any that within her
    reach descended.
He, an ancestress discerning, ere for council he implored
    her,
Touched her eyes, a charm repeating, and to sight at
    once restored her.
Then they found a creeper rooted, finely for his pur-
    pose suited.
Up he went exultingly, bold-hearted, joyous-eyed, firm-
    footed.
At the tree-top, see ! a tiny spider-thread upshooting
    shiny,
Wavering, viewless half, yet ever held aloft by mere
    endeavour.
With a beating heart, Tawhāki, muttering many an
    incantation—
Wild with hope so high it takes the very hue of
    desperation,
Clasps the clue so evanescent; then with yearnings
    deep, incessant,
Seeing in the vault above him only Hapae's eyes that
    love him,
Up and up, for ever upwards mounts he dauntless,
    nothing scares him,
Up through azure bright abysses still that thread in
    triumph bears him.

Suddenly a sunny grove is round him—cheery people
    working

THE LEGEND OF TAWHAKI.

At a great canoe, appear. All day he keeps the thicket, lurking,
Till when balmy shadow veils them, and serenest sleep assails them,
Stripping off his youthful glory, **out** he steals, **an old man hoary** ;
Strikes a few swift strokes, and magic-like **the work is ended.**
Graceful with its lofty stern, with open-circled fretwork splendid,
Lo ! the **great** canoe completed ! To his copse he then retreated.
On **another** hollowed trunk next night **the wonder-work** repeated—
Those Celestials marvelled **greatly** ; yet reflecting in their pleasure
Such a worker were a treasure as a slave beyond **all measure,**
Watched and **clutched that old man wilful—so decrepit, yet so skilful,**
And to their great ruler **bore him.—O delight !** who sits before him ?
'Tis his beautiful **benign one, 'tis his downy-plumed divine** one,
Hapae ! will he now deride her, or **the subtle Elf beside her !**
Kindly greeted, with caresses he **the child allures and presses**
To his heart, no more to sever. Then as he flings off for **ever**
That disguise's dim defilement, **Hapae smiles sweet reconcilement ;**
Swift the child they **bathe, baptize it, lustral waters** o'er it dashing ;
And **Taháki**—breast **and brow sublime insufferably flashing,**

Hid in lightnings, as he looks out from the thunder-
 cloven portals
Of the sky—stands forth confest—a God and one of the
 Immortals!"

THE HAUNTED MOUNTAIN.

"Shall we run into the cloudlet, love, so luminous and
 white,
That is crouching up in sunshine there on yonder lofty
 height.
We could step out of the splendour all at once into the
 mist,
Such a sunny snowy bower where a maiden might be
 kissed;
From the woody lower terrace we could climb the russet
 steep,
O'er that chasm gorged with tree-tops still in shadow
 —dewy-deep,
Where another slip of vapour, see! against the purple
 black,
Set on fire by the sunbeam which has caught it there
 alone,
Like a warrior-chief inciting his adherents to attack,
Has upreared itself upright with one imperious arm
 out-thrown!
Up that slope so smooth and ruddy we could clamber
 to the crags,
To the jutting rim of granite where the crouching
 cloudlet lags:
In and out the bright suffusion up above there in the
 skies,

I would follow my fleet darling by the flashing of her
　　eyes,
O'er that lofty level summit, as they vanish vapour-
　　veiled,
Or would glitter out rekindling and then glance away
　　to seek,
Like swift meteors seen a moment, for some other silver
　　streak,
Now bedimmed and now bedazzling, till each dodge
　　and double failed,
And I caught her—O would clasp her! such delicious
　　vengeance wreak—
On those eyes—the glad, the grand ones! on that
　　laughter-dimpled cheek,
Till with merciless caresses the fine damask flushed
　　and paled,
And, half quenched in burning kisses, those bewitching
　　lustres quailed!"

"Nay, but Rano, my adored one—O my heart and
　　soul's delight!
Scarce with all your love to lead me—fold me round
　　from all affright—
Would I dare ascend that mountain! Woody cleft and
　　fissure brown
Are so thick with evil spirits—it has such a dread
　　renown!
Such a hideous lizard monster in its gloomy shade it
　　screens,
That as rugged as the rocks are, winds along the close
　　ravines—
E'en asleep lies with them sinuous like a worm in
　　twisted shell—
And has eaten up more people in old days than I can
　　tell!

Would you go and wake that Taniwha! O, not at
 least to-day :
Look how lovely calm the Lake is!—'twill be sweeter
 far to stray
In the blue hot brilliant noontide to each secret shadowy
 bay,
And afloat on liquid crystal pass the happy time
 away!"

ALFRED DOMETT.

THE PINK TERRACES, N.Z.

I.

" *How beautiful! how wonderful! how strange!* "
Such words, less thought than mere emotion, well
Might Ranolf with abated breath, in tone
That wonder-stricken to a whisper fell,
For Amo's looks of triumph now exchange :
So fair a vision charmed our loiterers lone,
As at the closing of a sultry day,
In search of some good camping ground
They paddled up Mahána's Lake,
Where they a small canoe had found
(Which Amo settled they might take),
With little care half hid in sedge,
Flax-fastened to the water's edge—
Its owners clearly far away.
From the low sky line of the hilly range
Before them, sweeping down its dark-green face
Into the lake that slumbered at its base,
A mighty cataract—so it seemed—
Over a hundred steps of marble streamed

And gushed, or fell in dripping overflow ;
Flat steps, in flights half-circled—row o'er row,
Irregularly mingling side by side ;
They and the torrent-curtain wide,
All rosy-hued, it seemed, with sunsets glow.
But what is this !—no roar, no sound,
Disturbs that torrent's hush profound !
The wanderers near and nearer come,
Still is the mighty cataract dumb !
A thousand fairy lights may shimmer
With tender sheen, with glossy glimmer,
O'er curve advanced and salient edge
Of many a luminous water ledge ;
A thousand slanting shadows pale
May fling their thin transparent veil
O'er deep recess and shallow dent
In many a watery stair's descent ;
Yet mellow bright, or mildly dim
Both lights and shades—both dent and rim—
Each wavy streak—each warm snow tress—
Stand rigid, mute, and motionless !
No faintest murmur—not a sound—
Relieves that cataract's hush profound ;
No tiniest bubble, not a flake
Of floating foam is seen to break
The smoothness where it meets the lake ;
Along that shining surface move
No ripples ; not the slightest swell
Rolls o'er the mirror darkly green,
Where, every feature limned so well—
Pale, silent, and serene as death—
The cataract's image hangs beneath
The cataracts—but not more serene,
More phantom-silent than is seen
The white rose-hued reality above.

II.

They paddle past, for on the right,
Another cataract comes in sight,
Another, broader, grander flight
Of steps all stainless, snowy bright!
They land, their curious way they track,
Near thickets made by contrast black;
And then that wonder seems to be
A cataract carved in Parian stone,
Or any purer substance known—
Agate or milk-chalcedony.
Its showering snow cascades appear
Long ranges bright of stalactite,
And sparry frets and fringes white,
Thick-falling, plenteous, tier o'er tier;
Its crowding stairs in bold ascent,
Piled up that silvery glimmering height
Are layers, they know, accretions slow
Of hard silicious sediment.
For as they gain a rugged road,
And cautious climb the solid rime,
Each step becomes a terrace broad—
Each terrace a wide basin brimmed
With water, brilliant yet in hue
The tenderest delicate harebell-blue
Deepening to violet!

     Slowly climb
The twain, and turn from time to time
To mark the hundred paths in view—
Crystalline azure, snowy rimmed—
The marge of every beauteous pond,
Curve after curve—each lower beyond

The higher—outsweeping white and wide,
Like snowy lines of foam that glide
O'er level sea-sands lightly skimmed
By thin sheets of the glistening tide.
They climb those milk-white flats incrusted
And netted o'er with wavy ropes
Of wrinkled silica.   At last—
Each basin's heat increasing fast—
The topmost step the pair surmount,
And lo, the cause of all!   Around,
Half-circling cliffs a crater bound;
Cliffs damp with dark green moss—their slopes
All crimson stained with blots and streaks—
White-mottled and vermilion—rusted.
And in the midst, beneath a cloud
That ever upward rolls and reeks
And hides the sky with its dim shroud,
Look where upshoots a fuming fount—
Up through a blue and boiling pool
Perennial—a great sapphire streaming,
In that coralline crater gleaming.
Upwelling ever, amethystal,
Ebullient comes the bubbling crystal
Still growing cooler and more cool
As down the porcelain stairway slips
The fluid flint, and slowly drips,
And hangs each basin's curling lips
With crusted fringe, each year increases,
Thicker than shear-forgotten fleeces;
More close and regular than rows,
Long rows of snowy trumpet-flowers
Some day to hang in garden-bowers,
When strangers shall these wilds enclose.

III.

But see! in all that lively spread
Of blue and white and vermeil red,
How, dark with growths of greenest gloss
Just at the ledge of that first ledge,
Calcareous string to cliff-formed bow
(O'er which the hot pool trickles slow)
A little rocky islet peeps
Into the crater-caldron's deeps.
Along the ledge they lightly cross,
And from its midway islet gaze
O'er all the scene, and every phase
The current takes as down it strays.
They note where'er, by step or stair,
By brimming bath, on hollow reef,
Or hoary plain, its magic rain
Can reach a branch, a flower, a leaf.
The branching spray, leaf, blossom gay
Are blanched and stiffened into stone!
So round about lurks tracery strewn
Of daintiest moulded porcelain ware,
Or coral wreaths and clusters rare,
A white flint foliage rather say
Such fairy work as frost alone
Were equal to, could it o'erlay
With tender crust of crystals fair,
Fine spikes so delicately piled—
Not wintry trees leaf-stripped and bare,
But summer's vegetation rich and wild,

CHRISTMAS GUESTS.

"The loneliest night of all the lonely year!"
　　The sick man murmured with a weary moan;
"And I shall spend, without a creature near,
　　Another dreary Christmas-tide alone!"

A wooden shanty, common, rough, and bare,
　　Rude shelter offered to a suff'ring man;
Its door flung open to the warm night air,
　　Courting, in vain, a breeze his cheek to fan.

A man well on in years; deep-lined and grey
　　His brow, and those scant locks which o'er it hung;
One who had lost, he had been heard to say,
　　All that he lived for while he still was young.

A world-worn wand'rer on the face of earth,
　　Whom Death and Sorrow, in an evil time,
Had driven from the country of his birth
　　To lonely labour in an Austral clime.

Where, toiling without heart, to keep alive
　　A life he did not cherish, he had failed,
As hopeless toilers fail 'mid those who strive;
　　For sorry life alone his gains availed.

Half-dressed, and flung upon his restless bed,
　　He, burning-eyed, gazed out upon the night—
Gazed from the glowing darkness overhead
　　To where the distant township's lamps shone bright.

"Full many kindly souls," he muttered low,
　"Feasting and laughing on this Christmas Eve,
Did they my dire extremity but know
　Would gladly seek my suff'rings to relieve.

"And who am I, to wrap me in my pride,
　Scorning to ask what would be freely given?
Yet, no! I *cannot* beg!" he feebly cried,
　"Help, to be help for me, must come from Heav'n!"

E'en as he spoke, high in the vast dark blue,
　A meteor, loosened from its viewless ties,
Across the star-flow'red fields of ether flew,
　Like some grand, fired-winged bird of paradise.

Its trailing lustre shed a transient gleam
　Upon two figures at the open door,
Whose faces brightened with a tender beam
　The lonely hut that was so dim before.

A woman and a child! Was he distraught,
　That neither fear nor wonder held him bound
To welcome beings who, his reason taught,
　Had slept for twenty years in English ground?

Why should he fear them. Were they not his own—
　The wife, the child—with whom his heart had died?
What wonder if, when he was sick and lone,
　They left their Heaven for service at his side?

Hand clasped in hand, they crossed his threshold now,
　Smiling upon their loved one as they came;
They spoke no word, but kissed his pain-dewed brow,
　And coolness fell upon his fevered frame.

How 'twas he knew not—but within a space
   That seemed no longer than a moment's flight—
A happy change had come upon the place,
   And all around him streamed a soft, clear light.

The child was hanging garlands ev'rywhere,
   Familiar wreaths of holly's glossy green,
Of laurel and of bay; while here and there
   Gleamed marv'llous unknown blooms of snowy sheen.

The mother spread the table for a feast,
   As though resuming old sweet household care;
And he, in whom all sense of pain had ceas'd,
   Was gently led this wondrous meal to share.

What was his fare, that Eve of Christmas morn?
   He cannot tell us, and he only could;
But, if 'twere not a dream of weakness born,
   He, for the first time, tasted angels' food!

Then, smiling still, they held his feeble hands,
   And sweetly raised that old, old hymn of praise,
That echoes on through widest-sundered lands,
   In Christian hearts all earthly Christmas days,

"Come, all ye faithful!" Were they calling him?
   Bidding him seek a heavenly Bethlehem?
He smiled in answer as his eyes grew dim,
   And strove to rise that he might follow them.

"Joyful and triumphant!" Ah! such harmonies
   Thrilled through the humble hut, as human ear,
Unhelp'd by angel-teachers from the skies,
   Has never heard, may never hope to hear.

Grandly it rose and swelled, that Christmas song!
   Surely all choirs of Heaven joined the strain—
That mighty stream of praise that bore along
   Upon its flood a being freed from pain!
     .   .   .   .

When his next neighbours, on the Christmas Day,
   Some friendly impulse to his shanty led,
Calm, placid, still, upon his bed he lay,
   A smile was on his face——and he was dead!
              LINDSAY DUNCAN (Mrs T. C. Cloud).

FROM MIDAS.

THEN are there Gods indeed?
Or was it a fantastic creed
Dreamed of our doting fathers long ago,—
Which peopled the blue space
With an immortal race,
Who mixed their thoughts with things below
And recked of human weal and human woe?
Was it a poet's dream
That power and will supreme
Possess the thrones above?
That infinite wisdom, strength, and love
Fulfil themselves in days and years
And motions of the spheres?
That from the central core
To the uttermost outward rim
Of this round sea without a shore,
Which men with senses weak and dim
Pretentiously explore,
   And through disastrous ages puzzle o'er,

This multiform mysterious shell
And curtain of material seeming
Which nature, like a conscious maiden innocently teeming
With many a thought she loathes yet longs to tell,
Before her secret wonders coyly holds,
And save to those who love her well
Or win her by transcendent dreaming,
Or painful study of her laws,
Never unfolds,
Or loosely lifts, or amorously withdraws—
That through creation's cosmic course,
Through first effect and final cause,
Through fashioning Will and plastic Force,
Through molecules made warm
With harmony of growth and form,
When pulse of mystic motion first
The shell of Chaos burst,
Through germs of birth and breath,
Through life and death,
One universal soul
Informs and fills the whole—
That still through water, earth, and air
God lives and flows, and Heaven is everywhere?
If such a Heaven there be,
If earth and air and sea,
If all around, beneath us, and above,
Thrill with the eternal pulse of Love;
If universal life,
With Godhead, and with Gods be rife,
Why mock they man's persistent prayer,
Why groan and fret we thus for ever and in vain,
Why find our woes no echo there,
And our tremendous pain
Awaken but indifference and disdain?

The race of beasts I reckon blest:
Their dream of life, though passing brief,
The labour and alternate rest
Is yet their own for joy or grief;
Their own, and naught beyond, they know;
They revel in the right possessed;
They taste the pleasures undepressed
By shadows of impending woe;
No spirit shocks their tranquil moods molest,
Nor phantom fears infest,
Nor spectral memories haunt their happy hours
Amid the ephemeral flowers
That on their pathway grow;
No black foreboding rears its serpent crest;
Unconscious to their goal they go.
What ills they suffer in their meek estate,
Exhaust the rage of fate.
The torture swift or slow,
The burden and the blow,
The heat, the cold, the hunger, and the thirst—
These ills are in their suffering all,
And suffered, then have done their worst.
But whether great or small,
They bring no rankling sore,
They leave no sting behind,
They cast no shade before.
Man, man alone, whose conscious mind
The eternal doubt devours,
With all his boasted knowledge blind,
The creature of contrarious powers,
Ever from his birth oppressed
By the accumulating hours,
With the inherited unrest,
Like a baleful shadow cast
From the dimness of the past,

Which above the future towers,
Breathing on the life to come
Presages of poison-bloom,
And for ages yet unfurled
Fatally foredooms the world,
And through each succeeding morrow
Piles up sorrow upon sorrow.
We dig, we delve, we crush, we tear,
We ransack ocean, earth, and air—
All forms of ill, all shapes of suffering brave,
To build fresh heaps for those who have
Already in excess, yet dare
Still more to covet, more to crave,
Wherewith to swell the unearned superfluous share,
Who have not borne what we must bear,
Nor owned their wealth by toil, and misery and despair.

For them, not for ourselves we toil.
Like forked fires that desolate the plain,
Their tyrant tongues lick up spoil
We gather with our sweat and labour's bloody pain.
For them we strive, for them we pine,
For them from forest, field, and mine,
We wring the golden grain.
For them, with life and strength accursed,
Through heat and cold, through drought and rain,
Through hunger and through thirst,
We perish piecemeal to sustain
Their lives which out of ours like parasites are nursed.
To give them strength we drain
And empty heart and brain;
We bleed to give them blood
From every quivering vein;
Our very flesh unnatural food,

A horrid hunger draws
To their insatiate jaws.
And this, even this, we seem to give,
Whereby the old saying is made good,
However little understood,
The many perish that the few may thrive,
And thus from age to age the labourer's lot,
While all around him changes, changes not;
And griefs that were the burden of old chimes,
The pangs our fathers felt, the wrongs they bore,
   Like an eternal sore,
Eat fostering to the heart of our familiar times.

WILLIAM FORSTER.

THE WIND AND THE SHE-OAK TREE

O, WOULD that I could translate
Each untranslateable tone
Of the wind in the she-oak's leaves,
   As it maketh its plaintive moan.

Nor only moan doth it make;
It knoweth the subtlest speech
To waft the attuned soul afar
   'Yond mortal things and their reach.

And, oh mournful and dark-hued tree,
With thy myriad pendant leaves,
That like slender reeds make the strings
   For those airs that the wind-soul weaves.

THE WIND IN THE SHE-OAK TREE.

   Thou fittest of instruments art
For the pathos that lies in the strain!
For knowest thou not all that mystery dark
   Whose haunts are the bush and the plain?

   And wind stealing over the grass,
With a sound like soft rustling of sheaves,
Brought ye not sighs, from the dying lips
   Of some traveller lost, to these leaves.

   For see, as your fingers touch,
Tho' e'er so lightly the strings,
There ariseth the look of the burning day,
   And the sound of the whirr of wings.

   The steep range stands in the blaze
Of the noon; and the dry creek-bed
Is panting and white 'neath the pitiless sky;
   The birds are awatch for the dead.

   And this dying note is the hush
Of the night's swift fall—of the awe
Of the man's spent soul as he sinks to the grass,
   Whence he knows he shall rise no more.

   And this other sound like a sob,
Fell perchance on the ear of the night,
While the speechless stars looked down
   On the solemn and woeful sight.

   Wild longings and memories fond,
And anon most passionate pain,
The calm of despair and the sense of the dark,
   All mingle and speak in the strain.

For the loving, a world away,
Who watch for the wanderer's face,
Thro' the mystic thrill of the spirit bond
Are troubled in soul in their place.

For nature doth speak thro' the air,
Thro' the flowers, the fields, and the sea,
And Her wind is composer and player both
In the leaves of the she-oak tree.

FRANCES TYRRELL GILL.

BENEATH THE WATTLE BOUGHS.

THE wattles were sweet with September's rain,
He drank in their breath and the breath of the spring,
" Our pulses are strong with the tide of life,"
I said, " and one year is so swift a thing ! "

The land all around was yellow with bloom ;
The birds in the branches sang joyous and shrill ;
The blue range rose 'gainst the blue of the sky ;
Yet she sighed, " But death may be stronger still ! "

Then I reached and gathered a blossomy bough,
And divided its clustering sprays in twain,
" As a token for each " (I closed one in her hand)
" Till we come to the end of the year again ! "

Then the years sped on, strung high with life ;
And laughter and gold were the gifts they gave,
Till I chanced one day on some pale dead flowers,
And spake, shaking and white, "One more gift I crave."
" Nay," a shadow voice in the air replied,
" 'Neath the blossoming wattles you'll find a grave ! "

FRANCES TYRRELL GILL.

LOVE'S LOYALTY.

DAY.

With the magpie for the nightingale,
  The wattle for the beech,
And for the woodland warbler's notes
  The wild bush-parrot's screech—

With unknown range and gorge to scan,
  Unbounded land to roam,
And for the changeful English seas,
  The long Australian foam!

For afternoons of dreaming fond,
  In old leaf-hidden lanes,
Is the long sure stride of my swift-limbed horse
  Across the short-grassed plains.

I drink the golden morning air,
  And, as the returnèd tide
Of full life bounds along my veins,
  I crave for naught beside!

I hear the loud creek plunging down,
  The slope just freshed with flood—
Its wild song keeps triumphant time
  With the rapture of my blood.

"This sense of new untrammeled life,
  This sense," I cry, "of space,
Hath cured me of the fever wrought
  By one enchanting face!"

LOVE'S LOYALTY.

NIGHT.

Now evening falls upon the land,
   The magpie's parting strain
Dies out along the ti-tree marge;
   My tired horse crops the plain.

Half dreamily the faint blue line,
   That marks the farthest range,
Takes in the hill's familiar form
   That rose behind the grange.

The English scents steal in the air;
   A rush of liquid notes
Fills all the leafy copse—poured forth
   Unnumbered feathered throats.

Those lovely hazel eyes again!
   With their old haunting look—
That lithe light form—one dainty foot,
   Drawn backward from the brook!

The raging pain swirls thro' my soul;
   In fierce resolve and dire,
I shake me from the glamour free
   Beside the red camp fire.

My comrade's laughter fills the hours,
   Night claims her toll of sleep,
The large soft southern stars gaze on,
   The hush is close and deep.

From dreams I wake to find my soul
   A captive to the past.
Tho' all the seas are wide between,
   My freedom could not last!

Oh love! Love-loyal I remain!
  For tho' some spirit bar
Constrained thy soul, thy face for aye
  Lives on—my guiding star!

FRANCES TYRRELL GILL.

WHILE THE BILLY BOILS.

WHILE the ruby coals in the dull grey dust
  Shine bright as the daylight dies;
When into our mouths our pipes are thrust,
  And we watch the moon arise;
While the leaves, that crackle and hiss and sigh,
  Feed the flames with their scented oils,
In a calm content by the fire we lie,
  And watch while the billy boils.

A desire for rest, a wash in the creek,
  And a seasoned bit of clay,
With a chum who knoweth the time to speak,
  And who singeth a jovial lay,
Though our pants are moles and apparently made
  With the aid of a tomahawk,
Though we are not in fashion's garb arrayed,
  We can revel in tea and talk.

Old Toucher, look up at those gum trees old—
  They're not lovely, but will be soon;
They are ugly enough in the sunlight bold,
  But look well by the silver moon.
The light in which life is viewed on earth
  Makes it better or greatly worse;
And hardship is often but food for mirth,
  And trial a boon or curse.

Just now the sun in its glory sank
  At the back of the slow creek's fringe,
On a sapphire, ruby, and crimson bank—
  Even now there is left a tinge—
Just a tinge to soften the sombre hue,
  'Till the banners of night unfurl,
'Till the flowers shall be drenched with silver dew,
  And the moon mount the path of pearl.

They can't bottle the sunset up, old boy,
  And cart it away to town—
Yes, even their gold has some alloy—
  It won't buy the desert's crown.
Though the rich lie soft, yet we sleep well
  On our bed of the fragrant leaves ;
And we're better than those who in mansions dwell
  In this—that we fear no thieves.

We have no turtle in grand tureens,
  But, with hunger to serve as sauce,
We can relish the bacon and wholesome beans,
  The damper and salted horse.
One thing we have which is always good—
  Which poverty can't destroy—
Though our meals be made of the coarsest food,
  Through hunger we still enjoy.

Some look on our lives as wasted, true,
  And our views are the same as theirs—
At present we've scarcely enough to do,
  They are worried with business cares.
We have elegant leisure and time for thought—
  Had we something to think about—
They have lots of wealth, and business fraught
  With a constant care and doubt.

THE SICK STOCK-RIDER.

Not all the good things are reserved for one
 In this wonderful world of ours—
We each have our share of the shade and sun—
 We must take the thorns with the flow'rs;
To make the best of the hardest fate,
 Is a maxim that cannot be wrong;
So, Fred, as for tea we have not to wait—
 Suppose you attempt a song?
                          KEIGHLEY GOODCHILD.

THE SICK STOCK-RIDER.

Hold hard, Ned! Lift me down once more, and lay
  me in the shade.
Old man, you've had your work cut out to guide
Both horses, and to hold me in the saddle when I
  swayed,
  All through the hot, slow, sleepy, silent ride.
The dawn at "Moorabinda" was a mist rack dull and
  dense,
  The sun-rise was a sullen, sluggish lamp;
I was dozing in the gateway at Arbuthnot's bound'ry
  fence,
  I was dreaming on the Limestone cattle camp.
We crossed the creek at Carricksford, and sharply
  through the haze,
  And suddenly the sun shot flaming forth;
To southward lay "Katâwa," with the sand peaks all
  ablaze,
  And the flushed fields of Glen Lomond lay to north.
Now westward winds the bridle-path that leads to
  Landisfarm,
  And yonder looms the double-headed Bluff;

From the far side of the first hill when the skies are
    clear and calm,
  You can see Sylvester's woolshed fair enough.
Five miles we used to call it from our homestead to
    the place
  Where the big tree spans the roadway like an arch ;
'Twas here we ran the dingo down that gave us such
    a chase
  Eight years ago—or was it nine ?—last March.
'Twas merry in the glowing morn among the gleaming
    grass,
  To wander as we've wandered many a mile,
And blow the cool tobacco cloud, and watch the white
    wreaths pass,
  Sitting loosely in the saddle all the while.
'Twas merry 'mid the blackwoods, when we spied the
    station roofs
  To wheel the wild scrub cattle at the yard,
With a running fire of stock whips and a fiery run of
    hoofs ;
  Oh ! the hardest day was never then too hard !

Aye ! we had a glorious gallop after " Starlight " and
    his gang,
  When they bolted from Sylvester's on the flat ;
How the sun-dried reed-beds crackled, how the flint-
    strewn ranges rang,
  To the strokes of " Mountaineer " and " Acrobat,"
Hard behind them in the timber, harder still across
    the heath,
  Close beside them through the tea-tree scrub we
    dash'd ;
And the golden-tinted fern leaves, how they rustled
    underneath :
  And the honey-suckle osiers, how they crash'd.

We led the hunt throughout, Ned, on the chestnut
    and the grey,
  And the troopers were three hundred yards behind,
While we emptied our six-shooters on the bush-rangers
    at bay,
  In the creek with stunted box-trees for a blind !
There you grappled with the leader, man to man, and
    horse to horse,
  And you roll'd together when the chestnut rear'd.
He blazed away and missed you in that shallow water-
    course—
  A narrow shave—his powder singed your beard !

In these hours when life is ebbing, how those days
    when life was young
  Come back to us ; how clearly I recall
Even the yarns Jack Hall invented, and the songs
    Jem Roper sung ;
  And where are now Jem Roper and Jack Hall?

Aye ! nearly all our comrades of the old colonial school,
  Our ancient boon companions, Ned, are gone ;
Hard livers for the most part, somewhat reckless as a
    rule,
  It seems that you and I are left alone.

There was Hughes, who got in trouble through that
    business with the cards,
  It matters little what became of him ;
But a steer ripp'd up Macpherson in the Cooramenta
    yards,
  And Sullivan was drown'd at Sink-or-swim ;
And Mostyn—poor Frank Mostyn—died at last, a fear-
    ful wreck,
  In the "horrors" at the Upper Wandinong,

And Carisbrooke, the rider, at the Horsefall broke his neck
Faith! the wonder was he saved his neck so long!
Ah! those days and nights we squandered at the Logans' in the glen—
The Logans, man and wife, have long been dead.
Elsie's tallest girl seems taller than your little Elsie then;
And Ethel is a woman grown and wed.

I've had my share of pastime, and I've done my share of toil,
And life is short—the longest life a span;
I care not now to tarry for the corn or for the oil,
Or for wine that maketh glad the heart of man.
For good undone, and gifts misspent, and resolutions vain,
'Tis somewhat late to trouble. This I know—
I should live the same life over, if I had to live again;
And the chances are I go where most men go.

The deep blue skies wax dusky, and the tall green trees grow dim,
The sward beneath me seems to heave and fall;
And sickly, smoky shadows through the sleepy sunlight swim,
And on the very sun's face weave their pall.
Let me slumber in the hollow where the wattle blossoms wave,
With never stone or rail to fence my bed;
Should the sturdy station children pull the bush-flowers on my grave,
I may chance to hear them romping overhead.

ADAM LINDSEY GORDON.

AN EXILE'S FAREWELL.

I.

The ocean heaves around us still
  With long and measured swell,
The autumn gales our canvas fill,
  Our ship rides smooth and well.
The broad Atlantic's bed of foam
  Still breaks against our prow;
I shed no tears at quitting home
  Nor will I shed them now.

II.

Against the bulwarks on the poop
  I lean, and watch the sun
Behind the red horizon stoop—
  His race is nearly run.
Those waves will never quench his light,
  O'er which they seem to close;
To-morrow he will rise as bright
  As he this morning rose.

III.

How brightly gleams the orb of day
  Across the trackless sea!
How lightly dance the waves that play
  Like dolphins in our lee.
The restless waters seem to say,
  In smothered tones to me,
How many thousand miles away
  My native land must be.

IV.

Speak, ocean! is my home the same,
  Now all is new to me?
The tropic sky's resplendent flame,
  The vast expanse of sea?
Does all around her, yet unchanged,
  The well-known aspect wear?
Oh! can the leagues that I have ranged,
  Have made no difference there?

V.

How vivid Recollection's hand
  Recalls the scene once more!
I see the same tall poplars stand
  Beside the garden door;
I see the bird-cage hanging still,
  And where my sister set
The flowers in the window-sill—
  Can they be living yet?

VI.

Let woman's nature cherish grief,
  I rarely heave a sigh,
Before emotion takes relief
  In listless apathy.
While from my pipe the vapours curl
  Towards the evening sky,
And 'neath my feet the billows whirl,
  In dull monotony!

VII.

The sky still wears the crimson streak
  Of Sol's departing ray.
Some briny drops are on my cheek,
  'Tis but the salt sea spray!

Then let our bark the ocean roam,
  Our keel the billows plough,
I shed no tears at quitting home,
  Nor will I shed them now!
                    L. G. (Adam Lindsey Gordon.)
Ship "Julia," Sept. 1853.

ADAM LINDSEY GORDON.
HENRY HALLORAN.
R. H. HORNE.
  Vide Introduction.

THE CLOUD.

ONE summer morn, out of the sea-waves wild,
A speck-like Cloud, the season's fated child,
Came slowly floating up the boundless sky,
And o'er the sun-parched hills all brown and dry.

Onward she glided through the azure air,
Borne by its motion without toil or care,
When looking down in her ethereal joy,
She marked earth's moilers at their hard employ;

"And oh!" she said, "that by some act of grace
'Twere mine to succour yon fierce-toiling race,
To give the hungry meat, the thirsty drink—
The thought of good is very sweet to think."

The day advanced, and the cloud greater grew,
And greater likewise her desire to do

Some charity to men had more and more,
As the long sultry summer day on wore,
Greatened and warmed within her fleecy breast,
Like a dove fledging in its downy nest.

The heat waxed fiercer, until all the land
Glared in the sun as 'twere a monstrous brand;
And the shrunk rivers, few and far between,
Like molten metal lightened in the scene.
Ill could Earth's sons endure their toilsome state,
Though still they laboured, for their need was great,
And many a long beseeching look they sped
Towards that fair cloud, with many a sigh that said—
" We famish for thy bounty ! For our sake
O break thou ! in a showery blessing, break !"

" I feel, and fain would help you," said the cloud,
And towards the earth her bounteous being bowed;
But then remem'bring a tradition she
Had in her youth learned from her native sea,
That when a cloud adventures from the skies
Too near the altar of the hills, it dies,
Awhile she wavered and was blown about
Hither and thither by the winds of doubt;
But in the midst of heaven at length all still
She stood; then suddenly, with a keen thrill
Of light, she said within herself, " I will !
Yea, in the glad strength of devotion, I
Will help you though in helping you I die."

Filled with this thought's divinity, the cloud
Grew world-like vast as earthward more she bowed.
Oh, never erewhile had she dreamed her state
So great might be, beneficently great !

THE CLOUD.

O'er the parched fields in her angelic love
She spread her wide wings like a brooding dove:
Till as her purpose deepened, drawing near,
Divinely awful did her front appear,
And men and beasts all trembled at the view,
And the woods bowed, though well all creatures knew
That near in her, to every kind the same,
A great predestined benefactress came.

And then wide-flashed throughout her full-grown form
The glory of her will! the pain and storm
Of life's dire dread of death whose mortal threat
From Christ Himself drew agonising sweat,
Flashed seething out of rents amid her heaps
Of lowering gloom, and thence with arrowy leaps
Hissed jagging downward, till a sheety glare
Illumined all the illimitable air ;
The thunder followed, a tremendous sound,
Loud doubling and reverberating round ;
Strong was her will, but stronger yet the power
Of love that now dissolved her in a shower
Dropping in blessings to enrich the earth
With health and plenty at one blooming birth.

Far as the rain extended o'er the land,
A splendid bow the freshened landscape spanned,
Like a celestial arc, hung in the air
By angel artists, to illumine there
The parting triumph of that spirit fair :
The rainbow vanished, but the blessing craved
Rested upon the land the cloud had saved.

CHARLES HARPER.

THE CREEK OF THE FOUR GRAVES.

A SETTLER in the olden times went forth
With four of his most bold and trusted men
Into the wilderness—went forth to seek
New streams and wider pastures for his fast
Increasing flocks and herds.   O'er mountain routes,
And over wild wolds clouded up with brush,
And cut with marshes perilously deep,—
So went they forth at dawn; at eve the sun,
That rose behind them as they journeyed out,
Was firing with his nether rim a range
Of unknown mountains, that like ramparts towered
Full in their front; and his last glances fell
Into the gloomy forest's eastern glades
In golden gleams, like to the angel's sword,
And flashed upon the windings of a creek
That noiseless ran betwixt the pioneers
And those new Apennines—ran, shaded o'er
With boughs of the wild willow, hanging mixed
From either bank, or duskily befringed
With upward tapering feathery swamp-oaks,
The sylvan eyelash always of remote
Australian waters, whether gleaming still
In lake or pool, or bickering along
Between the marges of some eager stream.

Before them, thus extended, wilder grew
The scene each moment and more beautiful;
For when the sun was all but sunk below
Those barrier mountains, in the breeze that o'er
Their rough enormous backs deep-fleeced with wood
Came whispering down, the wide up-slanting sea
Of fanning leaves in the descending rays
Danced dazzlingly, tingling as if the trees

Thrilled to the roots for very happiness.
But when the sun had wholly disappeared
Behind those mountains—O, what words, what hues,
Might paint the wild magnificence of view
That opened westward! Out extending, lo!
The heights rose crowding, with their summits all
Dissolving as it seemed, and partly lost
In the exceeding radiancy aloft;
And thus transfigured, for awhile they stood
Like a great company of archaeons, crowned
With burning diadems, and tented o'er
With canopies of purple and of gold.

Here halting wearied now the sun was set,
Our travellers kindled for their first night's camp
A brisk and crackling fire, which seemed to them
A wilder creature than 'twas elsewhere wont,
Because of the surrounding savageness.
And as they supped, birds of new shape and plume
And wild strange voice came by; and up the steep
Between the climbing forest growths they saw,
Perched on the bare abutments of the hills,
Where haply yet some lingering gleam fell through,
The wallaroo look forth. Eastward at last
The glow was wasted into formless gloom,
Night's front; then westward the high massing woods
Steeped in a swart but mellow Indian hue,
A deep dusk loveliness, lay ridged and heaped,
Only the more distinctly for their shade,
Against the twilight heaven—a cloudless depth,
Yet luminous with sunset's fading glow;
And thus awhile in the lit dusk they seemed
To hang like mighty pictures of themselves
In the still chambers of some vaster world.
At last, the business of the supper done,

The echoes of the solitary place
Came as in sylvan wonder wide about
To hear and imitate the voices strange,
Within the pleasant purlieus of the fire
Lifted in glee, but to be hushed ere long,
As with the darkness of the night there came
O'er the adventurers, each and all, some sense
Of danger lurking in its forest lairs.

But, nerved by habit, they all gathered round
About the well-built fire, whose nimble tongues
Sent up continually a strenuous roar
Of fierce delight, and from their fuming pipes
Drawing rude comfort, round the pleasant light
With grave discourse they planned the next day's deeds.
Wearied at length, their couches they prepared
Of rushes, and the long green tresses pulled
From the bent boughs of the wild willows near;
Then the four men stretched out their tired limbs
Under the dark arms of the forest trees
That mixed aloft, high in the starry air,
In arcs and leafy domes whose crossing curves,
Blended with denser intergrowth of sprays,
Were seen in mass traced out against the clear
Wide gaze of heaven; and trustful of the watch
Kept near them by their master, soon they slept,
Forgetful of the perilous wilderness
That lay around them like a spectral world;
And all things slept; the circling forest trees,
Their foremost boles carved from a crowded mass,
Less visible by the watch-fire's bladed gleams
That ran far out in the umbrageous dark
Beyond the broad red ring of constant light;
And even the shaded mountains darkly seen,
Their bluff brows looming through the stirless air,

Looked in their stillness solemnly asleep;
Yea, thence surveyed—the universe might have seemed
Coiled in vast rest; only that one dark cloud,
Diffused and shapen like a spider huge,
Crept as with crawling legs along the sky,
And that the stars in their bright orders, still
Cluster by cluster glowingly revealed,
As this slow cloud moved on, high over all,
Peaceful and wakeful, watched the world below.

Part II.

Meanwhile the cloudless eastern heaven had grown
More luminous, and now the moon arose
Above the hill, when lo! that giant cone
Erewhile so dark, seemed inwardly aglow
With her instilled irradiance, while the trees
That fringed its outline, their huge statures dwarfed
By distance into brambles, and yet all
Clearly defined against her ample orb,
Out of its very disc appeared to swell
In shadowy relief, as they had been
All sculptured from its surface as she rose.
Then her full light in silvery sequence still
Cascading forth from ridgy slope to slope,
Chased mass by mass the broken darkness down
Into the dense-brushed valleys, where it crouched,
And shrank, and struggled, like a dragon-doubt
Glooming a lonely spirit.

     His lone watch
The master kept, and wakeful looked abroad
On all the solemn beauty of the world;
And by some sweet and subtle tie that joins
The loved and cherished, absent from our side,

With all that is serene and beautiful
In nature, thoughts of home began to steal
Into his musings—when, on a sudden, hark!
A bough cracks loudly in a neighbouring brake!
Against the shade-side of a bending gum.
With a strange horror gathering to his heart,
As if his blood were charged with insect life
And writhed along in clots, he stilled himself
And listened heedfully, till his held breath
Became a pang. Nought heard he: silence there
Had recomposed her ruffled wings, and now
Deep brooded in the darkness; so that he
Again mused on, quiet and reassured.
But there again—crack upon crack! Awake!
O heaven! have hell's worst fiends burst howling up
Into the death-doomed world? Or whence, if not
From diabolic rage could surge a yell
So horrible as that which now affrights
The shuddering dark! Beings as fell are near!
Yea, beings in their dread inherited hate
Awful, vengeful as hell's worst fiends, are come
In vengeance! For behold from the long grass
And nearer brakes arise the bounding forms
Of painted savages, full in the light
Thrown outward by the fire, that roused and lapped
The rounding darkness with its ruddy tongues
More fiercely than before, as though even it
Had felt the sudden shock the air received
From those terrific cries.

      On then they came
And rushed upon the sleepers, three of whom
But started, and then weltered prone beneath
The first fell blow dealt down on each by three
Of the most stalwart of their pitiless foes;

But one again, and yet again, rose up,
Rose to his knees, under the crushing strokes
Of huge clubbed nulla-nullas, till his own
Warm blood was blinding him. For he was one
Who had with misery nearly all his days
Lived lonely, and who therefore in his soul
Did hunger after hope, and thirst for what
Hope still had promised him, some taste at least
Of human good however long deferred ;
And now he could not, even in dying, loose
His hold on life's poor chances still to come,
Could not but so dispute the terrible fact
Of death, e'en in death's presence. Strange it is,
Yet oft 'tis seen, that fortune's pampered child
Consents to death's untimely power with less
Reluctance, less despair, than does the wretch
Who hath been ever blown about the world,
The straw-like sport of fate's most bitter blasts ;
So though the shadows of untimely death,
Inevitably under every stroke
But thickened more and more, against them still
The poor wretch struggled, nor would cease until
One last great blow, dealt down upon his head
As if in mercy, gave him to the dust,
With all his many woes and frustrate hopes.

The master, chilled with horror, saw it all ;
From instinct more than conscious thought he raised
His death-charged tube, and at that murderous crew
Firing, saw one fall ox-like to the earth,
Then turned and fled. Fast fled he, but as fast
His deadly foes went thronging on his track.
Fast! for in full pursuit behind him yelled
Men whose wild speech no word for mercy hath !
And as he fled the forest beasts as well

In general terror through the brakes ahead
Crashed scattering, or with maddening speed athwart
His course came frequent. On, still on, he flies;
Flies for dear life, and still behind him hears,
Nearer and nearer, the light rapid dig
Of many feet, nearer and nearer still.

Part III.

So went the chase. Now at a sudden turn
Before him lay the steep-banked mountain creek;
Still on he kept perforce, and from a rock
That beaked the bank, a promontory bare,
Plunging right forth and shooting feet-first down,
Sunk to his middle in the flashing stream,
In which the imaged stars seemed all at once
To burst like rockets into one wide blaze.
Then wading through the ruffled waters, forth
He sprang, and seized a snake-like root that from
The opponent bank protruded, clenching there
His cold hand like a clamp of steel; and thence
He swung his dripping form aloft, the blind
And breathless haste of one who flies for life,
Urging him on; up the dark ledge he climbed,
When in his face—O verily our God
Hath those in His peculiar care, for whom
The daily prayers of spotless womanhood
And helpless infancy are offered up!—
There in its face a cavity he felt,
The upper earth of which in one rude mass
Was held fast bound by the enwoven roots
Of two old trees, and which, beneath the mound,
Over the dark and clammy cave below,
Twisted like knotted snakes. 'Neath these he crept,
Just as the dark forms of his hunters thronged

The steep bold rock whence he before had plunged.
Duskily visible beneath the moon
They paused a space, to mark what bent his course
Might take beyond the stream. But now no form
Amongst the moveless fringe of fern was seen
To shoot up from its outline, 'mid the boles
And mixing shadows of the taller trees,
All standing now in the keen radiance there
So ghostly still as in a solemn trance;
But nothing in the silent prospect stirred;
Therefore they augured that their prey was yet
Within the nearer distance, and they all
Plunged forward till the fretted current boiled
Amongst their crowding forms from bank to bank;
And searching thus the stream across, and then
Along the ledges, combing down each clump
Of long flagged swamp grass where it flourished high,
The whole dark line passed slowly, man by man,
Athwart the cave!

     Keen was their search but vain;
There grouped in dark knots standing in the stream
That glimmered past them moaning as it went,
They marvelled; passing strange to them it seemed;
Some old mysterious fable of their race,
That brooded o'er the valley and the creek,
Returned upon their minds, and fear-struck all
And silent, they withdrew. And when the sound
Of their retreating steps had died away,
As back they hurried to despoil the dead
In the stormed camp, then rose the fugitive,
Renewed his flight, nor rested from it, till
He gained the shelter of his longed-for home.
And in that glade, far in the doomful wild,

In sorrowing record of an awful hour
Of human agony and loss extreme,
Untimely spousals with a desert death,
Four grassy mounds are there beside the creek,
Bestrewn with sprays and leaves from the old trees
Which moan the ancient dirges that have caught
The heed of dying ages, and for long
The traveller passing then in safety there
Would call the place—The Creek of the Four Graves.

CHARLES HARPER.

A STORM ON THE MOUNTAINS.

A LONELY boy, far venturing from home
Out on the half-wild herd's faint tracks I roam ;
'Mid rock-browed mountains, which with stony frown
Glare into haggard chasms deep adown ;
A rude and craggy world, the prospect lies
Bounded in circuit by the bending skies.
Now at some clear pool scooped out by the shocks
Of rain-floods plunging from the upper rocks
Whose liquid disc in its undimpled rest
Glows like a mighty gem brooching the mountain's breast,
I drink and muse, or mark the wide-spread herd,
Or list the tinkling of the dingle-bird ;
And now towards some wild-hanging shade I stray,
To shun the bright oppression of the day ;
For round each crag, and o'er each bosky swell,
The fierce refracted heat flares visible,
Lambently restless, like the dazzling hem
Of some else viewless veil held trembling over them.

Why congregate the swallows in the air,
And northward them in rapid flight repair?
With sudden swelling din, remote but harsh,
Why roar the bull-frogs in the tea-tree marsh?
Why cease the locusts to throng up in flight
And clap their gay wings in the fervent light?

Why climb they, bodingly demure, instead
The tallest spear-grass to the bending head?
Instinctively, along the sultry sky,
I turn a listless, yet inquiring, eye;
And mark that now with a slow gradual pace
A solemn trance creams northward o'er its face;
Yon clouds that late were labouring past the sun,
Reached by its sure arrest, one after one,
Come to a heavy halt; the airs that played
About the rugged mountains all are laid:
While drawing nearer far-off heights appear,
As in a dream's wild prospect, strangely near!
Till into wood resolves their robe of blue,
And the grey crags rise bluffly on the view.
Such are the signs and tokens that presage
A summer hurricane's forthcoming rage.

At length the south sends out her cloudy heaps,
And up the glens at noontide dimness creeps;
The birds, late warbling in the hanging green
Of steep-set brakes, seek now some safer screen;
The herd, in doubt, no longer wanders wide,
But fast ongathering throngs yon mountain's side,
Whose echoes, surging to its tramp, might seem
The mutter'd troubles of some Titan's dream.
Fast the dim legions of the muttering storm
Throng denser, or protruding columns form;

A STORM ON THE MOUNTAINS.

While splashing forward from their cloudy lair,
Convolving flames, like scouting dragons, glare:
Low thunders follow, labouring up the sky,
And as fore-running blasts go blaring by,
At once the forest, with a mighty stir,
Bows, as in homage to the thunderer!

Hark! from the dingoes' blood-polluted dens,
In the gloom-hidden chasms of the glens,
Long fitful howls wail up; and in the blast
Strange hissing whispers seem to huddle past;
As if the dread stir had aroused from sleep,
Weird spirits, cloistered in yon cavy steep,
(On which, in the grim past, some Cain's offence
Hath haply outraged heaven!) who rising thence
Wrapped in the boding vapours, laughed again
To wanton in the wild-willed hurricane.
See in the storm's front, sailing dark and dread,
A wide-winged eagle like a black flag spread!
The clouds aloft flash doom! short stops his flight!
He seems to shrivel in the blasting light!
The air is shattered with a crashing sound,
And he falls, stonelike, lifeless, to the ground.
Now, like a shadow at great nature's heart,
The turmoil grows. No wonder, with a start,
Marks where right overhead the storm careers,
Girt with black horrors and wide-flaming fears!
Arriving thunders, mustering on his path,
Swell more and more the roarings of his wrath,
As out in widening circles they extend,
And then—at once—in utter silence end.

Portentous silence! Time keeps breathing past,
Yet it continues! May this marvel last?

This wild weird silence in the midst of gloom
So manifestly big with coming doom?
Tingles the boding ear; and up the glens
Instinctive dread comes howling from the wild-dog's
    dens.

Terrific vision! Heaven's great ceiling splits,
And a vast globe of withering fire emits,
Which pouring down in one continuous stream,
Spans the black concave like a burning beam,
A moment;—then from end to end it shakes
With a quick motion—and in thunder breaks!
Peal rolled on peal! while heralding the sound,
As each concussion thrills the solid ground,
Fierce glares coil, snake-like, round the rocky wens
Of the red hills, or hiss into the glens,
Or thick through heaven like flaming falchions swarm,
Cleaving the teeming cisterns of the storm,
From which rain-torrents, searching every gash,
Split by the blast, come sheeting with a dash.

On yon grey peak, from rock-encrusted roots,
The mighty patriarch of the wood upshoots,
In those proud-spreading tops' imperial height
The mountain eagle loveth most to light;
Now dimly seen through tempestuous air,
His form seems harrowed by a mad despair,
As with his ponderous arms uplifted high,
He wrestles with the storm and threshes at the sky!
A swift bolt hurtles through the lurid air,
Another thundering crash! the peak is bare!
Huge hurrying fragments all around are cast,
The wild-winged, mad-limbed monsters of the blast.

The darkness thickens! With despairing cry
From shattering boughs the rain-drenched parrots fly;

Loose rocks roll rumbling from the mountains round,
And half the forest strews the smoking ground;
To the bared crags the blasts now wilder moan,
And the caves labour with a ghostlier groan.
Wide raging torrents down the gorges flow
Swift bearing with them to the vale below
Those sylvan wrecks that littered late the path
Of the loud hurricane's all-trampling wrath.

The storm is past. Yet booming on afar
Is heard the rattling of the thunder-car,
And that low muffled moaning, as of grief,
Which follows with a wood-sigh wide and brief.
The clouds break up; the sun's forth-bursting rays
Clothe the wet landscape with a dazzling blaze;
The birds begin to sing a lively strain,
And merry echoes ring it o'er again;
The clustered herd is spreading out to graze,
Though lessening torrents still a hundred ways
Flash downward, and from many a rocky ledge
A mantling gust comes quick and shining o'er the edge.

'Tis evening; and the torrent's furious flow
Runs gentlier now into the lake below.
O'er all the freshened scene no sound is heard,
Save the short twitter of some busied bird,
Or a faint rustle made amongst the trees
By wasting fragments of a broken breeze.
Along the wild and wreck-strewed paths I wind,
Watching earth's happiness with a quiet mind,
And see a beauty all unmarked till now,
Flushing each flowery nook and sunny brow;
Wished peace returning like a bird of calm,
Brings to the wounded world its blessed healing balm.

* * * * * *

On nerveless, tuneless lines how sadly
Ringing rhymes may wasted be,
While blank verse oft is mere prose madly
Striving to be poetry :
While prose that's craggy as a mountain
May Apollo's sun-robe don,
Or hold the well-spring of a fountain
Bright as that in Helicon.
CHARLES HARPER.

AN ABORIGINAL MOTHER'S LAMENT.

STILL farther would I fly, my child,
  To make thee safer yet,
From the unsparing white man,
  With his dread hand murder-wet !
I'll bear thee on as I have borne
  With stealthy steps wind-fleet,
But the dark night shrouds the forest,
  And thorns are in my feet.

    O moan not ! I would give this braid—
      Thy father's gift to me—
    But for a single palmful
      Of water now for thee.

Ah ! spring not to his name—no more
  To glad us may he come !
He is smouldering into ashes
  Beneath the blasted gum !
All charred and blasted by the fire
  The white man kindled there,
And fed with our slaughtered kindred
  Till heaven-high went its glare !

> O moan not! I would give this braid—
>   Thy father's gift to me—
> For but a single palmful
>   Of water now for thee.

And but for thee, I would their fire
  Had eaten me as fast!
Hark! Hark! I hear his death-cry
  Yet lengthening up the blast!
But no—when his bound hands had signed
  The way that we should fly,
On the roaring pyre flung bleeding—
  I saw thy father die!

> O moan not! I would give this braid—
>   Thy father's gift to me—
> For but a single palmful
>   Of water now for thee.

No more shall his loud tomahawk
  Be plied to win our cheer,
Or the shining fish pools darken
  Beneath his shadowing spear;
The fading tracks of his fleet foot
  Shall guide not as before,
And the mountain-spirits mimic
  His hunting call no more!

> O moan not! I would give this braid—
>   Thy father's gift to me—
> For but a single palmful
>   Of water now for thee.

CHARLES HARPUR.

IDEAL BEAUTY.

Absolve me for a while, undo
The links that bind me as your thrall,
So I be more myself, more worthy you;

Let me forget you too in dreams,
   Your lang'rous waist and musical
Soft ways, like cadences of streams
Unlooked for, strange, but sweetly rhythmical;

The morning freshness of the rose,
The suave strong motion of the sea,
The strenuous splendour and repose
Of marble, and the lily's purity;

All these are types that symbolize
The secret charm, the subtle grace,
The music as of paradise
That plays about your lissom limbs and face;

Let me forget all these and be
Once more self-centred, circumspect,
And of dædalian longings free,
Let me a fuller, stronger life elect;

So may I on a windy shore
See screaming seagulls flying near,
And hear the hollow channels roar,
Nor seek in every breeze your voice to hear;

Or where the glints of sunshine steal
Through clust'ring clematis and fern,
There let me roam alone and feel
The simple joys of sense for which I yearn;

The lights and shadows of the bush,
The prattling music of the creek,
The stir of insects and the hush
Of solitude,—these are the joys I seek

Oh idle words! since Marsyas died,
How many has Apollo slain?
And ah! how many too have tried
To win you, or to shun you—but in vain.

E. S. Hay.

THE HUT ON THE FLAT.

You've heard of Warradgery Run, he said, where old Morris
Died a while back; I was stockman there, years ago now.
Morris had an old shepherd up there, God knows his name, I don't.
There's many a man in these parts whose right name nobody knows.
We called him old Jack; he wasn't so old, but quiet and queer in his ways,
And for a station hand uncommonly steady. You know
If we work hard in the bush, when we get a chance of enjoyment,
We take our pleasure like work, as much as we can at a spell;
Perhaps we'd do better to take our sport as I've heard some do with their wine,
Drinking to taste and not to be drunk. Well, it's our way.

Jack had little to say, the same as most of the shepherds.
Often I've thought when a man has no one to talk to,
Nothing but sheep and his dogs around him day after day and for ever;
Silence becomes so familiar at last, that his voice is strange to himself.
You may think he is shy, but his silence is ignorance and habit.
All he learns is the news of the run in a yarn with a stockman or rider,
And nought of the world "inside" he knows, save when he gets from a shearer
Or some of the station hands a newspaper, months after date.
He doesn't dislike a yarn, but he must do most of the listening,
That is the way with the most, but Jack liked to keep to himself.
If he noticed you coming his way, he would drive off the sheep if he could;
But if he must stay, he would merely answer your questions.
"Going wild," they said on the run, and he was left to himself.
His hut was out on Dingo Flat, three miles or more from the station—
A lonely place; between the hut and the station lived no one.
A gunyah of slab the hut, bark-roofed; the walls within lined with sacking.
Only one room it had, and the fireplace took up a side.
Opposite, raised on short posts and built in the slabs of the wall
Was a bunk for his bed, planked up at the head and the foot.

From the top of the bunk to the wall a part of the
 hut had been ceilèd,
And in the loft thus made he kept his bridle and saddle.
The floor was the earth flattened well by tramping
 and beating.
Under the window, unglazed and closed with a strong
 wooden shutter,
Stood his table, uneven and rudely made of deal casing
Supported on saplings short that sunk in the earth of
 the floor ;
He had made it himself ; between table and fireplace
 a campstool.
Beside the window his cupboard was placed, a gin case
 nailed to the wall ;
On it rested some pipes, and a bushman's various
 trifles,
Scattered about the hut were his simple household
 utensils,
And save himself and his dogs, in the place was never
 a living creature.

This hut stood down at the end of the Flat ; behind it
 a pen for the sheep.
A hundred yards from the door ran a little creek, and
 about it
Here and there, grew a she-oak, tall and sombre of
 foliage.
Black and green wattles and pines and gum trees
 covered a hillock
With a thick scrub to the summit. This in the front
 to the east.
Behind the gunyah were flats with low bare hills
 alternated,
Bare were both flats and hills save for here and there
 a huge gum.

THE HUT ON THE FLAT.

Riding one day by Warraman Creek, amongst the scrub on the hillside
And over the flats by the water, I saw Jack's sheep were astray.
Neither Jack nor his dog responded when loudly I cooeyed,
So I rode on to his hut. The door was closed; not dismounting,
I struck on the door with my stockwhip handle and listened—no answer.
Again I struck, and a faint voice said, "For God's sake, come in."
The door was locked, and I broke the hasp with repeated blows of a log,
Entered, and saw in the twilight Jack lying still in his bunk
So like a dead man that at first I scarcely believed he was living.
Shrunken and ghastly pale was his face, unmoving among the blue blankets.
He had not the strength to rise, but when he saw who it was entered
A change came on his face as he found relief from some terror;
And when I stood at his side he stretched forth weakly yet eager
His wasted hands to grasp mine, and strove, though they could not, to hold me,
And sitting beside him he told me the tale I will tell you.
It was long hearing for me; though he seemed impatient to tell it;
His strength would fail, and long he would lie unwillingly silent;
When he spoke 'twas with many a groan and pause between the words that he gasped.

Stay by me, Jim, for the time is not long to my death.
A week have I lain, and the sickness threatened before that.
As I grew feeble and worse, fearing my strength would utterly fail me,
I turned the sheep loose; better lost than starved in the yard.
And never the face of one living I saw, but only a face that I wished not;
For whether I slept or whether I waked, or opened mine eyes were or closed,
Ever a dreadful vision burned through my sense to my soul—
Eyes with a terrible threat and reproach in their passionless sameness—
Living eyes in a dead wan face that was gapped with a ruinous blow.
And I thought it the judgment of God, the face of my victim should haunt me,
And the eyes of him whom I slew should witness my doom without pity.
Three years ago it is now, one wild night a man weak and ailing,
Wandered up to the hut and asked shelter! O, God! that he had not!
But this is hell—to do crime and gain not, yet never undo it.
He entered and lay that night in a bed I made on the hearthplace,
He was worse in the morning, and wandered much in his mind,
And in his madness he talked of his money, and bade me
Open his swag to be sure it was there; from that day I wished for his death,

THE HUT ON THE FLAT. 99

But I thought not yet of a crime, expecting he would
    not recover.
When the delirium passed he lay so feeble and help-
    less,
I thought some day to return and find he had died in
    his sleep;
Then I might hide his swag, and give them word at the
    station
A sick man came to the hut and after a day or two
    died.
But one day he rose by himself and thenceforth grew
    stronger.
He knew it as well, and said that I would find he was
    grateful,
"You will not lose by me," he declared, "I am not so
    poor as I look."
Forgetting—how should he remember? when mad
    alike we gazed on his wealth.
And daily I brooded about the chance of his money
    escaping.
Though I tried not to show my desire he might have
    perceived it,
For I was afraid he would leave some time and find his
    way to the station.
Nightly I brought back the sheep, and while I penned
    them, our ration
He cooked and laid our meal; in silence we ate it.
Then he would sit at one side of the fire, I at the other,
    nor speak,
For I was never a talker, and he got tired of every
    thing soon.
If he began to talk I'd say, "aye" or "no," and all
    the while I was thinking
Of the notes in his swag I had seen when first he came
    to the hut.

When the fire burnt down he went to the bunk, while
    my bed I made on the hearth.
One night, coming back, I got tired of it all; shall I
    wait, I said to myself,
Till he gets strong and goes off, and all his money goes
    with him?
You have a right to it, too; but for you he had died
    on the flat.
So the mischief had worked, while I knew not whither
    my thoughts were leading,
And the deed I must do to possess his wealth then first
    arose in my mind;
For a moment I shrank, then my purpose was deadlier
    strengthened.
When he turned in, I listened till I heard his steady,
    low breathing,
Then rose, took the axe, gently felt in the dark for his
    face,
Struck once, and he loudly groaned, shuddered, and
    then he lay still.
Mad to conceal him, then with the axe I hewed a
    grave under the bunk,
And wrapping his body, yet warm, in the bedclothes
    he lay in,
Hurried it into the hole, threw the earth back, and
    placed the box over.
I burnt the swag, and his money you'll find it all in
    the box.
When he began, I thought him by sickness and loneli-
    ness maddened,
And the story some dream of his fever; but as he pro-
    ceeded
Without a pause, save that which his illness commanded,
In spite of myself I believed. When he ceased, he lay
    silent;

Almost I feared to stay there; the murdered man
  lying beneath us,
Above him his murderer dying at night in that hut on
  the flat.
He asked me for water at length, and I went for it
  down to the creek;
Never did night seem more lovely to me, every star
  stood out from the blue,
There was no wind, and the air was cool and fresh,
  and the scene most silent—
Perfectly silent, but for the distant wailing of curlews.
The very trees seemed asleep, and my steps broke
  harsh on the quiet.
The water was calm as the air, and when I disturbed it,
Danced in the ripples the shimmering stars as if de-
  lighted with motion.
There was no moon, and the starlight showed no
  horizon;
And the world stretched out to the stars in that
  shadow all landscape of twilight.
Back I turned to the hut. I gave the man drink and
  sat by his bedside,
And waited there through the dreary hours knowing
  him past any help.
Uneasily slept he a while with many a shudder and
  groan,
Sometimes sobbing, then delirious waked, and towards
  the morning he died,
All his face working and shrieking; "I didn't do anything with it."
Suddenly broke his shriek to a groan, and passed
  through his limbs a strong shudder,
Then like a blow from a hand unseen the death change
  smote all his face.
So he died, and at once I rode back to the station.

Morris was down in Melbourne, and I told the manager
    Benson.
At daylight he sent off a man to round up the sheep,
    and later
He and I rode down and fastened the hut till a magis-
    trate came.
Then I went over to Wirra, and Jackson and his
    overseer
Came the same day to Warradgery. The hut never
    saw such a muster,
For the story had spread and every one wished to
    attend.
Below the bunk the floor was dug up; not four feet
    under the surface
We found what had been a man, with rotting blue
    blankets about it.
And when all proceedings were over no shepherd
    could be persuaded
To live near the spot. A stranger soon heard of the
    story.
A new hut was built farther on, and the old one
    abandoned left standing.
So little by little the place went all to destruction,
The shutter was torn away, and the door fell, hung by
    one hinge,
The sacking got torn away down within, and the rain
    beat in through the cracks,
Fallen wholly, one slab left a ruinous gap in the
    front,
The roof was loosed by the wind, and the bark frayed
    out into ribbons.
So looked the hut on that desolate flat the last time I
    saw it,
Late in a stormy day in August; the sun was not
    sunken,

THE HUT ON THE FLAT.

Yet was the landscape darkened by cloud; the creek was swollen by rains;
Over the flat a heavy wind blew and whistled among the she-oaks,
Bringing now and again a shower of thick stinging sleet.
While my mare stopped for a drink, I turned in my saddle and gazed
Up to Jack's gunyah standing desolate there as I tell you.
I have seen some places unholy in different parts of the country,
But the God-forsakenest spot that ever mine eyes were set on
Was the scene of Jack's crime, that stormy evening in August—
Blasted as if the place shared in the curse on a pitiless murder.
Soon after the coach came up, and we set off again on our journey;
Neither spoke to the other, each in a corner sat down silent;
We two the passengers only; what my comrade was thinking I know not;
But the damp wind, blowing hard through the trees by the roadside,
Was ever in my sad thoughts as the moaning wind in the she-oaks,
And the driver's song, and the rhythmic fall of horse's feet on the highway,
The ring of the wheels, and the clash of harness, and sound of the threatening whip,
Made an accompaniment to "I didn't do anything with it,"
To the shriek of a deathful voice, "I didn't do anything with it."
THOMAS HENRY.

MY QUEEN OF DREAMS.

In the warm-flushed heart of the rose-red West,
When the great sun quivered and died to-day
You pulsed, O star, by yon pine-clad crest,
And throbbed till the bright eve ashened grey.
      Then I saw you swim
      By the shadowy rim
Where the grey gum dips to the western plain,
      And you rayed delight
      As you winged your flight
To the mystic spheres where your kinsmen reign!

O star, did you see her? My queen of dreams!
Was it you that glimmered the night we strayed
A month ago by these scented streams?
Half-checked by the litter the musk-buds made?
      Did you sleep or wake?—
      Ah, for love's sweet sake,
(Though the world should fail, and the soft stars wane!)
      I shall dream delight
      Till our souls take flight
To the mystic spheres where your kinsmen reign!

                        Philip J. Holdsworth.

STATION HUNTING ON THE WARREGO.

An Episode of Australian Frontier Life.

(Just what the bushmen told, while raging rains
Whirled tempests round our hut at Stockyard Flat,—
Just what he told that night—the self-same tale,
Yet not the self-same words—I tell to-day.
I change his rough to smooth, and simply touch
His bare blunt speech with certain chimes of verse.)

Hedge round the fire (he said), and while yon blasts
Blow out their gusty summons, friends, give heed!
I speak of griefs and perils felt and faced
While station-hunting on the Warrego.

Two seasons had been parched, sirs, and a third
Flamed, droughtier than its fellows, till the grass,
The green, lush grass, grew spoilt by baneful days
And nights that came uncoupled with cool dews.
And musing much on decimated flocks,
And gaunt herds thinned by dearth of sustenance,
Paul cried, one day, to Oscar: "Are we men?
Ay, men, I say, or marble? Plagues and droughts
Smite the sick land with horrors,—yet we stand
Slave-like, and smile at buffets! Comrade, rouse!
And, ere some wide-mouthed ruin swallow all,
Let's seek, far west, some richer pasturing ground!"

So—spurred by strong compulsive need—they went.

Five days the comrades, journeying horse by horse,
Passed herbless plains, and clay-flats cracked with heat;

And crossed dry blackened beds, where twisting creeks
And runnels once had brawled. But loath (stout hearts!)
To leave that waste with failure in their hands,
They slacked no rein, till, checked by hostile ground,
Their maimed steeds fell,—disabled utterly!

Now, mid those sterile tracts unhorsed, and vexed
With leagues of drought and travail, toiled the friends,
Till Oscar, though the brawnier-limbed, laid hands
(Weak, feverish hands) on Paul, and groaned,—
  "Enough!
"Slow torpor numbs my strength, and arduous hours
Seem changes rung on one perpetual pain.
Were Heaven's pearled gates in sight, I can no more!"
"Nay, nay," said Paul, "take heart! To-day, I slew
A sulphur-coloured snake that doubtless slid
Due west, toward water-shallows! Courage, friend."

Courage? The phrase fell profitless as grief;
Lost, like a stream, sand-swallowed; vain as tears
That waste, in sleep, when sharp dreams dominate.
Courage the man possessed, but supple thews
And sinewy limbs, he lacked. And so, perforce,
They camped beside some samphire-covered hills
That reddened with the sunset.

                    All that night
Strong fever marshalled hosts of pains, and plagued
The sick man's flesh; and when next dawn rayed out
God's liberal light, Paul strode where lines of scrub
Buttressed with brushwood-yellow mounds of sand—
And roughly reared a screen of boughs, to foil
Noon's fiery edge, and shield his anguished friend.
Six days Paul watched, slow days that lagged to nights,
And loitered into morns; and, on the seventh,

When gathering glooms had sucked light's last faint
    flakes,
And keen white stars crept, palpitatingly,
Amid unfolding skies, the sick man moaned :—
"Comrade ! On, on to safety ! I am doomed,
Doomed utterly ! Forsake me, Paul, and fly !"

"May God forsake me, if I do !" said Paul ;
"Though thirst and famine come, and sweeping storms
Clamour and brawl, and shake the world's four walls,
Paul shall not flinch or budge ! Here lies my part,
Whatever be the issue !"

      But again,
Slowly the faint voice murmured :—"Death draws nigh !
Yea,—knells his certain summons, for my veins
Burn, and grow sapless as the dead loose leaves
That clog the forest aisles in bleak July !
Heed dying lips ! turn, Paul ! O turn and fly !"

"Nay, turn and sleep !" Paul answered, "twice accursed
By Heaven and Earth are cowards. Sleep ! I say,
May God forsake me if I faint and fly !"

Thus spoke a brave heart's friendship : yet, once more,
With passionate persistence wailed the voice :—
"'Mid prosperous realms, and cities thronged with life,
Where millions toil and grovel (soul and flesh
Bond-slaves to Belial and the Hunger-God),
While Fortune's favourites heap red gold like mire,—
There too, again, 'mid plains that stretch and show
Illimitable tracts, whose furnaced sands
Gasp languidly, and mock the day !—alas,
These have I paced, a mateless, childless man ;
A solitary soul.   For me, no wife,
(When dry December scorched or Augusts wept

Their windy way through ranks of rain-black clouds)
Cheered, like a seraph, life's vicissitudes:
For me no babes, with glib bewitching speech,
Lisped the sweet prate that charms the silent sire
As bird-psalms charm the bard. O Paul, O Paul,
On me these heaven-gleams glint not, but on you!
Close-barred from me, God's largess showers on you!
Spare, spare the guiltless far ones: pause and fly!"

Here first the stout heart faltered: for the thin
Strained voice had struck one master chord of life,
Man's vehement love of quiet household joys,
His heart aches for the witching charms of home:
But Paul, perplexed and tearful, cried, "Forbear,
"Forbear, Heaven frowns when cravens faint and fly!"
Now darkness circled round them like a spell:
And Oscar drowsed, while Paul yearned, moodily,
To pierce the vast void stillness. Fitful winds,
Like melancholy night-gasps, waxed, and then
Waned noiselessly, and timorous brush birds wailed
From out the mallee-scrub and salt-bush clumps
That flanked the dun base of the sand-ridge near.
At times, far dolefuller sounds vexed Paul, for lo,
Sonorous curlews scudded past, with shrieks
And dismal lamentations, wofuller
Than those dread groans which daunt the woodman's
   heart,
When strong north-easters sweep through swamp-oak
   groves.
Forlornly shrilled these wasteland cries, while Paul
Sat, hour by hour, and marvelled if God's Hand,
Past the fierce limits of that wild lone land,
Would guide them to a havened peace again.

So passed the night, that long and desolate night!—
Throned mid its infinite retinues of stars,

It passed, and gradual day, with stealthy strides,
Stalked slowly, broadly, on.

      Now drifts of cloud,
Showed dawn's soft rose-prints deepening in the east,
And melting mists made visible far hills.
Huge battlemented crags were they, whose fronts
And fractured summits, grappled by ruthless time,
And scarred by rains and tempests, frowned on Paul,
Like hell's grim cliffs, and rocks unscalable.
Keen anguish pierced his soul, that brave strong soul,
With toils sore spent, and vexing vigils wrung ;
And, glancing where his friend supinely lay,
Paul saw the languid eyes grow luminous
With strange mysterious light, and soon the voice
Spake hollowly :—

      (As when, mid cavernous chasms,
Some lost foot-wanderer wails for succouring aid,
Distinct at first, his shrill voice volleying flies,
Till, checked where wide rifts gape, and huge rocks jut,
It wanes and wastes, and echoes hopelessness ;
Meanwhile, high up, (a-drowsing mid their flocks),
Dull hinds catch hints of deep sepulchral cries
That surge like death-sighs from a world of graves :
So thin, so worn, so hollow, ached that voice :—)

"Midway 'twixt dusk and dawn," it wailed, "I heard
The cry of crested pigeons, wheeling low,
And thrice the air grew black with clanging wings,
And hoarse with marsh-fowls clamours ; (Peace ! I know
When famished spoonbills, shrieking, scent lagoons !)
Moreover, at that hour, when conquered night
Shrinks shuddering from the dawn, cold winds arose,
And breathed soft benedictions, soothing me
With sounds like babbling brooks ; and then my pangs

Ceased, for I heard far torrents! Paul, be urged!
Strike south, and seek assistance for us both!"
So moaned the dying Oscar.

           Paul took up
These last weak words, and thus considered them:—

"Cooped here, man's bones might bleach till Doom's
  dead trump
Thundered confusion on all flesh that lives!
Christian, or Christless, what man treads these wastes?
Here no oases bloom: no springs outgush:
Some curse mars all, and battles with mankind!"
So muttering, he unslung the water-flask,
And drew with niggard hand their daily dole.

(Ah God! what fierce extremes encompass life.
Note yon plump Sybarite, whose moons are feasts,
Whose midnight dainty banquets! Hedged with gold,
He sucks abundance from earth's shores and seas;
He drains the wine of life from jewelled cups,
And fattens well for grave-worms!

           Different fares
Yon child of pain that treads dry, furnaced tracts!
Above, stretch skies of fire: around him, plains,
Bare, moistureless: beneath him, earth—his grave!
For him no rich looms play with curious skill;
No menials crook and cringe; no tempting cates,
No rare wines glisten; at Fate's Sibyl hands
He plucks desire, mistrust, hope, fear, and death!
Ah God! what fierce extremes encompass life!)

Now thirst, that deadly desert-foe, stalked near;
For, nestling in their flasks, alas, remained
Scarce three days' water for the body's need:
And Paul, though staid, and nowise fooled by dreams,
Sat piecing Oscar's talk. He knew, right well,
That dying eyes have strength to see and pierce
Those dim, dark realms, which border Death, and knew
That hands, just loosening from the world, may gain
Their firmest, godliest, grasp of things Divine;
And thus, perturbed and vexed with hopes and fears,
He mused, well-nigh to madness.

       Soon he cried,
"Turn, or turn not, Destruction dogs my heels!
Slow Death confronts, and Famine follows me,
Till, like some snared wild beast, bound limb and limb,
I fall—ignobly trapped! Nay, better, I say,
To face my fate with sinews braced and set
And make a manlike end! Ay, nobler far!
God help us: I must seek these water springs!"

With that, Paul's heart seemed some whit comforted;
For wise resolve both sanctifies and saves;
Nor do the clefts and caves of legioned hell
Hold souls more surely damned than wavering men
Who, like light leaves 'mid windy buffetings,
Whirl restlessly, corrupting day by day!"

Here, gathering up what strength lay still unspent
In nerve and thew, Paul sought the patch of scrub,
And, hewing down broad boughs of close-leaved box,
Sped straightway back:—"Because," said he, "rough winds
May rave and fret the self-same hour I go,
And rains, perchance, may pelt persistently

That white wan face (ah, horrible rains!) and so
To match these possibilities, my hand
Must weatherfend the wurley!"

         This he did.
He bound the thick boughs close with bushman's skill,
Till not a gap was left where raging showers
Or gusts might riot. Over all he stretched
Strong bands of cane-grass, plaited cunningly.

By this high noon had passed, and eve's slant sun
With weak and yellowing gleam just topped the west.

Now stayed Paul's hand till dark;—for restful night,
In arid regions, makes cool journeyings,
While day's bewildering heats baulk man and beast.
He loitered, then, till dusk, and paced the camp,
With faint but kindling hope, in search of stores
For necessary travel.

      As he turned,
The sick man thrilled convulsively, and lo,
Half rose, stretched forward, clutched the flagon, poured
Their scant supply in Paul's own travelling-flask,
And swooning, reeled and fell.

        But Paul beheld!
That small sublime deceit Paul saw, unseen;
Tears sluiced his eyes, while, grasping Oscar's flask
He ran the liquid back, and scarcely kept
(To tread that trackless wilderness) as much
As, at a gulp, might ridge the smooth, soft, throat
Of some grey-breasted plover parched with thirst.
 Then, striding where the man lay, motionless,

He sobbed :—" If God's grace guide me—O my friend—
In yon great range may huddle billabongs ;
If not,—thy mightier need confutes mine own ! "
   Therewith he placed the flask by Oscar,—aye,—
And kissed his white wan brows with that strained
    kiss,
His bloodless brows with that strained passionate kiss,—
Which strong men, in a lifetime moved, kiss once :
And, shouldering back the fringe of leaves, again
He gazed at Oscar ; then heart-agonized,
Crossed the green threshold.

            Thus went Paul his way !

(O Sovereign Love ! sublime 'twixt man and maid,—
But Christlike, more august, 'twixt man and man !
O Power that rules broad realms, and clans, and creeds,
And makes the world's heart jubilant ! O Love,
Majestic Love,—man's noblest attribute,—
In poor or rich, how beautiful art thou !
In hind or king how comely ! Yea, from Him
(The sinless, slain, miraculous Nazarene)
Whose red blood ransomed Man, to yon sad wretch,
Who, scorned and squalid, starved and desolate,
Feels, yet, compassionate pangs,—most beautiful !
O pure, O mystic Love, that thrives and spreads
Like some strange tree, whose far roots wrap Man's soul;
On whose vast boughs crowned Seraphs sit ; whose top
Thrones the veiled splendours of Omnipotence !—
How wonderful art thou ! How wonderful !)

Through night's long hours Paul trod that hopeless land,
Nor neared the peaks till dawn. Grim hills were they
Whose huge piled blocks seemed poised by giant hands
In high perpetual menace of mankind !
   Athwart their base rough gorges stretched, and past

Precipitous steeps, one large dry gum-creek, paved
With smooth round boulders, and worn gravel-stones.
Its banks were loose and blistered. Noon's strong heats
Had sucked the streams that once hummed hereabout
True desert music. So Paul drooped, forlorn
(Prone on a sandstone block) with head that bent
As bends some battered bulrush, maimed by rains,
And sapped by sudden storms.

     But what boots Grief
When Life craves action ! Therefore Paul arose,
And searched those stubborn sands with hot, keen eyes,
For some small glimpse of help.

      At length he scanned
A faint old sheep-trail, trending northwardly ;—
And as a cave-lost man, mid murk and gloom,
Grows wild with hope, and hails some distant gleam,
So Paul exulted then ! With frenzied eyes,
That often lost, but swiftlier found, the tracks
And feet that faltered rarely, on he pressed,
Till daylight waxed and waned, and dusk warned
 " Hold."

 With night came coupled Dread.
      For merciless thirst
Nipt the worn wanderer, till he drained the flask,
And hurled the shell afar. Then Sleep,—soft Sleep,—
Kind, pitiful Sleep—crept drowsily, and wrapt
The tough, racked body in dreamless rest.

       Next morn,
Fierce rose the sun, and smote him,—smote him,
 sirs,—
Till pains and throbbings roused him, whereupon
Up gathering to his feet, he searched anew.

By noon, the sandwaste altered,—for the ground
Grew strewn with splintered, flint-like stones that took
A dull and tawny hue i' the strong sun's glare.

  To plod long leagues of sand seemed hard ; but now,
More terrible toils were Paul's, his wayworn feet
Fared bitterly on sharp, unstable flints,
And slipped, and stumbled, till by prints of blood,
His limping way was land-marked.
                        Still brave heart,
His strong will urged him onward ; for he deemed
The flints might form that grinding stony zone,
Which oft in sterile regions, belts the plain ;
(Sand flanked on either side). He therefore aimed
To cross that strip with speed, and haply reach
More promising plains beyond.
                        But hope unhelped
Soon famishes man's flesh,—and, when Fatigue
Strangled the Trust that homed within his heart
Like some supernal guardian, Paul's faint strength
Waned with the westering sun, whose nether rim
Low-poised and luminous, reddened on the verge
Of sands far reaching westward. As it sank,
Prone, on the plain, he swooned without a cry,
And lay, outstretched, till dawn.
                        Throughout that night,
Cool dews came sallying on that rain-starved land,
And drenched the thick rough tufts of bristly grass,
Which, stemmed like quills (and thence termed porcu-
    pine)
Thrust hardily thin shoots amid the flints
And sharp-edged stones.
                    Soon fan-shaped spread the dawn :
And kinglike, pranked with pomps of ushering clouds,

The crimson cruel sun arose, and trailed
Swift through that sterile plain red skirts of fire!
Hell's grip was on his heart again!—Paul stirred—
Cried muttered cries, and woke right wearily
And seeing those coarse stalks diamonded with dew,
Yea, webbed and wet with beaded filaments,
He grovelled low, and scooped his black burnt mouth
To suck the dwindling drops, whereat, in truth
One small wood-swallow scarce could sip.

         Driven wild,
And desperate in his life's supremest need,
Once more he staggered on.

         And now the sun
Climbed to the topmost heaven, and steadfastly
Shone with consuming strength, until the air
Glowed like a thing incorporate with the flames
That scorched and stung Paul's brain. I tell you, sirs,
Through all earth's myriad tribes, God saw that day
No mournfuller sight than him! At length, alas,
Both plain and sky seemed suddenly to swirl
And plunge down dreamless deeps where Famine, Thirst,
And Anguish sank from sight,—far under worlds
Where death and silence reigned Lords Paramount.

 Even that swoon passed; for life was strong:—and then
Trooped dead delights which perished days had known!
For dreamscapes came and went of years when life
Was like some scroll, fast-shut, of wizard-lore
Mysterious and unknown, in dim vague dreams,
He roamed, once more, through haunts of innocent youth.
He saw Monaro's peaks whose kingly crests
Bulk skyward from the vales to glance at God:—

Hills robed in light, august, majestical,—
And fruitful vales, whose breadths of delicate green
Are dear to nibbling flocks, and herds that browse.
In visioned vista, too, its broad rich plains
And loamy meadows stretched,—and, chiefliest, one
(By Love, that subtle sleuth-hound, tracked) wherein
His father's homestead stood, like some fair Ark
'Mid seas of billowing grain.

       Beguiled he wept.
Anon, with sleep and memory, strode his sire,—
A gracious man, grave-browed with care and crowned
With meditative age's concomitant,
Experience ripely-garnered. By his side,
Girt with serenest grace, the mother gazed
Regardfully. Her eyes (two mournful moons
Made glorious with the love-light shrined in them)
Babbled tenderly from fond clear depths life's first
Unfathomable boon,—maternal love :—
That old perennial spell which still outcharms
The spurious lesser loves that fret mankind.

 Again came mortal pangs.

       Home's golden dreams
And pageants bulked once more to things of dread
That nightmared Paul. Myriads of monstrous hands,
Gaunt, claw-tipped, seemed to writhe out from fierce
 skies,
And pluck him back to life and agony ;—
At which, with terrible cries, the swooner woke.
He lay upon the plain, with limbs diffused ;—
Half-tombed by drifting sands. One down-stretched hand
Had delved a hollowed place some four spans deep,
Athirst, perchance, to grasp beneath parched plains,

Coolness, denied above.   Or, haply else
As though the soul's continual aches had warned
The weak, faint frame, to scoop its grassless grave
Past reach of kites and prowling warrigals.
  His bare right arm was flesh-torn to the bone,
As if by wild beasts' teeth ; and, on the wounds
Swarmed crawling crowds of small black ants, that
    cleansed
The thick and oozing blood-clots.   Aye, amid
Delirious hours, self-lacerating teeth
Had gnawed Paul's own shrunk limb ; and famished lips
Had fastened on impoverished veins and drawn
The oil that fuelled life's spasmodic flame.
(Though wrought in madness, this was horrible !)
And, weakening fast, Paul feebly cloaked his face
And waited for the end !

                      He felt that soon
His white and graveless bones would front the sun
In gleaming accusation of day's wrath :
That soon his dust would whirl unsepulchred
Nor requiemed, save by wails from those quick winds
That sink and swell about the night's mid-heart:
And, crushed by stress of suffering, he prayed
The hand of death—of dumb relentless death—
Might free his souL

                    Even this the enemy neared :
A ravenous presence—vague, intangible—
That blindly sucked his life.   Its clammy breath
(Like dews that reek and drip from charnel vaults)
Froze anguish into stupor ; and sharp films
Bleared his faint, heavy, eyelids as he gasped—
" Mother,—farewell,—farewell,—wife,—children,"—
  .   .   .   .

"Hold!
Quick—quick—my man! just tilt that water flask!
Leftwards: now drench him!—so; he's coming too!"
And Paul strained up;—beheld strong, bearded men,
Heard helpful words, and swooned to nothingness!

. . . .

Of Oscar, Friends, I kept my tale's straight march,
And so spared speech of Oscar, yet when Paul
Plucked, from a three months' fever, what remained
Of pristine health and strength,—he told at large,
Of desperate perils, faced where seldom rain
Cheers the baked earth;—told, too, of wastelands strewn
With keen-edged shards, and fragmentary flints,
Till rude, rough, bush-hands wept compassionate tears.
Ranging, he spoke of Oscar; hunger clung
Beneath the bough-piled gunyah. But, at this,
The plain rough listeners shook half-doubtful heads
And shrugged incredulous shoulder-shrugs and saying—
"Wild fever's seeds yet linger in the man!"
Put forth no hand to help.

Yet, sirs, they lie,
Who say Paul closed with such cold counsellings;
I say they lie! Through hazardous months of pain,
Paul sought his comrade's deathplace night and day—
But where these naked bones blanch, God, who knows
Has kept from friend and kin.
Sirs, I AM PAUL!

Abrupt, he ceased:—and grave thoughts chained us all
Till Reed cried, "Boys! bestir, the tempest's past."
Whereat each slipped to saddle, and was gone.

So ran that tale of risks and jeopardies
Which menace man amid our inland wilds—

And though Regret feigns hopefuller things and sighs
" 'Twas well with Oscar's soul," I know (alas)
Earth's banefullest pains and plagues rain thick on men
That waste amid untravelled tracts, consumed
By pestilent Thirst, and past-cure maladies.

From which dire straits protect us, O our Lord,
Who perished crosswise on the tree accursed !
P. J. HOLDSWORTH.

FROM THE CANTATA.

A FEW short rolling years have fled
    Down time's abysmal track,
Since o'er this pleasant land was spread
    The wild uncultured Black.
Now far beyond fair Torrens' stream,
    'Mid spires and gilded domes,
Like the sweet visions of a dream
Bursts on the raptured sight the gleam
    Of myriad happy homes.

The shades where earth's primeval cloak
    Hung round the native's lair,
Have vanished 'neath the woodman's stroke,
    Bloomed 'neath the ploughman's share.
Approving heaven our efforts crowned,
    Hope pointed to the goal ;
In faith a trusty friend we found ;
Prudence with soft endearment wound
    Contentment round the soul.
JOHN HOWELL.

TAHITI: THE LAND OF LOVE AND BEAUTY.

THE ARRIVAL AND WELCOME.

Yo-rana! *Yo-rana!* Our haven is reached,
   The perils of ocean are o'er;
Our anchor is cast, and our shallop is beached,
   We are treading that wonderful shore
Where scenes of enchantment bewilder the eyes,
From the emerald earth to the amethyst skies,
From the mountains resplendent with deep purple dyes
   To the ocean of beauty and calm.
'Tis the Isle of Tahiti—the fairest on earth;
It is gay Papeete—the palace of Mirth;
It is where all the Loves and the Graces have birth—
   The land of the Coral and Palm!

Yo-rana! We hail thee, thou Orient Queen,
   As thou sitt'st on thy coralline throne;
Adoring we gaze on thy beauties serene,
   And the charms that are wholly thine own.
Is it city or garden that greeteth our sight?
The luscious banana hangs ruddy and bright:
The bread-fruit and orange to feasting invite;
   The zephyr seems loaded with balm;
The lime and the shaddock are lovely to see;
The sweet golden papao hangs on the tree;
Rare spices and flowers grow uncultured and free,
   In the land of the Coral and Palm.

Yo-rana! Ye hills so fantastic yet fair,
   That rear your bold fronts to the sky;
All hail, lovely harbour, beyond all compare,
   Where fleets might at anchorage lie;

Where bright fishes dart from the deep coral cave
To glance in the sunshine that cleaves the blue wave;
Where the lingering tides, as the pebbles they lave
   Murmur soft a perpetual psalm;
Where the boatman spreads gaily his white lateen sail,
And his frail craft speeds lightly before the soft gale;
Yo-rana! fair city and harbour! All hail
   To the land of the Coral and Palm!
J. L. KELLY.

HENRY KENDALL.
(*Vide* Introduction.)

THE STORY OF ABEL TASMAN.

BOLD and brave, and strong and stalwart,
   Captain of a ship was he;
And his heart was proudly thrilling
   With the dreams of chivalry.
One fair maiden, sweet though stately,
   Lingered in his every dream,
Touching all his hopes of glory
   With a brighter, nobler gleam.

Daughter of a haughty father,
   Daughter of an ancient race,
Yet her wilful heart surrendered,
   Conquered by his handsome face;
And she spent her days in looking
   Out across the southern seas,
Picturing how his bark was carried
   Onward by the favouring breeze.

Little wonder that she loved him
  Abel Tasman, brave and tall;
Though the wealthy planters sought her,
  He was dearer than them all.
Dearer still because her father
  Said to him, with distant pride,
"Darest thou, a simple captain,
  Seek my daughter for thy bride?"

But at length the gallant seaman
  Won himself an honoured name;
When again he met the maiden,
  At her feet he laid his fame:
Said to her, "My country sends me,
  Trusted with a high command,
With the Zeehan and the Heemskirk,
  To explore the southern strand."

"I must claim it for my country,
  Plant her flag upon its shore;
But I hope to win you, darling,
  When the dangerous cruise is o'er."
And her haughty sire relenting,
  Did not care to say him nay:
Flushing high with love and valour,
  Sailed the gallant far away.

And the captain, Abel Tasman,
  Sailing under southern skies,
Mingled with his hopes of glory
  Thoughts of one with starlike eyes.
Onward sailed he, where the crested
  White waves broke around his ship,
With the lovelight in his true eyes,
  And the song upon his lip.

Onward sailed he, ever onward,
    Faithful as the stars above ;
Many a cape and headland pointing
    Tells the legend of his love:
For he linked their names together,
    Speeding swiftly o'er the wave—
Tasman's Isle and Cape Maria,
    Still they bear the names he gave.

Toil and tempest soon were over,
    And he turned him home again,
Seeking her who was his guiding
    Star across the trackless main.
Strange it seems the eager captain
    Thus should hurry from his prize,
When a thousand scenes of wonder
    Stood revealed before his eyes.

But those eyes were always looking,
    Out toward the Java seas,
Where the maid he loved was waiting—
    Dearer prize to him than these.
But his mission was accomplished,
    And a new and added gem
Sparkling with a wondrous lustre
    In the Dutch king's diadem.

Little did the gallant seaman
    Think that in the days to be,
England's hand should proudly wrest it
    From his land's supremacy.

                FRANCES SESCA LEWIN.

FROM THE STORY OF BALLADEÄDRO.

KOLORKOR (HOT BLOOD).

KOLORKOR rose, Mirbango's king—
And thus address'd the listening ring:—
"Sirs! Warriors! Children! hearken well
To all your king has come to tell.
Our fathers spirits, ill at rest,
Flit nightly o'er the mountain's breast;
Yon stream is troubled, and the flood
'Neath last night's moon seem'd curdling blood,
Birds of ill omen croaked on high,
The eagle swooning fled the sky.
Oh, would the oracles withheld,
The meaning sought by seers of eld
Strange portends dire of varied mien
Presage such ill as ne'er hath been.
Last night there crept athwart my frame
A shuddering sense of woe and shame;
Something—oh, would it were forgot—
'Tis day, and yet it leaves me not.
I sprang from out the evil dream,
And saw—extended through the beam,
The red moon cast upon the coals—
Consuming slow their burning souls
Two giant hands—one dark as night,
The other, "stained with blood," was white;
Opposed as 'twere in equal strife,
And nerved to struggle for the life.
The dark hand hovered o'er my head,
And all my trembling fears lay dead,
When sudden came within my clasp,
The spear you now behold me grasp.

I poised the reed; but ere I hurled,
The white hand vanished from the world;
And I, without the slumbering camp,
Shook from my brow big drops of damp.
Then, as morn's blossom burst the bud,
I saw, oh horror!—gouts of blood—
Blood on my hands, and woman's hair,
Blood fastened to my trusty spear."
He sate, and seemed beside the fire
Some victim of supernal ire;
But ghostly terror had not quenched
His soul, nor yet his visage blenched.

WADARO.

Wadaro rose, "of rugged face,"
Chief of the tall Darakong race;
And gathering on his arm his cloak,
To King Kolorkor fiercely spoke:—
"You marked, Kolorkor, ere was hurled
The spear sent from the spirit world,
The hand had vanished; but the blood—
'Twas ours—'twill surely swell the flood
That yet must with its darkening stain
Our greenest forest glades engrain.
Pour, mingled tide, thy kindred flood,
Darakong and Mirbango blood!
Join the hot flow, red Tapook rill!
And drink, war demon, drink thy fill!
Haste, twin-born tribes!—yon king, and I,
Across the hills must quickly fly;
And o'er our heads the darker hand
Shall point the way to Tapook land.
We'll send the war-sign through their camp,
And flat their turf with dancing tramp.

Speed thee, Ganook, with these swift spears—
This fire-brand weeping fiery tears;
And take this quandang's double plum,
'Twill speak alliance tho' 'tis dumb.

GANOOK (OR THE SWIFT MESSENGER).

The Ganook danced o'er hill and plain,
Ascending, toiled, "ran down like rain,"
Nor paused till at the Tapook's feet
He laid the brand aglow with heat.
So swept across yon purple plains,
At night o'erspread with starry chains,
Karakorok, the sacred crow,
That first brought fire to realms below,
And carried blazing in his bill
The brand that lights our camp fires still.

THE TAPOOK'S RECEPTION OF THE MESSENGER.

The lazy Tapook raised his head,
Regarding, as he gazed the red,
Whose warlike flash suffused each limb,
That flamed like fiery Seraphim;
The tinge of war, the tinct of blood
Figured the tide of ruby flood,
And called as loud as symbol might,
For helping hand in heady fight.
Alas! ere this the white man's dole,
Had bought the slavish Tapook's soul,
Who lost the dotted plains that spread
From Wando's mouth to fountain-head—
From those stern crags whence springs Matar
To ocean's tumbling waves afar,

Which, lost in distance, sun, and spray,
Melt mist-like into heaven away!
The pale face brought his bartering bread,
The Tapook gave him land instead;
Green hills, and hunting grounds, and vales,
Lakes virgin yet from ships and sails,
Were his for robing, raiment, food,
And axe of steel that felled the wood.
The faithful harbinger fell back,
But king Kolorkor on the track
Not far behind, with flaming brand,
And polished lance in either hand,
Came stalking tow'rds the royal Tapook.
As erst the swift but mute Ganook:—
" Tried ally (he began) of ours,
'Mid crash of clubs and spear-shafts showers—
Our stout and brave would join thy bold,
And mass their ranks on this green wold.
See! stout Wadaro's warriors near,
Me and my brave Mirbangos hear,
Be 't thine to lead thy stalwart clan—
A thousand, numbered man for man."
To him the Tapook, turning, sighed,
And with but half his soul replied,
" What need of all these marshall'd ranks?
Our nation owes the stranger thanks.
Our food, our shelter, is prepared,
His very blanket robes are shared
With us; and as for roots, instead
He sows broad-cast among us bread.
But tarry, brother king, awhile,
And rest, for many a weary mile
Hath plucked the sinews from thy heel,
And stiffened all thy nerves of steel."

THE TARRYING IN THE TAPOOK'S LAND.

Moons waned, and suns successive steered
Their course toward west horizon weird,
Yet no alliance made nor planned
Against the white aggressive hand.
No warriors fought—the sport and hunt,
Made all their battle weapons blunt;
And each returning from the chase,
With slower and spoil-burdened pace,
Cast longing eyes on Tapook maids,
That lay beneath the lengthening shades;
And many a brave transgressed the rule,
Framed in their twin-blood-allied school,
And, mating with the maid he chose,
Sought her green roof to find repose.
Kolorkor, one of these the first,
A fiercely-burning passion nurst;—
Balladeādro fired his brain—
Balladeādro with a chain
Unconscious bound his bursting heart,
And barred his wishes to depart.

KOLORKOR'S WOOING.

To her it seemed an easy thing—
Herself the daughter of a king—
To dally with Tangola's guest;
But when his suit with warmth he pressed,
She turned her laughing face away,
Heedless of all his love could say.
Then would Kolorkor's anger rise,
And flash like lightning from his eyes;
But, past the pang of wounded pride,

He sate him silent by her side,
Like some huge thunder-cloud expended,
The calmer when the storm is ended.
'Twas thus for days and afternoons,
For many waxing, waning moons,
Half trusted hope his only wage,
Neglect still spurred him on to rage,
And so the monarch's wooing sped,
With giddy brain and heart like lead.

WADARO'S COUNSEL.

One day it chanced, in pensive mood,
He sought Wadaro in the wood;
And finding him, his counsel sought,
With heart, and brain, and soul distraught.
"Kolorkor," thundered forth the king,
"You make yourself a little thing;
And me, your friend, a thing still less;
In counsel grave on nothingness.
Remember, who our tribes would rule,
Can never mate him with a fool!
Are not our maidens fair as they?
And formed from quite as pure a clay?
Their eyes, their hair, their winning looks,
Are more than match for these Tapooks.
Besides our wise ancestral laws
Bid all our manlier ones to pause,
Ere stepping o'er the sacred bounds
That mark our ancient hunting grounds;
And seek amid our virgins fair,
The solace sent to sooth our care."
To him Kolorkor thus replied,
In phrase that reason's front defied :—

"Wadaro, what I've said, I've said,
The rest—be that upon my head."

. . . . . .

Time with his train rolled on, and all
That paved the way towards his fall,
His warrior ways were all forgot,
His weapons now he heeded not.
Laid by some reedy river's brink,
Musing, he'd watch the bell-bird drink;
Thence rising, pace the pebbly marge,
Till dying day had dropped his targe,
And sinking with his latest blood
He reddened all the trembling flood:
Till night drew near and closed his eye,
And spread her mantle tenderly
Across his darkening rayless face,
And hid him in his resting-place,
Whilst wind-waved reeds his requiem sighed,
In wailing accents o'er the tide.

. . . . . .

Time's waters rolled towards the sea
(Dim ocean of eternity),
And hurried with the current all
That presaged proud Kolorkor's fall;
Each pebble bandied by the stream,
That caught betimes a golden gleam,
Seem'd some event by prescience willed—
Some ancient prophecy fulfilled.
Straight through his breast a sadness crept,
And as he mused Kolorkor wept;
He saw in every sinking targe,
That lit the river's shimmering marge,
The funeral of his hopes and fears—
The grave of unrewarded years.

Tangola's Refusal.

At sunset sad, at dawning wild,
His brain with failing plans he piled,
Till, tired with unavailing care,
He sought the father of the fair—
Sought him, who sold his birth-right land,
And sued him for his daughter's hand.
He paused.—Tangola silence broke,
And to the suitor thus he spoke :—
" Seest thou above with silvery sheen,
The evening star, pale Mirgabeen?
She looks with saddening eye towards earth,
Which holds the secret of her birth.
Couldst thou from heaven pluck out yon star,
That shines upon us from afar,
And lay her in her beauty's pride
Between me and my own fire-side—
I'd not yield up my daughter fair,
With flashing eyes and raven hair.
And know, proud king, that threats are vain—
Tho' spears should fall like summer rain,
Deem not Balladeādro's sire
Yet wanting all his ancient fire.
Up, go thy way, hot-blooded chief,
And seek at other hands relief.
Go get some mild Mirbango mate
To rear an heir to rule thy state ;
As for Balladeādro rare,
No stranger may that jewel wear ;
A father's joy, a camp-fire's pride,
To alien ne'er can be allied."

Murder of Tangola.

Short time for parley now remained,
The madden'd chief his feet regained,

Fierce hate from both his eyeballs gleamed,
A fiend in all his wrath he seemed,
"Take this," he hissed, and raising high,
The spear to his unerring eye
He hurled, and all his muscles shook,
As pierced his lance the tall Tapook ;
Who, bowing sudden to his fate,
Fell forward on his grizzled pate.
No time was lost—as quick as thought
The virgin to his arms he caught ;
Then dragged her to Trelinnay's bower,
And charged him with the new-plucked flower.
Fit gaoler ! less of man than creature,
And hard as flint in face and feature.

BALLADEADRO IN CAPTIVITY.

There flitted o'er the luckless maid
Th' uncertain wav'ring dappled shade,
As toyed the breeze with every flower
And leaf that decked the captive's bower.
With sad tho' joyous-seeming face,
And artless art dissembling grace,
She wrought in silence blues with greens,
And scarlet in her gilburneens ;
Thus would she sit, and work and muse,
From morning's dawn till evening dews,
While singing ever by her side,
Sat grim Trelinnay's ancient bride.
She weaved, and weaving trolled her song,
Sang on and weaved the rushes long,
And cast at times a furtive glance
From eyes that pierced like pointed lance ;
Outwards and toward where stranger's tread
Was heard, she raised her grisly head.

O, tyrant sex! to thine the same
'Neath tropic sunbeam's burning flame,
As where the arctic ice and snow
Baulk the swift river in its flow.
Give ye to guard a sister charge,
And say :—Who'll overstep the marge.

Mora-Mora (surnamed the Ganook or Swift Messenger).

Hard by the bower that held the maid,
Beneath the same dark forest's shade,
Through which the slanting sunbeam shot
Stood Mora-Mora's sylvan cot.
This youth, whose skill with axe of stone
Had made his father's badge his own,
Sate there amid the hunting gear,
Repairing broken net and spear.
Oft passing westward to the chase
The captive maiden's sadden'd face
Would haunt the hunter as he walked,
And trip him while his game he stalked.
His hand had lost (so many deemed)
Its cunning since those eyes had beamed
Their first bright rays into his own,
And taught him that he dwelt alone.
Henceforth, with throbbing heart on fire,
Possession was his sole desire;
And if love's eyes a language speak
The same to Roman, Celt, or Greek—
The same in France, or sunny Spain,
On Tartar steppes or Afric's plain—
Such flashed from captive maid to man,
And thus their burning loves began.
But still the king with stately tread,

And heron feathers in his head,
Approached at noon with presents rare,
To woo his drooping prisoner fair.
Kind his entreaty—half forlorn—
His only meed was smiling scorn.
Thus hours of unavailing praise,
With prayers, made up the sum of days,
And still nor hope nor joy beguiled
The suitor of the orphaned child.
She, when her tongue the silence broke,
These burning words in anguish spoke :—
" Strike, murd'rer, home ! she fears no pain
Whose father throbs in every vein !
What ! crouched at thy false feet to lie
Thy wife !—thy prisoner first she'd die !
Avaunt ! begone ! away, away—
With words that lie, and hands that slay."
Kolorkor's brow a cloud o'ercast,
His breath was coming " thick and fast,"
And fanned his anger-burning cheek,
As thus the chief essayed to speak:

KOLORKOR'S THREAT.

" Not by this spear, that lately stood
A sapling in Tor's sacred wood,
But by the keener point unseen
Of shaft whose bark ne'er budded green,
Hurled by the might of wizard spell,
With force resistless, fierce and fell—
Mine now the lock you lost when fright
Had mastered all your senses quite,
'Tis mine ! but Kolpo's be the charge
To weave the spell, and grave the targe,
To symbol forth those plaint limbs,

Depict each orb in tears that swims,
And trace the darkly flowing hair,
Forced gage to passion from despair!
Such be his play at dead of night
When the fair figure, fixed upright,
Shall fade and wither 'fore the fire,
While Kolpo, sings Kolorkor's ire;
And in the weird night-air shall wave
Thy hair from poison-dripping stave,
Nor dream, fond maid, of hope, escape,
Nor aid nor help in any shape.
Kolorkor swears! His heart is steeled!
And thou, thine awful doom is sealed.
Pity—forgiveness—hence!—remorse,
Farewell!—until thy withered corse
Shall rot upon the arid plain,
And whiten in the sun and rain.
There never shall the raven stoop
With shifting eye and quivering swoop;
The birds, the very beasts of prey,
Awestruck, shall shivering turn away;
And grass beneath and leaves above,
Shall wither with Kolorkor's love."
He turned, and turning, swiftly fled
Into the gloom the forest shed,
Nor paused till well beneath the roof
Whence all the tribe most held aloof,
And sought the ghoul whose peering eye
Seemed tracing out some mystery.

INCANTATION OF KOLPO THE WIZARD.

Within the wood, by weird fire-light
The Wizard plied his art at night;
And sitting with his palms outspread,

And palsied, forward-bending head,
Sang to the flames a dreamy stave,
That sounded like a half-spent wave.
" Lambent tongues of sacred fire,
That own the burning sun as sire;
And thou, oh sun! whose kindling ray,
Drives forth the night, begets the day;
Whose red and ever-glowing hearth,
Plundered for shivering suns of earth,
Conceived the heat that warms our hands
With blazing heav'n-enravished brands,—
Assist our spell—our incantation,
Nor heed a lover's lamentation.
   Bat and Bird,
   Lizard, Owl,
   Crow and Snake
   With hooded cowl,
Cast with me malignant eyes
On Kolpo's symboll'd sacrifice;
Circle, flit about the flames;
Fan the fire that aids our aims.
Night-jar, owl, and fluttering bat
Sail ye round and round. That fat
Came from a warrior's cloven side,
Grim trophy of a victor's pride:
This, and poison from the snake,
With juice of deadly herb, I take,
And, breathing wizard's withering curse,
Anoint the targe and work for worse.
Eat her, Pudgill,—gnaw her frame;
Burn her, leprous tongues of flame;
Wrinkle all of her that's round,
Nor leave a single sinew sound;
So shall each supple limb give way,
And shrink into a shrivelled spray;

So shall dull death, by slow degrees,
Her heart's swift-bounding current freeze.
Blast the twin blossoms of her breast,
Burn and gnaw—'tis our behest.
Quench you two stars—our sacrifice
Demands the light of beauty's eyes."

. . . .

'Twas thus the palsied wizard sang,
As Mora-Mora on him sprang.
All that long night he 'd watched the ghoul,
The lizard, bat, and large-eyed owl:
Had seen the raven fan the flame
That flickered, leapt, and went and came:
Had marked, with swift-increasing ire,
The loathsome hell-craft by the fire.
No longer to be held, he swung
His club aloft, it hissed and sung,
As falling on the wizard's pate,
It turned the wavering scale of fate.

THE BROKEN SPELL.

Thus the destroying Kolpo fell,
As all the camp traditions tell;
And Mora-Mora stooped to stretch
Across the quivering prostrate wretch,
And snatched, with all a lover's care
The streaming lock—the maiden's hair;
O'erturned the targe and quenched the fire,
And 'venged the maid, though not the sire.

THE RETURN, AND THE FULL-MOON DANCE.

To gain the camp, one day and night,
He westward sped on limbs of might;

And found the tribes with spear and lance
Preparing for the "full-moon" dance;
And tho' half-weary from the race,
He painted o'er his anxious face,
And joined the dancing joyous throng,
With mazy tread and sounding song.
The crowd advanced, the crowd retired,
In martial rank by music fired;
Anon sank softly, as the strain
Subsiding like the slumbrous main
Which, murmuring gently on the beach,
Breathes to the sky its failing speech.

THE TIDINGS OF REVENGE.

When all was still—and man and maid
Well wearied, wandered through the glade,
Or sought the hut and warm fireside
To rest awhile in painted pride—
Then Mora-Mora found the cot,
Seeming as tho' he sought it not,
The one that held his maiden's charms,
All trembling there with love's alarms;
And clasping her with wild embrace
He kissed the big tears from her face.
Short were their whispered words and few,
Beneath the bower-leaves wet with dew.
Swift he restored the ravished lock,
And 'gan the wizard's art to mock:
"Our tribe, my girl—will arm anon,
And thou must all thy bravery don,
To fly with me when all is won,
Or see me die ere next the sun
Shall crown yon mountain's sombre brow,
And seal or loose our plighted vow."

The Battle by Moonlight.

The song waxed loud—the dancers flew,
As Mora-Mora backwards drew,
Stealing towards the rocky ledge,
That fenced the towering plateau's edge;
Thence beckoning to his trusty clan,
He posted warriors, man by man.
"I go," he cried, "to join the king,
But when you hear my war-club ring
Against his shield, rush every man
Into the battle's bristling van,
And where you note the curlew's cry,
Press forward to the fray!—'tis I!"

. . . . . .

The shield was struck! The king amazed,
Upon the painted stripling gazed,
Then rushed upon him with the spear,
But found the foe devoid of fear;
Raised his stout arm, and thundered, "Die!"
When rose to heaven the curlew's cry,
And braves in masses forward press'd
With levelled spear and fluttering crest;
And lo! aloft, a giant arm,
Whose mailèd might with starry charm,
Was studded o'er at every joint,
That blazed with many a rivet point.
It held the moon! a silver shield
Outstretched above their battle-field,
And legioned stars in bright array,
Seem'd waiting for the coming fray;
Thence glanced the star-shaft launched in vain,
Thence it reeled wildering o'er the plain,

As point from boss was harmless turned,
And death impending swiftly spurned.
. . . . . .

The heavens knelled back the shouts and cries
Of warriors in their agonies;
And through the star-lit blue vault rang
The din of arms—the battle clang.
Host forth to host defiance hurled,
As the stern conflict shook the world;
The hissing spears sped on like levin,
Obscuring in their flight the heaven;
While circling thro' the air there sang
The swift careering boomerang.

THE DEATH OF MORA-MORA.

The victors left the mangled dead,
Unburied, as they onward sped
To gain ere earliest matin ray,
The track that marked their homeward way.
But ere the braves had cleared the wood,
Or made their victor footing good,
The king stole round, and blocked the pass,
Where, hid behind the tufted grass,
He rallied soon a faithful few,
To charge the foe that rose to view.
Onward in warlike rank they came,
With arms and limbs of symbolled flame;
But ah! too soon that marching throng,
Disordered, changed their triumph song
To one of wailing, woe, and grief,
When spear-transfixed their gallant chief,
Fell to the turf with heavy sound,
And all his blood bedewed the ground.

Death of Balladeadro.

Kolorkor's vengeance nigh complete,
He hurled again, and at the feet
Of bleeding Mora-Mora fell,
The maiden both had loved so well.
The shaft he urged, by fury prest,
Had pierced the virgin's yielding breast;
There the reed, blood-stained, trembling hung,
As died these last words on her tongue :—
"Alas! I die! and well 'tis so,
Since blood and love commingled flow!
Smile, Father! on this marriage-bed,
And bless the pair that death has wed.
Ah! happier thus by spearman's point
To fall, than wither root and joint,
A victim to the wizard's spell,
Insidious, cruel, dark, and fell!"
She folded in her last embrace
Her lord, and laid her dying face
Against his cheek, with eyes upcast,
And thus two loving spirits passed.

. . . . . .

She fell! Another spear in rest
Wrought the avenger's stern behest;
But whether this were deed of chance,
Or of some destined, chosen lance,
None knows, or no one cares to tell,
Save that the proud Kolorkor fell.
This much is known :—'tis breathed by night,
By many a dying camp-fire's light,
By watchers as they while away
The hours that usher in the day,
Or tell the children round the fires—
How trembled once their stalwart sires,

To find no kingly corpse next day,
Among the common warrior clay.
How from on high a bleeding owl,
With glaring eyes and snowy cowl,
Gazed on that field with fixed despair,
Shrieked, and so vanished into air!
But when the child makes bold to ask,
Some crone the mystery to unmask,
She only answers—"Trim the fire,
Or, pile the sticks a little higher,
And cuddle closer while we sing,
A story of some other king."

GEORGE GORDON McCRAE.

THE CYNIC OF THE WOODS.

I COME from busy haunts of men,
   With Nature to commune,
Which you, it seems, observe, and then
   Laugh out like some buffoon.

You cease, and through the forest drear
   I pace with sense of awe,
When once again upon my ear
   Breaks in your harsh guffaw.

I look aloft, to yonder place
   Where placidly you sit,
And tell you to your very face,
   I do not like your wit.

THE CYNIC OF THE WOODS.

I'm in no mood for blatant jest,
   I hate your mocking song,
My weary soul demands the rest
   Denied to it so long.

Besides, there passes through my brain
   The poet's love of fame—
Why should not an Australian strain
   Immortalize my name?

And so I pace the forest drear,
   Filled with a sense of awe,
When louder still upon my ear
   Breaks in your harsh guffaw.

Yet truly, Jackass, it may be,
   My words are all unjust:
You laugh at what you hear and see,
   And laugh because you must.

You've seen Man, civilized and rude,
   Of varying race and creed,
The black-skinned savage almost nude,
   The Englishman in tweed.

And here the lubra oft has stayed
   To rest beneath the boughs,
Where now, perchance, some fair-haired maid
   May hear her lover's vows.

While you, from yonder lofty height,
   Have studied human ways,
And with a satirist's delight
   Dissected hidden traits.

Laugh on, laugh on! Your rapturous shout
  Again on me intrudes;
But I have found your secret out,
  O Cynic of the Woods.

Well! I confess, grim mocking elf,
  Howe'er I rhapsodize,
That I am more in love with self
  Than with the earth and skies.

So I will lay the epic by
  That I had just begun;
Why should I scribble? Let me lie
  And bask here in the sun.

And let me own, were I endow'd
  With your fine humorous sense,
I, too, should laugh—aye, quite as loud,
  At all Man's vain pretence.

              ARTHUR PATCHETT MARTIN.

A ROMANCE IN THE ROUGH.

A STURDY fellow, with a sun-burnt face,
  And thews and sinews of a giant mould;
A genial mind, that harboured nothing base,—
  A pocket void of gold.

The rival's years were at fifty at the least—
  Withered his skin, and wrinkled as a crone;
But day by day his worldly goods increased,
  Till great his wealth had grown.

And she, the lady of this simple tale,
  Was tall and straight, and beautiful to view;
Even a poet's burning words would fail
  To paint her roseate hue.

The suitors came, the old one and the young,
  Each with fond words her fancy to allure.
For which of them should marriage bells be rung,
  The rich one or the poor?

She liked the young one with his winning ways,
  He seemed designed to be her future mate—
Besides, in novels and romantic plays
  Love has a youthful gait.

But well she knew that poverty was hard,
  And humble household cares not meant for her;
Nor cared she what the sentimental bard
  Might warble or infer.

She made her choice, the wedding bells rang clear;
  The aged bridegroom figured in the *Times*.
The young man, after some superfluous beer,
  Went forth to foreign climes.

And this is all I ever chanced to know,
  Told by my mate while digging on the Creek,
Who ended with his handsome face aglow,
  And with a verse in Greek.

ARTHUR PATCHETT MARTIN.

A BUSH STUDY, À LA WATTEAU.

HE.

See the smoke-wreaths how they curl so lightly sky
    ward
  From the ivied cottage nestled in the trees;
Such a lovely spot—I really feel that I would
  Be happy there with children on my knees.

SHE.

No, you wouldn't. These are merely idle fancies
  Of a gentleman much given to day-dreams.
These chimneys always smoke, and, then, the chance is
  You would have a scolding wife and babe that
    screams.

HE.

Ah! but look! just there, above that lowly cottage,
  Birds are flitting in the sunlight clear and pure;
And the three-score years and ten—man's poor allot-
    tage—
  Might be passed away with pleasure there, I'm sure.

SHE.

Now, pray listen, oh, vain wanderer from the city,
  And look bravely up and meet my searching eyes:
Would you give up all your town life, bright and witty,
  Just because the cottage smoke curls to the skies?

HE.

I regret to find you're one of those young ladies—
  Pet productions of this artificial age:
Rural solitude to you is simply Hades,
  And your paradise the ballroom or the stage.

She.

Yes, forsooth! and why?   Because, my airy dreamer,
   I can use my eyes as well as gaily dance—
See the Husband, Wife, the Lover, Dupe, and Schemer
   All whirling past and weaving a romance.

He.

You think, then, Miss, such dreadful social questions
   Are like cards, designed to pass away the time;
Do you not perceive that all these pseudo-Christians
   Are but moths that flutter round the candle Crime?

She.

At the play, too, where I oft with dear mamma go,
   There's the drama being acted on the boards;
And Othello, Desdemona, and Iago
   In the boxes, p'raps, without the paint and swords.

He.

Well, that may be, but the life of show and fashion
   You so prize above the simple joys around,
Is all false; more noble manhood and true passion
   In the daily lives of rustics may be found.

She.

Think you, then, that those who dwell in rural places
   Are quite free from every evil thought and deed?
Pray speak unto the swain who hither paces
   With slow steps, as though in pain, across the mead.

He.

If you will not sneer, I'll ask him for his story;
   But expect not that his daily life shall be
Full of famous deeds; he careth not for glory,
   But lives by honest labour pure and free.

A BUSH STUDY.

She.

Speak on ; speak ! and let me hear this modern idyll
   From the lips of yonder heavy-footed swain ;—
By-the-bye, his wild, erratic sort of sidle
   Seems to indicate that he the bowl doth drain.

He.

Hush—he'll overhear. . . . O tell me, gentle cottar,
   Dwellest thou here remote from carking care and
      strife?

Rustic.

What's that to you? Are you a bloated squatter?
   Better clear, old man [hic], 'companied by your wife.

He.

Thou mistakest me, thou toil-worn man and humble;
   I own no lands where graze the peaceful sheep.
Thou art stirred with deep emotion, and dost mumble—
   Speak up bravely, brother man, and do not weep.

Rustic.

Hot to-day, guv'nor; let's go and have a liquor;
   Lady take anything?—Bless you I can pay—
Haven't had one yet, and nothing makes me sicker
   Than abstaining altogether such a day.

Sings.

    Shearing sheep is dry work,
    Kissing girls is sly work;
    But drinking deep is my work.
    So, let's drink, boys, drink!

He.

Come, Mabel, come. He is worse than Turk or Bulgar,
   And his presence doth the very air pollute.

SHE.

Well, I must confess he is a trifle vulgar;
But what say you now, my dreamer?

HE.

I am mute.

ARTHUR PATCHETT MARTIN

THE STORM.

AYE, not a doubt 'twas dark without,
Dark and drear, and bitterly cold;
But we, within that quaint old inn,
Were out of the blast like sheep in the fold.
There sat we, old comrades three,
Telling our stories and singing our staves;
Little we recked that the sky was flecked
With the lightning's fury—light-hearted knaves.

It was not far to the harbour bar,
Where groaned in anguish a noble ship,
And a lady there, of beauty rare,
Gazed into the darkness with quivering lip.
In sight of the town the ship went down—
Went down, though they lifted up praying hands,
And at break of day all stark they lay,
Those storm-tossed ones, on the glittering sands.

While there we sat, old comrades three,
Till one, with the love-light fresh in his eyes,
Sang, "The morning breaks, and each bird wakes,
And to-day my bird to my bosom flies."

But the townsmen pale spake of wreck and gale,
As we sauntered out of the tavern door,
And the ebbing tide showed his fair young bride,
And he swooned on her breast by the hard, bleak
    shore.   ARTHUR PATCHETT MARTIN.

MY COUSIN FROM PALL MALL.

THERE's nothing that exasperates a true Australian
    youth,
Whatever be his rank in life, be he cultured or uncouth,
As the manner of a London swell. Now it chanced,
    the other day,
That one came out, consigned to me—a cousin, by the
    way.

As he landed from the steamer at the somewhat dirty
    pier,
He took my hand; and lispingly remarked, "How very
    queer,
I'm glad, of course, to see you—but you must admit
    this place,
With all its mixed surroundings, is a national disgrace."

I defended not that dirty pier, not a word escaped my
    lips;
I pointed not—though well I might—to the huge three-
    masted ships;
For, although with patriotic pride my soul was all
    aglow,
I remembered Trollope's parting words, "Victorians
    do not blow."

On the morrow through the city we sauntered, arm in
    arm ;
I strove to do the cicerone—my style was grand and
    calm.
I showed him all the lions—but I noted with despair
His smile, his drawl, his eye-glass, and his supercilious
    air.

As we strolled along that crowded street, where Fashion
    holds proud sway,
He deigned to glance at everything, but not one word
    did say ;
I really thought he was impressed by its well deserved
    renown
Till he drawled, " Not bad—not bad at all—for a pro-
    vincial town."

Just as he spoke there chanced to pass a most bewitch-
    ing girl,
And I said, " Dear cousin, is she not fit bride for any
    earl ?"
He glanced, with upraised eyebrows and a patronising
    smile,
Then lisped, " She's pretty, not a doubt, but what a
    want of style ! "

We paused a moment just before a spacious House of
    Prayer ;
Said he, " Dear me ! Good gracious ! What's this
    ugly brick affair—
A second-rate gin palace ?" " Cease, cease," I said ;
    " you must—
O spare me,"—here my sobs burst forth. I was
    humbled to the dust.

But, unmindful of my agonies, in the slowest of slow
    drawls,
He lisped away for hours of the Abbey and St
    Paul's,
Till those grand historic names had for me a hateful
    sound,
And I wished the noble piles themselves were levelled
    to the ground.

My young bright life seemed blasted, my hopes were
    dead and gone,
No blighted lover ever felt so gloomy and forlorn;
I'd reached the suicidal stage—and the reason of it
    all,
This supercilious London swell, his eye-glass and his
    drawl.

But, though hidden, still there's present in our darkest
    hour of woe,
A sense of respite and relief, although we may not
    know
The way that gracious Providence will choose to right
    the wrong,
So I forthwith ceased my bitter tears—I suffered and
    was strong.

Then we strolled into the Club, where he again com-
    menced to speak,
But I interrupted, saying, "Let us leave town for a
    week,
I see that Melbourne bores you—nay, nay, I know
    it's true ;
Let us wander 'midst the gum-trees, and observe the
    kangaroo."

My words were soft and gentle, and none could have
    decerned
How, beneath my calm demeanour, volcanic fury
    burned.
And my cousin straight consented, as his wine he
    slowly sipped,
To see the gay Marsupial and the gloomy Eucalypt.

Ah! who has ever journeyed on a glorious summer
    night
Through the weird Australian bush-land without
    feeling of delight?
The dense untrodden forest, in the moonlight coldly
    pale,
Brings before our wondering eyes again the scenes of
    fairy tale.

No sound is heard, save where one treads upon the
    leaf-strewn track;
We lose our dull grey manhood, and to early youth
    go back—
To scenes and days long passed away, and seem again
    to greet
Our youthful dreams, so rudely crushed like the leaves
    beneath our feet.

'Twas such a night we wandered forth; we never
    spoke a word.
(I was too full of thought for speech—to him no thought
    occurred),
When, gazing from the silent earth to the star-lit
    silent sky,
My cousin in amazement dropped his eye-glass from
    his eye.

At last, I thought, his soul was moved by the grandeur
    of the scene,
(As the most prosaic Colonist's I'm certain would have
    been),
Till he replaced his eye-glass, and remarked—"This
    may be well,
But one who's civilized prefers the pavement of Pall
    Mall."

  .   .   .   .

I swerved not, from that moment, from my purpose
    foul and grim ;
I never deigned to speak one word, nor even glanced
    at him ;
But suddenly I seized his throat . . . he gave one
    dreadful groan,
And I, who had gone forth with him, that night
    returned alone.

                    ARTHUR PATCHETT MARTIN.

HOW WE RAN IN THE BLACK WARRI-GAL HORSE, "THE PET OF THE PRAIRIES."

You must let me have Topsail to-day, boss,
If we're going for that Warrigal mob,
And let Edwin ride Bunyip, the bay 'oss,
And put Miller on Rory the cob.
Poor old Zillah's as stiff as a poker
Or we'd give her a bit of a show ;
So let Arthur ride steady old Stoker,
Who can last tho' he is a bit slow.
You've got Mischief in very good fettle,
And, by Jove, he'll be tried well to-day,

For them flyers will sound all our mettle
And we shan't have it all our own way.
Last night I was bilin' the billy
When I see the whole lot sailing past;
In the lead was that mealy-nose filly,
And, by gosh, boss, that filly is fast!
The "Pet of the Prairies" looked awfully grand
Spieling well out on the wing,
With five mares without ever a brand
Loping in to the "Warrigal Spring."
   Next morning was plenty of bustle,
And tackling was carefully placed
On beauties with bone and with muscle,
Whose sires and whose dams had all raced.
We soon sighted "The spring," and the pipe
Was by one and by all being lit,
When M'Dermott (of bushman a type)
Said he'd ride up the rise just a bit.
From a shout he could scarcely refrain,
Then slipped off as though he'd been shot,
And whispered, "They're on the big plain,
And, by Jingo, we'll bag the whole lot!"
"Now, boys, are you ready? keep cool and ride steady,
The beggars don't dream we have found 'em.
Boss and Ned to the right, keep well out of sight—
We'll make a big try to get round 'em.
And, Arthur and Miller, you see that big willer
In the gorge by the Currajong-hill?
To make that is your dart — sneak round and look smart,
Till I signal you, keep there quite still,
And I'll make a sweep until I can creep
To 'The Spring' right round the outside;
Then, when you see smoke by the forky she-oak,
You can ride as you never did ride."

THE BLACK WARRIGAL HORSE.

We put back our pipes in their cases,
And paired off, as old Jack had said,
With the fire of the sport in our faces,
For we all were colonial bred.
And now we have all reached our cover,
We can see the black horse sniff the breeze;
No maiden e'er looked for her lover
More than we for that smoke by the trees.
See at last the smoke curls up—hurrah!
They see it as soon as we do;
Jack's close on their heels with "houp-la!"
And we echo his rally-cry, too;
Straight down the big plain all together,
Then their necks are craned straight for the hills.
Now, Bunyip, just let us see whether
You can come in a pace which kills.
Yes! Edwin has turned them—cleverly done;
Once more towards the station we hit,
The mob shows distress, five miles have we run,
And they're trying their hardest to split.
Now we streak through a forest of box,
Leaving shreds of our shirts in our train;
Now flounder o'er smooth granite rocks,
Now o'er fissures cut deep by the rain.
Poor old Stoker goes straight at a whopper,
But the old horse is killed by the pace,
And Arthur comes down such a cropper
That he is put out of the race.
And Miller on Rory is tailing;
This game is too fast for a hack,
Even Bunyip's endurance is failing,
So it's left to the boss and old Jack.
They tackle the "Pet of the Prairies,"
They must have him dead or alive;
They rally him right down the level

That leads to the Warrigal "drive."
How he rushes and dodges and twists,
How vainly he tries to clear out;
But behind him are muscles and wrists,
And men who know what they're about.
See at last he grows blinded and fagged,
They hustle him down the home track,
So the "Pet of the Prairies" is bagged,
And is now Elliot's favourite hack.
And on grog nights we yarn of that run,
As we sit by the old fireside,
And talk tall of the deeds that were done
In that wonderful Warrigal ride.

E. G. MILLARD.

AUSTRALIA.

ALL the things that have been done, and all the things
 that are to be;
All the wonders wrought on land, and all the wonders
 on the sea;
All the victories of nations, all the triumphs of mankind;
All the grand and bold achievements over matter won
 by mind;
That which stirs and thrills our spirits in the closings
 of to-day;
Words that sweep the world like fire, acts that all the
 nations sway,
When to-morrow's sun has risen, smiling from the
 glittering sea,
All are with the dead past ages, parts of life's long
 history;

Wrought into the grand mosaic lying down the course
    of Time;
Bits caught up from all the nations, lights and shades
    from every clime.
Rise and fall of every nation, origin of empires
    vast,
Trace we back through creeping decades to the dim
    and shadowy past;
Every great majestic river flowing on to meet the
    sea,
Bearing on its stately bosom many a gallant argosy,
Owes its proud, resistless volume to ten thousand tiny
    rills,
Takes its rise in some low wood-spring hidden in the
    quiet hills;
So through dimness and through darkness rose our
    infant colony
On a continent of beauty, sleeping on a southern
    sea,
Lying all at rest and silent, never dreaming what should
    be,
Never looking through the future to the wonders that
    we see.
Many a battle has been fought, and many a victory has
    been won,
Since first the sable warrior drew the blood of Eng-
    land's gallant son;
Many a deed of blood has reddened, many a cry gone
    up to God,
Since first this southern land of light was by the foot
    of white man trod,
Still through all, through fights and bloodshed, inward
    strife and inward fear,
Through the wearying disappointments always coming
    year by year;

Through it all with dauntless courage, inborn power and inbred might,
Like the grass in spring-time pushes through the earth's crust into light,
Through intrigues of legislators, faction fight and party strife,
Bravely did the nation struggle, upward, onward, into life,
Bravely fought and fairly conquered till to-day we see her stand,
Not a tiny scarce-known handful, but a rich and mighty land ;
Strong, with all the strength that youth has Time's unending war to wage,
Mighty with the might of ages, hers by right of heritage,
Rich with stores of mineral wealth, and flocks and herds by land and sea,
Lo ! her white-winged messengers are sweeping over every sea.
Lo ! a young world, lo ! a strong world, rises in this distant clime,
Destined to increase and strengthen to the very end of time.
Here through veins with young life swelling, rolls the blood that rules the world ;
Here as hers, and dear as honour, England's banner floats unfurled.
Oh, Australia ! fair and lovely, empress of the southern sea,
What a glorious fame awaits thee in the future's history.
Land of wealth and land of beauty, tropic suns and arctic snows,
Where the splendid noontide blazes, where the raging storm-wind blows ;

Be thou proud, and be thou daring, ever true to God
    and man ;
In all evil be to rearward, in all good take thou the van !
Only let thy hands be stainless, let thy life be pure
    and true,
And a destiny awaits thee such as nations never knew !
AGNES NEALE.

THE BLUE LAKE—MOUNT GAMBIER.

LYING asleep in the golden light
    Fringed with a setting of emerald green,
Crowned with a majesty peerless and grand,
    Nature has surely made thee her queen.
The clouds that gathered above in the air
    Mirror themselves in thy sparkling eye,
Sending their beauty to swell thy store,
    Till we scarce can tell the lake from the sky.

Lying asleep in the shining light,
    Silent and calm as befits a queen ;
Like a giant sapphire, limpid and pure,
    Set in a border of golden green ;
How wondrous calm and fair it must be
    Here when the glorious moonbeams lie
In silver floods on thy shining face
    And the soft winds wander in whispers by—

When the long fantastic shadows creep out
    And wander about in their silent way,
Giving a beauty weird and strange
    That will fade in the sober light of day.

And then in the solemn stillness of night,
  When the white stars burn from their thrones on high,
Does ever a moan steal up from thy heart
  To the far-off arch of the listening sky?

Down in that wonderful heart of thine,
  Does some awful secret of suffering lie—
Some tale of a dreadful tragedy,
  Wrought in the years that have long gone by?
O, beautiful picture of calmness and peace,
  I can see in fancy a terrible day,
When the very fiend of the bottomless pit
  In thy quiet nest held riotous sway.

When a bubbling cauldron of molten fire
  Seethed where thou sleepest in beauty now,
And a storm-cloud blacker than midnight dark
  Hung low on the shuddering mountain's brow;
When the lurid glare of destruction's light
  Flared red and wild in the face of heaven,
And the trembling earth in her agony
  By mighty earthquakes was rocked and riven;

When here, where the grass is velvet now,
  And the radiant golden sunlight lies,
A torrent of living fire swept down,
  And darkened the face of the noontide skies,
And the mountain reeled in the demon's clutch,
  As he belched forth scorching fire for breath;
And wherever his scathing footsteps trod
  There fell the shadow of darkness and death.
And when the rage of the fiend was spent,
  And the awful work of the day was done,
I can see the blackened and blasted land
  Lie stricken and dead in the light of the sun.

THE BLUE LAKE—MOUNT GAMBIER.

The land is smiling and emerald now,
  And the glorious sunlight's golden gleam
Lies warm on the stern old mountain's side,
  And the past seems only a hideous dream.
But that vision of horror is real and true—
  As real as this lovely summer scene—
Real as this mount with its sapphire heart,
  And its delicate border of golden green.

But why art thou lying there, oh, gem—
  Lying so solemn, and calm, and still?
Dost thou hold in thy beautiful azure bonds
  The strength of the raging fire-fiend's will?
No hand but the hand of the Lord of Heaven
  Could have laid thee here in thy quiet nest,
Could have cradled thee deep in a mountain's heart,
  With the sunlight kissing thy radiant breast.

Was it for this that He set thee here,
  To work out in silence His mighty will?
So that the earth from her trouble should rest,
  And the seething tempest of fire lie still?
Was it for this thou art cradled here?
  Or art thou the wonderful well of truth,
Or the fabled fountain whose waters hold
  The priceless treasure of fadeless youth?

Art thou only the work of enchantment? Say,
  Has thy beauty been wrought by some magic spell?
Will this wonderful vision vanish and fade,
  Leaving nothing behind but this empty well?
Or a grand old mountain, proud and high,
  Crowned to the summit in living green,
Bathed by the sunlight, and drenched by the rain,
  Just in the way that it often has been?

No answer comes up from thy silent lips,
   Thou holdest thy secret closely and well,
And whatever the future, no whisper will breathe
   From the azure depths of that rock-bound cell.
Farewell to thee, glorious mountain gem,
   Though thy beauty I never again may see,
Yet often in fancy I'll wander back
   To sit in the sunlight and dream of thee.

AGNES NEALE.

SOLITUDE.

WHERE the mocking lyre-bird calls
To its mate among the falls
Of the mountain streams that play,
Each adown its tortuous way;
When the dewy-fingered even
Veils the narrowed glimpse of heaven,
Where the morning re-illumes
Gullies full of ferny plumes,
And the roof of radiance weaves
Through high-hanging vault of leaves;
There 'mid giant turpentines,
Groups of climbing clustering vines,
Rocks that stand like sentinels
Guarding native citadels,
Lowly flowering shrubs that grace
With their beauty all the place,
There I love to wander lonely
With my dog companion only;
There, indulge unworldly moods
In the mountain solitudes;
Far from all the gilded strife
Of our boasted "social life,"

Contemplating, spirit-free,
The majestic company,
Grandly marching through the ages—
Heroes, martyrs, bards, and sages—
They who bravely suffered long,
By their struggles waxing strong,
For the freedom of the mind,
For the rights of humankind.

Oh, for some awakening cause,
Where we face eternal laws,
Where we dare not turn aside,
Where the souls of men are tried—
Something of a nobler strife,
Which consumes the dross of life,
To unite to truer aim,
To exalt to loftier fame,
Leave behind the bats and balls,
Leave the racers in the stalls,
Leave the cards forever shuffled,
Leave the yacht on seas unruffled,
Leave the haunts of pampered ease,
Leave your dull festivities—
Better far the savage glen,
Fitter school for earnest men.

(Sir) HENRY PARKES.

ON THE RIVER.

Our boat and we drift down the stream—
    Down the stream :
My love is seated facing me,
With blue eyes that welling beam,
Lustrously as in a dream,
    Full and shadowy.

Sultry grows the tropic sun,
    But we two
Feel no whit the summer heat,
Floating where the shade is sweet,
Down the river's rippling flow,
Where the red-brown rushes grow,
    Nodding in their cool retreat—

Floating in our fairy skiff,
    Where we list,
All in the hot Australian noon,
What time we see a dim white moon
And languid nature sinks to rest,
Slumbering with unruffled breast
    In a death-like swoon.

Down the river's curving reaches
    Drifting slow,
Underneath a fragrant shade
By low drooping she-oaks made;
While in the purple tide below
Chequered shadows come and go—
    Flush and flit and fade.

Oh! the warm Australian day—
    Golden fair!
Blue, stainless skies! and over all
A drowsy stillness seems to fall,
A perfect hush is everywhere,
And the waveless charmèd air
    Is held in dreamy thrall.

May, with flitting summer smiles
    On her lips,

ON THE RIVER.

Rows one hand, all lily white,
Through the waters blue and bright,
And from her rosy finger tips
The crystal water sparkling drips
    In liquid gems of light.

Deftly, my love, you touch the helm,
    Clever May !
And on my lazy oars I bide,
While all unhelped of sail we slide
Adown the river's peaceful tide,
Like that maid of olden day,
Pictured in the poet's lay,
Whom the stream bore far away
    By Camelot's rocky side.

Your broad-brimmed hat too jealously
    Hides, in good sooth,
All the sweet beauty of your eyes
Where the melting lustre lies,
And the laughter lives and dies ;
While on your cheek and on your mouth
Flushes the red blood of the South,
    And the warmth of Austral skies.

As on we glide come liquid strains
    Our ears to greet ;
Sweet chords from many a hidden throat
On the drowsy stillness float.
The fluting magpie, clear and sweet,
And the purple lorikeet,
    A sharp, fantastic note.

But mute for very happiness
    You and I

Watch the braided ripples run
     On and on, on and on,
Or follow with a lazy eye
The circles of the dragon-fly,
Now darting with a glitter by,
Now poising bright against the sky,
     Blazing golden in the sun.

O that we may thus for ever
     And for ever,
While a changeless life away
In an endless summer day,
Where the world's rude shock could never
Come between our loves to sever,
Floating down the dreaming river,
     On from aye to aye.

ROBT. RICHARDSON, B.A.

MUSK GULLY, DROMANA.

Far o'er the mountain summit lies
    A vale of gladness, ever green,
    Where feathery ferns and moss have been
From long-forgotten centuries.
There Beauty lives, nor ever dies;
    But summer after summer comes,
    And clothes again the mountain domes
With sweetness; and a soft wind sighs,
While down the valley runs a rill
    Of pearly water, leaping, falling,
    O'er rocks and stones, and singing, calling,

To ferns and wild-musk of the hill.
    Unto the gentle voice they bow,
    Saying for ever, saying now,
"Behold us! here is Nature still!"

Here Nature singeth, loud and strong,
    A strain begot of lovely places;
    And woodland elves show laughing faces—
To them the place doth still belong.
It knows not right, it knows not wrong,
    But singeth, aye, a song of gladness;
    To it there cometh one in sadness,
And sadness flieth at the song.
He sees and straight of Eden thinks;
    His woes are lost in woodland runes;
    His soul with Nature's soul communes;
His mind the draught of Lethé drinks.
    He thanks the Power who reigns above,
    Who left to join us, in his love,
To Heaven, spots like this as links.
                    J. STEELE ROBERTSON.

IN MEMORIAM: HENRY KENDALL.

THE singer is dead. But his mystical song
  Echoes back from the gloom of the tombs,
With words for the weak, and the wise, and the strong,
  And the light of a love that illumes
      The darkest of days,
      In the wearisome maze
Of a world, that with Death as a goal,
      Yet may garner relief
      For its harrowing grief

In the song of the poet's soul,
In the love that is life to his soul.

The singer is dead. And a requiem song
  Is heard in the wail of the wind,
In the croon of the creek as it creepeth along,
    A dirge of the dead we may find,
      For a poet whose rhymes
      In these practical times,
  Of a world with a cyphering brain,
      Are consumed in the fire
      Of a grasping desire,
That jeeringly jibes at the pain—
At the poet's most passionate pain.

The singer is dead. Whose notes were as sweet
  And as pure as the masters of song;
Who sang of the pangs of the hope incomplete
  That must ever and ever belong
      To the wanderers born,
      For the alien scorn
  Of a world that doth ruthlessly roll
      The Juggernaut weight
      Of a pitiless fate
On the hopes of a poet's soul,
On the strength of his exquisite soul.

But out of the crush and the wreck of the life
  Of the poet comes incense sublime;
A sweet-smelling savour that softens the strife,
  A lofty and redolent rhyme,
      Echoing back from the surges
      And wind-haunted verges,
  Of this world of the Antarctic pole,
      Strange words of the waves
      And the voices of caves,

Written deep on the poet's soul—
On the pathos and ruth of his soul.

Our Kendall is dead, but his song shall remain,
  Though the singer for ever is mute,
And the world shall yet honour the marvellous strain
  That flowed from his laureate lute.
    And though wings of the years
      With their burden of tears
Hurry earth to its ultimate goal,
    Pray the evergreen hours,
      With their guerdon of flowers,
Bring peace to the poet's soul—
A merciful rest to his soul.

J. HOWLETT ROSS.

THE BIRTH OF AUSTRALIA.

Not 'mid the thunder of the battle guns,
Not on the red field of an Empire's wrath,
Rose to a nation Australasia's sons;
Who tread to greatness Industry's pure path.
Behold a people, thro' whose annals runs
No damning stain of falsehood, force, or fraud;
Whose sceptre is the ploughshare—not the sword—
Whose glory lives in harvest-ripening suns!
Where 'mid the records of old Rome or Greece
Glows such a tale? Thou canst not answer, Time.
With shield, unsullied by a single crime,
With wealth of gold, and, still more golden fleece,
Forth stands Australia, in her birth sublime,
The only nation from the womb of Peace!

PERCY RUSSELL.

THE PROCLAMATION TREE.

[The Colony of South Australia was proclaimed on December 28th, 1836, by Capt. Hindmarsh, R.N.—the first Governor—under the shadow of a gum-tree. Of the identity of this tree there appears to be some doubt.]

" Long years ago, in that Gum-tree's shade,
I stood when the famous speech was made ;
Still to my memory strong it sticks,
Though that was in eighteen thirty-six ;
I'm certain of its identity—
I swear it's the Proclamation Tree !

" And grieved I am that in slow decay
The people allow it to fall away ;
Soon not a wrack of it will remain
To mark the spot on that sandy plain.
Relics like these should protected be—
You can't *make* a Proclamation Tree."

Some correspondents thus write, when, lo !
Another, who also "ought to know,"
Informs the Editor he was there,
And the right Gum wasn't old and bare ;
" And was it likely they'd choose "—says he—
" A shadeless Proclamation Tree ? "

" I remember well on that summer's day
The sun beat down with a blazing ray,
And the *real* tree's drooping foliage green
Threw a grateful shade o'er the pleasant scene.
From those who've written I disagree,
This isn't the Proclamation Tree ! "

THE PROCLAMATION TREE.

But now to the rescue another comes
To settle the claims of the rival gums.
He's certain the tree was old and bent,
For it partly upheld Mr Gouger's tent,
And he had a little refreshment free
Under the same Proclamation Tree.

Another, the son of a pioneer,
Wishes to make the matter clear.
Says he—" My father was also there,
And I'm certain he told me the Gum was bare ;
And often he's taken me down to see
The original Proclamation Tree."

Ah ! Memory's played a good many tricks
Since eighteen hundred and thirty-six.
Some cases, likely, have gone to rust,
And it's very certain that some one must
Get lavishing sentimentality
Over the wrong Proclamation Tree !

And Death's cold finger has beckoned away
Nearly all who stood on the spot that day.
They've left their hardships and weary toil—
Gone to select on a richer soil ;
Their tenure will there have a fixity,
Those knights of the Proclamation Tree !

No Ridley reaper nor double plough
They need to work on the holding now,
No Goyder's line can their course debar,
But they settle wherever the angels are ;
There's a harvest that lasts through eternity
For the boys who stood under the old Gumtree !

But never, O never, shall be forgot
Those pioneers, though their bones shall rot !
Grand old boys ! Though the tree may fall,
And the relic-hunters take root and all,
They shall live as long as the colony,
Those knights of the Proclamation Tree !

When before the Great White Throne there stand
The Sheep and the Goats on either hand,
And the Shepherd's Proclamation's read
Before the millions of risen dead,
His "Come, ye blessed !" we trust shall be
For those knights of the Proclamation Tree !

J. SADLER.

THE BELL-BIRDS.

MID-NOON IN AN AUSTRALIAN FOREST. FROM "THE HUMAN INHERITANCE."

A LYRE-BIRD sang a low melodious song
Far off, then ceased : a soft wind swept along
The lofty gums and breathless died away :
And Silence woke and knew her dream was day.

. . . . . .

Hush, from the trackless depths comes what sweet sound
Ineffable ? do spirits underground
In hollow caverns ring phantasmal chimes
For elfin deaths in fairy sunless climes—

Or does some sad aërial spirit high
In serene air suspend the listening sky
With sweet remember'd music of joy-bells
Changing for death? Hush, how it swells and swells
Still sweet and low and sad,—as tho' the peal
Were chimed in forest-depths where never steal
Sounds from the world beyond, and where no noise
Breaks ever the long dream. It is the voice
Of the mysterious bird whose bell-like note
Chimes thro' the Austral noon as church-bells float
O'er lonely slopes and pastures far at home.

. . . . . .

Sometimes but once it sang, as when the foam
On northern seas sleeps on the ebbing tide
And scarcely stirs the Inchcape's sounding side
To one faint clang: then ceased: then once again
Tolled out with silver sweetness its part pain,
Part reverie over some beloved thing.
At last it too was still, recovering
Some dream to brood upon with voiceless peace.

WILLIAM SHARP.

THE STOCK DRIVER'S RIDE.

O'ER the range and down the gully, across the river bed,
We are riding on the tracks of the cattle that have fled:
The mopokes all are laughing and the cockatoos are screaming,
And bright amidst the stringy-barks the parrakeets are gleaming.

The wattle-blooms are fragrant, and the great magnolias fair
Make a heavy, sleepy sweetness in the hazy morning air,
But the rattle and the crashing of our horses' hoofs ring out,
And the cheery sound we answer with our long repeated shout.—

Coo-ee-coo-ee-eee! Coo-ee-coo-eee—Coo-ee—Coo-ee!
"Damnation Dick" he hears us, and he shrills back whoo-ee-ee!
"Damnation Dick" the prince of native trackers thus we call,
From the way the swigs his liquor, and the oaths that he can squall.

Thro' more ranges, thro' more gullies, down sun-scorched granite ways
We go crashing, slipping, thundering in our joyous morning race—
And the drowsy 'possums shriek, and o'er each dried-up creek
The wallaroos run scuttling as if playing hide-and-seek:

And like iron striking iron do our horses' hoofs loud ring
As down the barren granite slopes we leap, and slide, and spring;
Then one range further only, and we each a moment rein
Our steaming steads as wide before us stretches out the grassy plain!

And "Damnation Dick" comes running like a human Kangaroo,
And he cries the herd have bolted o the creek of Waharoo!

THE STOCK-DRIVER'S RIDE.

So we swing across the desert and for miles and miles we go
Till men and horses pant athirst i' the fierce sun's fiery glow.
And at last across the plains, where the Kangaroos fly leaping,
And the startled emus in their flight go circularly sweeping,
We see the trees that hide the spring of Waharoo, and there
The cattle all are standing still—the bulls with a fierce stare!

Then off to right goes Harry on his sorrel "Pretty Jane,"
And to the left on "Thunderbolt" Tom scours across the plain,
And Jim and I well mounted, and on foot "Damnation Dick,"
Go straight for Waharoo and our stockwhips fling and flick!

Ho! there goes old "Blackbeetle," the patriarch of the herd,
His doughty courage vanish'd when Tom's long leash cracked and whirred,
And after him the whole lot flee, and homeward head-long dash—
What bellowing flight and thunder of hoofs as thro' the scrub we crash!

Back through the gum-tree gullies, and over the river-bed,
And past the Sassafras Ranges whereover at dawn we sped,
With thunderous noise and shouting the drivers and driven flee—
And this was the race that was raced by Tom, Jim, Harry, and me!   WILLIAM SHARP.

IN THE RANGES.

Through a dark cleft between two hills
A narrow passage leads the way
Close by a lonely lake; two rills,
Its children, sing the livelong day,
And from the water's lapping edge
The low tones of the long reeds come—
No other sound, save in the sedge
A black swan crooning; all the heights are dumb.

This cleft leads to an open space
Where arching tree-ferns grow around,
A still and solitary place:
Long waving grass grows from the ground,
And great green lizards half awake
Lie silent hours, and in the light
The fiery glances of a stealthy snake
Keep glinting, glinting, like twin stars at night.

Beyond, a wooded gully lies—
A greenstone on the topaz plain;
In its deep shade no glaring skies
E'er shine, so thick are overlain
The branches of the ancient trees;
Within its depths the lyre-bird hides,
And, save at mid-noon, never cease
The bell-birds singing where the streamlet glides.

Far off on higher uplands grow
The spicy gum and hardy box,

The delicate acacias throw
Their feather-leafings o'er the rocks,
And grey-green mistletoe doth creep
Till tree by tree is overlaid—
While in the noonday stillness sleep
The bright rosellas 'mid the wild vine's shade.
WILLIAM SHARP.

AUSTRALIAN TRANSCRIPTS.

I.—AN ORANGE GROVE (*VICTORIA*).

THE short sweet purple twilight dreams
Of vanished day, of coming night;
And like gold moons in the soft light,
Each scented drooping orange gleams
From out the glossy leaves black-green
That make through noon a cool dark screen.
The dusk is silence, save the thrill
That stirs it from cicalas shrill.

II.—BLACK SWANS ON THE MURRAY LAGOONS.

THE long lagoons lie white and still
Beneath the great round Austral moon:
The sudden dawn will waken soon
With many a delicious thrill:
Between this death and life the cries
Of black swans ring through silent skies—
And the long wash of the slow stream
Moves as in sleep some bodeful dream.

III.—BREAKING BILLOWS AT SORRENTO (*VICTORIA*).

A SKY of whirling flakes of foam,
A rushing world of dazzling blue:
One moment, the sky looms in view—
The next, a crash in its curv'd dome,
A tumult indescribable,
And eyes dazed with the miracle.
Here breaks by circling day and night
In thunder the sea's boundless might.

IV.—SHEA-OAK TREES ON A STORMY DAY (*S.E. VICTORIA*).

O'ER sandy tracts the shea-oak trees
Droop their long wavy grey-green trails:
And inland wandering moans and wails
The long blast of the ocean-breeze:
Like loose strings of a viol or harp
These answering sound—now low, now sharp
And keen, a melancholy strain:
A death-song o'er the mournful plain.

V.—MID-NOON IN JANUARY.

UPON a fibry fern-tree bough
A huge iguana lies alow,
Bright yellow in the noonday glow,
With bars of black,—it watcheth now
A gorgeous insect hover high
Till suddenly its lance doth fly
And catch the prey—but still no sound
Breathes 'mid the green fern-spaces round.

VI.—IN THE FERN (*GIPPSLAND*).

The feathery fern-trees make a screen,
Wherethrough the sun-glare cannot pass—
Fern, gum, and lofty sassafras :
The fronds sweep over, palely green,
And underneath are orchids curl'd
Adream through this cool shadow-world ;
A fragrant greenness—like the noon
Of lime-trees in an English June.

VII.—SUNSET AMID THE BUFFALO MOUNTAINS (*N.E. VICTORIA*).

Across the boulder'd majesty
Of the great hills the passing day
Drifts like a wind-borne cloud away
Far off beyond the western sky :
And while a purple glory spreads,
With straits of gold and brilliant reds,
An azure veil, translucent, strange,
Dreamlike steals over each dim range.

VIII.—THE FLYING MOUSE—NEW SOUTH WALES (*MOONLIGHT.*)

The eucalyptus-blooms are sweet
With honey, and the birds all day
Sip the clear juices forth : brown-grey,
A bird-like thing with tiny feet
Cleaves to the boughs, or with small wings
Amidst the leafy spaces springs,
And in the moonshine with shrill cries
Flits batlike where the white gums rise.

IX.—THE WOOD-SWALLOWS (*SUNRISE*).

The lightning-stricken giant gum
Stands leafless, dead—a giant still
But heedless of this sunrise-thrill:
What stir was this when all was dumb?—
What seem like old dead leaves break swift
And lo, a hundred wings uplift
A cloud of birds that to and fro
Dart joyous 'midst the sunrise glow.

X.—THE BELL-BIRD.

The stillness of the Austral noon
So broken by no single sound—
No lizards even on the ground
Rustle amongst dry leaves—no tune
The lyre-bird sings—yet hush! I hear
A soft bell tolling, silvery clear!
Low soft aërial chimes, unknown
Save 'mid those silences alone.

XI.—THE ROCKY-LILY (*NEW SOUTH WALES*).

The amber-tinted level sands
Unbroken stretch for leagues away
Beyond those granite slabs, dull grey
And lifeless, herbless—save where stands
The mighty rock-flow'r towering high
With carmine blooms crowned gloriously:
A giant amongst flowers it reigns,
The glory of these Austral plains.

XII.—THE FLAME TREE (NEW SOUTH WALES).

For miles the Illawarra range
Runs level with Pacific seas:
What glory when the morning breeze
Upon its slopes doth shift and change
Deep pink and crimson hues, till all
The leagues-long distance seems a wall
Of swift uncurling flames of fire
That wander not nor reach up higher.

XIII.—MORNING IN THE BUSH (DECEMBER).

The magpie 'midst the wattle-blooms
Is singing loud and long:
What fragrance in the scatter'd scent,
What magic in the song!
On yonder gum a mopoke's throat
Out-gurgles laughter grim,
And far within the fern-tree scrub
A lyre-bird sings his hymn.
Amongst the stringy-barks a crowd
Of dazzling parrakeets—
But high o'er all the magpie loud
His joyous song repeats.

XIV.—JUSTICE (*UNCIVILISED AND CIVILISED*).

Ling-Tso Ah Sin, on Murderer's Flat,
One morning caught an old grey rat:
"Ah, white man, I have got you now!
But no—dust be upon my brow
If needless blood I cause to fall—
So go, there's world-room for us all!'

That night Ah Sin was somewhat shot—
By accident! For he had got
From earth a little gold—black sin
For *thee*, though not for us, Ah Sin!

WILLIAM SHARP.

Murderer's Flat, Feb. 1878.

SOLACED.

The river banks glitter with white wild flower
    And feathery grasses wild,
While spring woos the wattle from hour to hour,
In the gleaming guise of a golden shower—
As Jove woo'd, in spite of her brazen tower,
    Eurydice's lovely child.

And fairy-like flow'rets, of azure and pink,
    And amber and scarlet, glow
Through the green and white on the river's brink,
Above where the cattle come down to drink—
But laughing jackasses laugh to think—
    Of only a year ago.

SOLACED.

Twelve months have passed since a man and a maid
    Walked over the fallen tree,
That bridged the stream, where of old they strayed,
When the game of love was the game they played,
And when he of the future was little afraid,
    And sanguine of heart was she.

They loved in the spring when the wattles bloomed,
    And the river banks gleamed white ;—
With the birth of summer she slept entombed
In the darksome grave, to which all are doomed,
And the spring-day visions that brightly loomed,
    Grew black in the murky night.

In the autumn days he had wandered there,
    Alone with his lonely heart,
When the banks of the stream were brown and bare,
After months of scorching summer air—
And dreamt of the days when his fate seemed fair,
    Ere death had bidden them part.

In the winter time, when the floods were high,
    And watered the arid plain,
Less often he came, and the banks grew dry,
While the face of a new love caught his eye,
And the heart that was weary ceased to sigh
    When the grass took heart again.

The spring is as bright, and the sky as clear
    As though she had never died,
Who gathered the blossoms and flowers last year,
And playfully tickled her lover's ear
With the feathery grasses ; and he is here,
    Alone on the river side.

The kingfisher sits with his folded wing
    And eyes him strangely, as though
Little birds could tell of the last year's spring
To the bride, that the morrow's sun will bring,
And jackasses' laughter seem to ring
    With, "Only a year ago."

He seeks for the flowers that she loved of old,
    And plucks them with gentle hands,
And weaves them deftly with blossoms of gold
Into a wreath that is fair to behold—
A wreath, to be lain on the grass-grown mould,
    Where the dead love's head-stone stands.

The bells have rung out, and the sound of glee
    Has echoed where wild flowers grow,
The love of last year must forgotten be,
For this year's love has been wedded—and she
Ne'er dreams the laughter of birds in a tree
    Means, "Only a year ago.
                  CHARLES ALLAN SHERARD.

LOST IN THE MALLEE.

FRAUGHT with flame, and clad in crimson, ride the heralds of the morn;
While the sun-god jousts with darkness, at the tournament of dawn:
And gleams of gauntlets glittering through lists of azure glance;
And the golden-armoured champion showers sunbeams from his lance;
Till some starry queen of beauty bids night's vanquisher advance.

A glorious golden glamour through the gloomy wildwood glints
Till the sombre scrub is sparkling in a galaxy of tints ;
And the morning in the Mallee, is suffused with genial glow ;
While the dying hound is watching o'er the sleeper lying low,
Who is dreaming at the day-birth of the days of long ago,
Of the days of deep desire and dreams of doing doughty deeds ;
Ere the flowers of hope were strangled with a multitude of weeds—
Of the morning of his springtime where his fancy-teaming brain
To the field of his ambition promised crops of golden grain ;
Ere he planted seeds of folly for a harvesting of pain.
Of the days when gallant comrades shared the glory of his youth
And his bright ideal of woman seemed a warm and living truth—
Ah ! that one love ne'er forgotten through the good days or the ill !
On his earth-bed in the Mallee he is dreaming of her still ;
Though what-might-have-been was never, and what-might-be never will.
And his sleeping fancy mocks him with the vision of a bride,
Tall and slender, golden-headed, snowy-browed, and violet eyed,
Robed in white and orange blossoms—as he saw her in the aisle

That day he sent his papers in, with a curse for
    woman's guile
And the Jews who long lamented his departure for the
    Nile.
Not a murmur breaks the silence in the solitude of
    scrub,
Where lies the whilom favourite of the messroom and
    the club,
With a ragged blanket round him, and the earth his
    only bed—
Not a murmur breaks the silence, as he lifts his weary
    head,
To find his dumb companion on the ground beside him
    —dead.

. . . .

Through the madding maze of Mallee, while the sun is
    at its worst,
Slowly staggers in a circle one, whose throat is parched
    with thirst—
Miles and miles he wanders onward, hearing nothing
    but the sound
Of the crackling of the deadwood on the broiled and
    burning ground,
And the dusk beholds him dying, when the dawn
    beheld the hound.
Had the Russian spilt his life-blood in the fury of the
    fight—
Had the savage sepoys shot him on that dark and
    deadly night,
When, as moment followed moment, came the whistling
    past his ears
Of the leaden rain that rattled from the murderous
    mutineers—
He had fallen as a hero, and been requiemed with
    tears.

Did the Angel of Destruction pass him by with dour
    disdain,
As unworthy of his sickle, when the bright and brave
    were slain,
So the voiceless bush might fold him in her arms of
    gruesome gloom?
Ah! a still small voice is asking, as the Stygian waters
    loom,
"Have you lived the life heroic that deserves the hero's
    doom?
Was the faith, or was the falsehood of a callous, cold
    coquette
Worth the mad trust of your manhood, or the years
    of long regret?
Was the world without her worthless, that you travelled
    down the hill?"
In his death-throes, in the Mallee, he is raving of her
    still,
Though what-might-have-been was never, and what-
    might-be never will.
Cloud-shed tears in silver torrents, wash the sombre
    stunted shrub
That sepulchres the stranger in the solitude of scrub—
Long-forgotten by his comrades in the charge or in the
    camp,
He has dreed his doom in darkness, dreary, desolate,
    and damp—
Who twice 'scaped dying a hero, ere he perished as a
    tramp.

                    CHARLES ALLAN SHERARD.

SATAN'S GANYMEDE.

Roughly clad, yet picturesquely
Through the woodland, where grotesquely
   Sombre shadows fall,
Rides a bushman, mighty chested,
Strong with strength by trials tested,
   Bearded, bronzed, and tall.

From the forest-land he passes
Over fields, where yellow grasses
   Shrivel in the sun;
Past the prison'd river, yearning
For the winter's floods returning
   With its freedom won;

Past where plundered wattles cluster
Bathed no longer in the lustre
   Of their golden rain;
Past the homestead garden, flowerless
In the wrath of summer showerless
   When all glories wane.

Backward looks he once and lingers,
As his swarthy sun-burnt fingers
   Ope the station gate,
Then, o'er dusty roads and gritty
Southward rides he to the city—
   Southward to his fate.

Cities swallow many strangers,
Beaten tracks are strewn with dangers
   Howsoever wide,
Whether 'tis for worse or better
Little knows he, doubly debtor
   To the country side.

Health and strength the bush has guerdoned
To the exile, long unburdened
  From the drink-disease;
Seldom can the city render,
In its many-tower'd splendour,
  Richer gifts than these.

Prizes won by years of labour,
With the wild-dog for a neighbour,
  Solitary time!
Days of toiling, nights of dreaming
Of the past with pleasures teeming
  In a cooler clime—

Saving stock from drought and looting,
Water-storing, dingo-shooting—
  Twice, a grim exchange,
Lead for lead in deadly battle
With the reivers of the cattle
  In the mountain range.

Work-achieving, danger-scorning—
Prompt to greet the birth of morning
  By the sun caressed—
When the dusk the sky was cloaking,
Musing in his hut, and smoking,
  With the world at rest—

Years of honest service-giving,
Sanctified by manly living
  And by healthful thought,
Reft of reveries resentful,
Howsoever uneventful,
  Are not lived for naught.

Better such an isolation
Than his early dissipation
  Or his later gloom.
Seven years of life unspotted,
Many sins, perchance, have blotted
  From his book of doom.

   .   .   .   .   .   .

Hoof strokes on the roadway clatter,
  Back-flung dust-clouds rise and scatter
In the bushman's wake.
Thirsty throats have wisdom scanty;
Speeds he onward to the shanty
  Olden vows to break.

Travel-stained and tired and dusty,
What are man and charger trusty
  To the landlord's eyes!
Wearied steed and foolish rider
Views he as the bloated spider
  Looks upon the flies.

Through both head and heart be steady
He has drugged the drink already
  For the shameful deed.
Such the welcome that he offers,
Poison taints the cup he proffers,
  Satan's Ganymede!

Little time in talk is wasted;
Once the tiger blood has tasted
  He must have his fill.
Flesh is weak and skin is porous;
Midnight hears a drunken chorus,
  Daylight hears it still.

SATAN'S GANYMEDE.

To a lower depth yet sinking,
Days and nights of deadly drinking
   Leave the man of toil
Racked with fire and senses deadened,
Nerves unstrung and eyelids reddened
   Soaked with fusel-oil.

Days and nights of poisoned madness,
Honest grief and lying gladness
   Alternating fast
With the senseless shameless revel
Comes the old deluding devil
   Back to him at last;

Comes he with his curst suggestions
Wrapped in soul-destroying questions,
   Feebly answered now;
Comes he with his mocking laughter
At the struggle followed after
   By the broken vow.

Greedy poison-vendor, leering
At your work! the end is nearing,
   Drive him from your door!
Though your parrot, not as stingy
Screeches, in your parlour dingy,
   "Only one drink more!"

Though your victim sinks yet deeper,
" You are not your brother's keeper!"
   Mouth your hateful creed.
Cain, than you, was fairer fighter.
Do you dream your guilt is lighter,
   Satan's Ganymede?

All is squandered ; all is ended,
From a leafless tree suspended
　Rots a wasted frame.
For that sudden deed of evil
Neither suicide nor devil
　May be most to blame.
　　　　　CHARLES ALLAN SHERARD.

THE SQUIRE'S BROTHER.

I.

"You, sitting in your ancient hall, before a beech-log fire,
Think that the elder should have all—of course you do—you're squire ;
I, sitting on a three-rail fence, beneath a Queensland sun,
Think that the law shows little sense to give the younger none.

Nell wouldn't know me, I suppose, were she to see me now
A Bushman to the very toes and bearded to the brow ;
I didn't wear a flannel shirt when I was courting her,
Or mole-skin pants engrained with dirt and shiny as a spur.

I daresay that she pictures me in patent leather boots,
A tall white hat (an L and B), and one of Milton's suits—
That was the Charlie whom she knew before the old man died ;
I wonder if she'd take this view if she were by my side.

How beautiful she was that night!—she seldom
  looked so fair;
And how the soft wax candle-light show'd up her
  auburn hair!
She was a bit inclined to tease, to stand on P's and Q's,
To 'Keep your distance, if you please,' until I told
  my news.

Then she rose up and took my hand and looked me in
  the face,
And when in turn her face I scanned, I saw a tell-tale
  trace
Of dew-drops from the brave blue eyes along the
  dimpled cheek,
The while she told in simple sighs the tale she would
  not speak.

She never let me kiss before, but now she gave her
  mouth
So frankly, that I almost swore I would forswear the
  South—
The sunny South of prospect vast—and hug the barren
  North,
Had not she held me to it fast, and, weeping, sent me
  forth.

So here I am—a pioneer, and work with my own hands
Harder than any labourer upon my brother's lands,
Far from the haunts of gentlemen in this outlandish
  place;
I wonder if I e'er again shall see a woman's face.

I couldn't stand it, but for this, that, when I first
  came out,
I used to see the carriages in which men drove about,

Who'd tended sheep themselves of old 'mid Highland
    moors and rocks,
And now were lords of wealth untold, and half a
    hundred flocks.

I laid this unction to my heart, that, if a Scottish herd
Could play so manfully his part, I should not be de-
    terred :
And so I slave and stay and save, and squander nought
    but youth :
Nell sometimes writes and calls me brave, and knows
    but half the truth.

Do you suppose that old Sir Hugh, who won your lands
    in mail,
Showed half the valour that I do in sitting on this rail?
He tilted in his lordly way, and stoutly, I confess ;
But I stand sentry all the day against the wilderness.

There isn't much poetical about an old tweed suit,
And nothing chivalrous at all about a cowhide boot ;
Yet oft beneath a bushman's breast there lurks a
    knightly soul,
And bushman's feet have often pressed towards a
    gallant goal.

So here I am, and, spite of all, I hope in long years
    more
To stand within my brother's hall, my quest of fortune
    o'er.
And so I slave and stay and save, and squander nought
    but youth ;
And if Nell said that I was brave she only told the
    truth."

II.

"And is it true, or do I dream? is this the dear old
  hall?
These the old pictures? Yes! I seem to recognise
  them all;
That is my father in his pink upon his favourite hack,
I wonder what would Nellie think knew she that I
  were back?

That is my brother—he is changed, and heavier than
  he was
When years ago the park he ranged with me on 'Phiz'
  and 'Boz;'
His figure is a trifle full, his whiskers edged with
  grey;
And yet at Oxford he could pull a good oar in his day.

The portrait in that frame is Nell—why, *I* gave Dick
  that frame,
And doesn't the old pet look well? I swear she's just
  the same
As when I left her years ago to cross the southern
  foam;—
I wonder if they've let her know that I'm expected
  home.

How well the artist coloured it; he caught the sunny
  shades
That ever and anon would flit across her auburn braids;
But no!—that isn't quite the blue that shone in Nellie's
  eyes;
Their light was nearer in its hue to our Australian skies.

White suits her best—she wore a white of some soft
  silky weft
Upon that memorable night, the night before I left;
Just such a graceful flowing train then rippled as she
  moved;
I'd like to see her once again, the lady that I loved.

I wonder what I'm staring at; this is a real dress-
  coat;
A veritable white cravat is tied about my throat;
I've had a dress-suit on before, and yet, I'm sure, I feel
Just like an awkward country boor ask'd to a Sunday
  meal.

I can't bear sitting here alone, it seems so strange and
  sad,
Now that my father there is gone, and I'm no more
  a lad.
'Twas here he nursed me on his knee in that old high-
  backed chair;
I'd give ten thousand down to see the old man sitting
  there.

What was that footstep?—not old John's? his boots
  have such a creak;
I'd almost swear I knew the tones, and heard a woman
  speak;
The steps come nearer, and the door—what is it stirs
  my heart?
Why should a footstep on the floor cause every nerve
  to start?

A lady scans with tear-bright eye a letter in her hand,
And bends her way unconsciously almost to where I
  stand:

I think I know that writing well: of course—for it's
    my own,
And she who reads it thus is Nell.—Together and
    alone!"

III.

A lady in her boudoir stands before a faded carte,
Wistfully folding her white hands, her sweet lips just
    apart;
"Yes, he is back," she said at last, "I thought he'd
    never come;
Yet now when all these years are past since first he
    left his home,

It seems as if 'twas yesterday on which I bade him go.
He never would have gone away if I had borne his 'No.'
And yet eleven years have flown :—I did not hear him
    come,
And went to read his note alone unvexed by gossip's
    hum.

I wonder if I laughed or cried, my eyes were full of
    tears,
To find my lover by my side and past the lonely years:
He took my hands, we dared not speak for full a
    minute's space;
I could not be the first to break the silence of the
    place.

Charlie is altered: he was once a *blasé*—little more—
Who thought it fine to be a dunce, and everything a
    bore;
Who wore the closest-fitting coats of any in 'The Row,'
And patent-leather button'd boots—a kind of Bond-
    street beau;

Yet capable of better things when out of Fashion's swim,
Or I, who scorn mere tailorlings, should not have borne with him:
But Charlie's heart was of good stuff, and of the proper grit;
Men always found it true enough when they had tested it.

He is much altered;—when I saw his dignified dark face,
I knew that changes had come o'er his life in that wild place:
I read the story in his eyes, I heard it in his voice,
The glad news that she ought to prize, the lady of his choice.

He must be more than dull of soul who in the open West
Sees leagues on leagues of prairie roll, and is not soul impressed;
Who knows that he may hold for his as far as he can see
Into the untamed wilderness from top of highest tree;

Who feels that he is all alone, without a white man near
To share or to dispute his throne o'er forest, plain, and mere;
With nought but Nature to behold, no confidante but her:
He must be of the baser mould or feel his spirit stir.

I'd rather marry him than Dick, though Dick is an
   'M.P.'
Lord of the manor of High Wick, a 'D.L.' and 'P.C.'
'Right Hon.' before your name, I know, is coveted by
   all,
And one needs courage to forego a gabled Tudor hall.

But then I wish Dick would not seem so like a well-
   fed dog,
And on his life's unruffled stream float so much like a
   log ;
The world has been so good to him that he has never
   known
How hard it sometimes is to swim when shipwrecked
   and alone.

Now Charlie's very different, he's seen the real world,
And where no white man ever went his lonely flag unfurled ;
He went to slave and stay and save, and squander
   nought but youth ;
And when I said that he was brave I knew but half
   the truth ;

For there in intermittent strife, with hostile 'natives'
   waged,
He spent the early noon of life in hum-drum toil en-
   gaged ;
Or galloping the livelong day under a Queensland sun,
To head the bullocks gone astray or stolen off the run.

He's handsomer, I think, to-day, although he is so
   brown,
And though his hair is tinged with grey, and thin upon
   his crown,

Than in the days when he was known at 'White's'
    as Cupid Forte,
And in good looks could hold his own with any man at
    Court.

Well, he has come and asked again that which he
    came to ask
The night before he crossed the main upon his uphill
    task :
I answered as I answered then, but with a lighter
    heart ;—
Who knew if we should meet again the day we had to
    part ? "

IV.

"'Neath a verandah in Toorak I sit this summer morn,
While from the garden at the back, upon the breezes
    borne,
There floats a subtle, faint perfume of oleander bow'rs,
And broad magnolias in bloom, and opening orange
    flow'rs.

A lady picking flowers I see draw near with footsteps
    light,
And when she stoops she shows to me a slipper slim
    and bright,
An ankle stocking'd in black silk and rounded as a palm,
Her dress is of the hue of milk, and making of
    Madame.

I wonder is that garden hat intended to conceal
All but that heavy auburn plait, or merely to reveal
Enough to make one long to catch a glimpse of what is
    there,
To see if eye and feature match the glory of the hair?

That is my Nellie—she is here and Mrs Cupid Forte:
We came to Melbourne late last year; I hate to be
    the sport
Of snow, and sleet, and slush, and rain, and yellow
    London fogs:
An English winter, I maintain, is only fit for frogs.

The night when first again we met—alone, by some
    good luck—
I asked if she repented yet the bargain we had struck?
She answered that she was too old, that what few
    charms she'd had
Had faded in the years that rolled since we were girl
    and lad.

And all the while she was as fair as ever she had
    been;
Years had not triumphed to impair the beauties of
    eighteen;
The same slight figure as of yore, the same elastic
    gait
I prized in her ten years before, were hers at twenty-
    eight.

And had her girlish loveliness lost aught of its old
    grace,
And had there been one shade the less of *esprit* in her
    face,
I had no calling to upbraid, and tell the bitter truth,
For whom she let her beauty fade and sacrificed her
    youth.

Look at her as she stoops to pull that rosebud off its
    briar;
Do you not think her beautiful as lover could desire?

Heard you that laughter light and sweet, that little
    snatch she sung?
Are they the tinkling counterfeit of one no longer
    young?

Here 'neath the clear Australian sky I lead the life of
    kings,
'Mid everything that tempts the eye or soothes the
    sufferings,—
Wealth, and a woman kind and fair, fine horses and
    fine trees,
Children, choice fruits and flowers rare, and health
    and hope and ease.

DOUGLAS B. W. SLADEN.

OUT WEST IN QUEENSLAND.

COIFI, the priest of King Edwin, likened the life of
    man,
Unto the flight of a sparrow with snow and the storm-
    wind wan,
Out of the frost and the darkness, into the warmth
    and light,
Filling the hall of the King's house, when it was
    wassail night.

And sojourning there for a moment, type of the life of
    men,
Into the frost and the darkness fluttering out again,
Sprung from the womb of the darkness, back on her
    breast we sink,
Knowing no whence and no whither, shivering on the
    brink.

Oft like the flight of a sparrow, lured, on a winter night,
Out of the frost and the darkness into the warmth and light,
Found we the coming of strangers out on the "runs" far west,
Coming to-night, and to-morrow gone, after food and rest.

Just riding up to the homestead, weary on weary horse,
Asking for food and a lodging, given as matter of course,
A shaking of hands and then supper, a smoke, and a yarn and bed,
Then saddle, and ere the sun's up, the stranger has gone God-sped.

DOUGLAS B. W. SLADEN.

TO AUSTRALIA.

O LAST of the Earth's children ! O latest born to Time !
Long hidden by the ocean in solitude sublime,
Your future and your greatness are still within the womb,
While, awed in expectation of high imperial doom,
The worn old Earth is waiting with anxious eyes to see
Cast in what mould the fortune of you, her last, shall be.

Yes! you were born to greatness, with your immense estates
In one compact block severed, with oceans for its straits,
From every race and country of puissance to compete,
And rich with every climate from equatorial heat

To mildness as delicious as breathes on Devon's sands,
And dow'red by grace of heaven with health above all
   lands.

Upon the sunny pastures of your unpeopled west,
The fleet, majestic chargers of Araby the blest,
Famed for their lightning courses and hardihood, at
   length
Are rivalled in their fleetness, outrivalled in their
   strength,
While to the virgin grasses of your far-stretching north
The short-horned steers of Durham have thriving
   wandered forth.

Look southwards o'er the paddocks of wealthy New
   South Wales,
And over young Victoria's world-famous western dales,
To where the pure merino, of royal Saxon birth,
French-noble and hidalgo, crops close the fertile earth,
In lustrous coat, long-stapled, and close as wild swan's
   down,
Fleeced to below the fetlock from sun and storm-wind's
   frown.

From Gippsland's hop-lined gardens to Carpentaria's
   bay,
The rocks and river channels disgorge the yellow
   clay,
That gladdens men or maddens, now turned to clothes
   and food,
Now melted in strong liquor, and oft with blood
   imbrued,
While every range of mountains is rich with coal or tin,
Or beds of solid copper, or crystals opaline.

Look once again far northwards, and see the sugared cane
Spread out in vast plantations along the Queensland main ;
Look once again far southwards, and see the leagues of corn
From Adelaide's broad bosom to honest labour born,
And eastwards to the orchards, where myriad orange-trees
With show'rs of snow-white blossom bewitch the harbour breeze.

Beside the stately Murray, the sunburned dwellers crush
Each autumn gold or purple grape-bunches sweet and lush,
That rival hothouse clusters in their luxuriance,
And press into a vintage as pure as that of France :
While further north, banana and pomegranate and pine
Their tropic richness mingle with orange and with vine.

Nor is't alone in gardens with hop or orange stored,
And wealth of sheep or vineyards, or sugar-bearing sward ;
Nor is it in swift horses, or mammoth fields of wheat,
Or sands or quartz-reefs golden, or range of cold and heat,
That you are counted happy, for you have children fair,
Whom you with proudest mother's may fearlessly compare.

For yours are bright-haired daughters, frank-eyed and fair of face,
Endowed with lissom bodies and gallant native grace ;

And they are not mere beauties in lace and silk
    arrayed,
Called, as they have been often, in battle unafraid,
To meet the venomed serpent, or wage a mortal strife
With flames and with starvation, in back-block station
    life.

Your sons might not pass muster in Bond Street or
    Pall-Mall,
But when bush fires are raging, they go to face the hell
With courage as undaunted as those who led the van
Right up to mouths of cannon, at San Sebastian;
Nor fisher of the Cinque Ports, with more unblench-
    ing cheek,
To save—even beasts—could venture to stem a winter
    creek.

The spirit of the Norman shone brightly in his breast,
Who with a single shepherd rode out into the west,
Regardless of the perils of undiscovered lands
(Of being bushed, or stricken by serpents, or the hands
Of swarming swarthy natives, who moved with ghostly
    stealth),
To lay the first foundations of all our fleecy wealth.

And something of the Norman must mingle in their
    blood,
Who emulate old England by fence and field and flood—
Who take their four-rail fences to hunt the kangaroo,
As well as would the Pytchley for all their view-halloo,
And, standing at the wickets, the cricket-bat can
    wield
With any that broad Yorkshire can send into the
    field.

TO AUSTRALIA.

The worn old Earth is waiting with anxious eyes to see
Cast in what mould the fortune of you, her last, shall be,
When grown into a nation, at length Australia's best
Have to meet doughty Europe, in face to face contest
Sterner than playing cricket and taking flying leaps,
Or beating both worlds' oarsmen upon smooth river-
    sweeps.

When you are a great nation, with free rule of your
    own,
Will you give ear to duty, as oft in every zone
Your elder sisters yearned to, though reared from
    youth in strife,
Though with no past to teach them a royal rule for life,
Though fostered in the ages, when Earth was young
    and rude
And could not school her children to paths of rectitude?

But you are heir and scholar to all the lore of Time,
Born of the Earth in flower, born in a golden clime;
You must profit by the errors of all your sisterhood;
You must purge away the evil and cleave unto the
    good;
Your reign must be the first-fruits of better years to
    come,
An earnest of the dawn of the true millennium.

The worn old Earth is waiting with anxious eyes to see
How steady the demeanour of you, her last, would be,
If the red foot of warfare were planted on your soil
And sword-blade put for ploughshare before the hand
    of toil,
Or the gulf-stream of commerce diverted to your ports,
And fleets of all the nations at anchor 'neath your forts.

Will Wellingtons and Nelsons come forward in your
    hour,
Or Washingtons discover a heaven-born leading-power?
Will you rule vast possessions with honest wish to do
Their right to all, as England so long has striven to?
And will you free the good gifts of Earth from land to
    land,
That everywhere the hungry may know her bounteous
    hand?

Go forth, young Queen, and prosper! may millions
    yet unborn
Cry blessings on Australia! teem you with gold and
    corn,
And sheep and kine and horses, and canes and hops
    and fruit!
May England's ancient greatness strike everlasting
    root
In our great Southern isle, and new continents obey
The greater Britain reared in the cradle of the day!

DOUGLAS B. W. SLADEN.

MRS WATSON.

A QUEENSLAND HEROINE.

YES! bury this woman as heroes are buried—
    A daughter and type of the conquering race—
With bayonets sheathed and with ranks unserried;
    For she fought with the savages face to face,
And conquered. There's many a chapter in story
    With heroines' names writ in characters fair,
But never a one that outglitters in glory
    The wife of the fisher of Bêche-de-mer.

The Maid of Arc, had she not chivalrous French-
    men
  Impatient to follow wherever she led?
The Countess of Brittany, had she no henchmen?
  And Hennebon Castle was battlemented.
Brave Mary Ambree had a company merry
  Of roystering English, one thousand and three;
And Grace Darling pulled in a good stout wherry
  In her perilous feat on the wild North Sea.

This wife, just a mother, had little to aid her—
  No fosse or escarpment or rampart of stone
To shelter her breast from the savage invader,
  With a babe and two Chinamen living alone
Within weatherboard walls on a desolate island
  Off the far away northerly Queensland coast;
While the wild blacks were swarming from delta and
    highland
  To swell and to aid the beleaguering host.

She left us her diary. Let it be printed:
  Let the heroine tell, in her own brave words,
How this one fell speared, and the other, sore-dinted,
  Could only just crawl to the sheltering boards.
She fought as her countrymen fought at Gibraltar
  The armies and navies of France and of Spain,
And made the fierce savages stagger and falter,
  And oft as they rallied repulsed them again.

They fled: but she knew what the flight of the foe
    meant,
  A ruse or a pause reinforcements to hail,
That if they withdrew it was but for the moment,
  That sooner or later her powder must fail.

So she stored a ship's boiler, her tank, with provision,
    And water enough, as she thought, for the while,
And, taking the firearms and ammunition,
    Launched out on the deep for a fostering isle.

This woman was born of a nation of freemen,—
    Their birthright to dare and to die on the wave;
Yet even to Britain's adventurous seamen
    'Twere hardly disgrace if they seemed not as brave.
What wonder if Gilbert who sank in the "Squirrel,"
    Or Davis, or Baffin, or Frobisher shrank
From facing the strange supernatural peril
    Of crossing the sea in a worn water-tank?

A pitiful story!—this valiant woman
    Who tempted the sea (here a dozen leagues wide),
Thus shipped, after routing the barbarous foeman,
    When she came to a haven to shelter her, died.
Eight days on the waves in a rust-eaten boiler—
    (She had better by half have been slaughtered at first),
And the foe that outflanked her, her only one foiler,
    Stands dim in her diary—"Dead with thirst!"*

No drain left to drink!—yet she would not be fearful,
    But in painful and feeble handwriting had writ
That her baby "was better and more cheerful,
    And condensed milk appeared to agree with it."
Not even the steamer when passing so near her,
    Unheeding the signals she hoisted in vain,
Could sicken the hope from her heart, or dis-cheer her;
    She noted it down, but she did not complain.

    * Literal Quotations from the heroine's diary. The story may be found in the Australasian Sketcher. Anno 1882-83.

If only a watch had been kept on that steamer!
   What has not that captain to answer for,
Sent hither by Heaven to be her redeemer?
   He will surely be haunted for evermore.
Were she living who fought then and wrought then so
     well, sons
  Might perchance have been born in our own far
     north
To match with the Drakes, and the Cooks and the
     Nelsons
  Whom the Mother of Continents has brought forth.
                 DOUGLAS B. W. SLADEN.

A CHRISTMAS LETTER FROM AUSTRALIA.

'TIS Christmas, and the north wind blows; 'twas two
   years yesterday
Since from the *Lusitania's* bows I looked o'er Table
   Bay,
A tripper round the narrow world, a pilgrim of the
   main,
Expecting when her sails unfurled to start for home
   again.

'Tis Christmas, and the north wind blows; to-day our
   hearts are one,
Though you are 'mid the English snows and I in
   Austral sun;
You, when you hear the northern blast, pile high a
   mightier fire,
Our ladies cower till it is past in lawn and lace attire.

I fancy I can picture you upon this Christmas night,
Just sitting as you used to do, the laughter at its height,
And then a sudden, silent pause intruding on your glee,
And kind eyes glistening because you chanced to think of me.

This morning when I woke and knew 'twas Christmas come again,
I almost fancied I could view white rime upon the pane,
And hear the ringing of the wheels upon the frosty ground,
And see the drip that downward steals in icy casket bound.

I daresay you'll be on the lake, or sliding on the snow,
And breathing on your hands to make the circulation flow,
Nestling your nose among the furs of which your boa's made—
The Fahrenheit here registers a hundred in the shade.

It is not quite a Christmas here with this unclouded sky,
This pure transparent atmosphere, this sun mid-heaven high,
To see the rose upon the bush, young leaves upon the trees,
And hear the forest's summer hush or the low hum of bees.

But cold winds bring not Christmastide, or budding roses June,
And while it's night upon your side we revel in the noon.

Kind hearts make Christmas ; June can bring blue sky
    or clouds above ;
The only universal Spring is that which comes of love.

And so it's Christmas in the South as on the North Sea
    coasts,
Though we are starv'd with summer-drouth, and you
    with winter frosts.
And we shall have our roast beef here and think of you
    the while,
Though all the watery hemisphere cuts off the mother
    isle.

Feel sure that we shall think of you, we who have
    wandered forth ;
And many a million thoughts will go to-day from south
    to north ;
Old heads will muse on churches old, where bells will
    ring to-day—
The very bells perchance which tolled their fathers to
    the clay.

And now good-night and I shall dream that I am with
    you all,
Watching the ruddy embers gleam athwart the
    panelled hall ;
Nor care I if I dream or not, though severed by the
    foam,
My heart is always in the spot which was my child-
    hood's home.

                        DOUGLAS B. W. SLADEN.

THE BUSHMAN.

HERE am I stretched, in careless ease,
  Outside my tent in this strange old wood;
The magpie chatters somewhere in the trees,
  And the curlew pipes in its dreariest mood;
The passion-flower's clinging leaves interlace,
  As a screen from the glare of the setting sun,
While phantoms of old flit past my face
  With the old year's hours dying out one by one.

Wattle-tree perfumes fall thick on the sense,
  And acacia blossoms whiten the ground,
While the silence around me, growing intense,
  Would lap my soul in a langour profound,
Save for the mosquitoes' unwelcome hum,
  Fanning their fires as the day grows cool,
Or "the muffled monotones" that come
  From a haunt of frogs in a neighbouring pool.

The forest is peopled with stiff stark forms
  That stare me like sentries in the face—
Not men, but grim, weird trees the storms
  Have thrown together devoid of grace—
And parasites climb the bald smooth sides,
  Hanging their tendrils from every bough,
Like my present life, that scantly hides
  The ghosts of hope that are ended now.

"Friends?" I had troops in my younger days—
  At least they appeared to be so to me—
They augured my future with smiles and praise,
  Faithful and steadfast they promised to be—

But now, like a withered leaf lightly whirled
  By the wind from some far-off flourishing stem,
I am blotted wholly out of their world,
  My very name is forgotten by them.

"Books?" Ah, well! I am not the dunce
  You may think me now, prosaic and slow—
Grave or gay, I loved them once,
  And they quickened my pulses long, long ago—
But useless now as these ringed old gums,
  To cheer or shade they have lost the art—
As vinegar upon nitre comes
  The singer of songs to a worn-out heart.

I was one time tempted to drown in drink
  The regrets that haunted me from the past—
But the fiend was conquered—I could not link
  Remorse to the shadows around me cast.
Hardly dealt with, I think, at times,
  I'll keep the innermost shrine unstained,
Hoping still that more generous climes
  May in God's universe yet be gained.

Aims, that formed the romance of youth—
  Hopes, that stirred me in earlier life—
The yearnings for undiscovered truth,
  With which my boyish days were rife—
The thirst to rise, excel, command—
  Seem only now to provoke a smile,
As I take my felling-axe in my hand,
  And hack at the forest with ceaseless toil.

Now for my pipe. The dying sun
  Darts its last rays through yon old shea-oak;
And the phantoms vanish, one by one,
  Before the ascending wreaths of smoke.

I have done an honest day's work, God knows—
  And when I turn in, and go to sleep,
All I ask for is deep repose
  In dreamless slumbers my soul to keep.
A. C. SMITH.

THE MIDNIGHT AXE.

THE red day sank as the Sergeant rode
  Through the woods grown dim and brown,
One farewell flush on his carbine glowed,
  And the veil of the dusk drew down.

No sound of life save the hoof-beats broke
  The hush of the lonely place,
Or the short sharp words that the Sergeant spoke
  When his good horse slackened pace,

Or hungrily caught at the ti-tree shoots,
  Or in tangled brushwood tripped,
Faltered amidst disrupted roots,
  Or on porphyry outcrop slipped.

The woods closed in; through the vaulted dark
  No ray of starlight shone,
But still o'er the crashing litter of bark
  Trooper and steed tore on.

Night in the bush, and the bearings lost;
  But the Sergeant took no heed,
For fate that morn his will had crossed,
  And his wrath was hot indeed.

The captured prey that his hands had gripped,
  Ere the dawn in his lone bush lair,
The bonds from his pinioned wrists had slipped,
  And was gone he knew not where.

Therefore the wrath of Sergeant Hume
  Burned fiercely as on he fared,
And whither he rode through the perilous gloom
  He neither knew nor cared,

But still, as the dense brush checked the pace,
  Would drive the sharp spurs in,
Though the pendent parasites smote his face,
  Or caught him beneath the chin.

The woodland dipped, or upward bent,
  But he recked not of hollow or hill,
Till right on the brink of a sheer descent
  His trembling horse stood still.

And when, in despite of word and oath,
  He swerved from the darksome edge,
The unconscious man, dismounting loath,
  Set foot on a yielding ledge.

A sudden strain on a treacherous rein,
  And a clutch on the empty air,
A cry in the dark, with no ear to mark
  Its accents of despair.

And the slender stream in the gloom below,
  That in mossy channel ran,
Was checked a space in its feeble flow,
  By the limbs of a senseless man.

II.

A change had passed o'er the face of night
  When, waking as from a dream,
The Sergeant gazed aghast on the sight
  Of moonlit cliff and stream.

From the shallow wherein his limbs had lain
  He crawled to higher ground,
And numb of heart and dizzy of brain,
  Dreamily gazed around.

From aisle to aisle of the solemn wood
  A misty radiance spread,
And, like pillars seen through incense, stood
  The gaunt boles gray and red.

Slow vapours, touched with a mystic sheen,
  Round the sombre branches curled,
Or floated the haggard trunks between,
  Like ghosts in a spectral world.

No voice was heard of beast or bird,
  Nor whirr of insect wing;
Nor crepitant bark the silence stirred,
  Nor dead or living thing.

So still—that but for his labouring breath,
  And the blood on his head and hand,
He might have deemed his swoon was death,
  And this the Silent Land.

Anon, close by, at the water's edge,
  His helmet he espied
Half-buried among the reedy sedge,
  And drew it to his side.

And ev'n as he dipped it in the brook,
  And drank as from a cup,
Suddenly, with affrighted look,
  The Sergeant started up.

For the sound of an axe, a single stroke,
  Through the ghostly woods rang clear;
And a cold sweat on his forehead broke,
  And he shook in deadly fear.

Why should the sound that on lonely tracks
  Had gladdened him many a day—
Why should the ring of the friendly axe
  Bring boding and dismay?

And why should his steed down the slope hard by,
  With fierce and frantic stride—
Why should his steed with unearthly cry
  Rush trembling to his side?

Strange, too—and the Sergeant marked it well,
  Nor doubted he marked aright—
When the thunder of hoofs on the silence fell,
  And the cry rang through the night,

A thousand answering echoes woke,
  Reverberant far and wide;
But to the unseen woodman's stroke
  No echoes had replied.

And while he questioned with his fear,
  And summoned his pride to aid,
A second stroke fell, sharp and clear,
  Nor echo answer made.

A third stroke, and aloud he cried,
   As one who hails his kind;
But nought save his own voice multiplied
   His straining sense divined.

He bound the ends of his broken rein,
   He recked not his carbine gone,
He mounted his steed with a groan of pain,
   And tow'rd the Sound spurred on.

For now the blows fell thick and fast,
   And he noted with added dread,
That ever as woods on woods flew past,
   The sound moved on ahead.

But his courage rose with the quickening pace,
   And mocked his boding gloom!
For fear had no abiding-place
   In the soul of Sergeant Hume.

III.

Where the woods thinned out, and the sparser trees
   Their separate shadows cast,
Waxing fainter by slow degrees,
   The sounds died out at last.

The Sergeant paused and peered about
   O'er all the stirless scene,
Half in amaze, and half in doubt
   If such a thing had been.

Nor vainly in search of clue or guide
   From trunk to trunk he gazed,
For, lo! the giant stem at his side
   By the hand of man was blazed.

And again and again he found the sign,
  Till, after a weary way,
Before him, asleep in the calm moonshine,
  A little clearing lay;

And in it a red slab tent that glowed
  As 'twere of jasper made,
The Sergeant into the clearing rode
  And passed through the rude stockade.

He bound his horse to the fence, and soon
  He stood by the open door.
With pallid face upturned to the moon
  A man slept on the floor.

Little he thought to have found him there,
  By such strange portent led —
His sister's son whom for many a year
  His own had mourned as dead,

Who had chosen the sundering seas to roam,
  After a youth misspent,
And to those who wept in his far-off home
  Token nor word had sent.

The face looked grim and haggard and old,
  Yet not from the touch of time;—
Too well the Sergeant knew the mould,
  The lineaments of crime.

And "Better," he said, "she should mourn him dead
  Than know him changed to this!"
Yet he kneeled, and touched the slumbering head
  For her, with a gentle kiss.

Whereat the eyelids parted wide,
   But no light in the dull eye gleamed;
The man turned slowly on his side
   And muttered as one who dreamed.

He stared at the Sergeant as in a trance,
   And the listener's blood ran cold
As he pierced the broken utterance
   That a tale of horror told.

For he heard him rave of murder done,
   Of an axe and a hollow tree,
And "Oh, God!" he cried, "must my sister's son
   Be led to his death by me!"

He seized him roughly by the arm,
   He called him by his name;
The man leaped up in mazed alarm,
   And terror shook his frame.

Then a sudden knife flashed out from his hip,
   And they closed in struggle wild;
But soon in the Sergeant's iron grip
   The man was as a child.

IV.

A wind had arisen that shook the hut,
   The moonbeams dimmed apace,
The lamp was lit, the door was shut,
   And the twain sat face to face.

As question put, and answer flung,
   A weary space had passed;
But the secret of the soul was wrung
   From the stubborn lips at last.

As one who resistless doom obeyed
   The younger told his sin,
Nor any prayer for mercy made,
   Nor appeal to the bond of kin.

" The quarrel? Oh, 'twas an idle thing—
   Too idle almost to name;
He turned up an ace and killed my king,
   And I lost the cursed **game.**

" And he triumphed and jeered, and his stinging chaff,
   By heaven, how it maddened me then!
And he left me there with a scornful laugh,
   But he never laughed again.

" We had long been mates through good and ill,
   Together we owned this land;
But his was ever the stronger will,
   And his the stronger hand.

" **But I** would be done with his lordly airs;
   I was weary of them and him;
So I stole upon him unawares
   In the forest lone and dim.

" **The** ring of his axe had drowned my tread;
   But a rod from me he stood,
When he paused to fix the iron head
   That had loosened as he hewed.

" Then I too made a sudden halt,
   And watched him as he turned
To a charred stump, in whose gaping **vault**
   A fire of branches burned.

"He had left the axe by the half-hewn bole,
   As whistling he turned away;
From my covert with wary foot I stole,
   And caught it where it lay.

"He stooped; he stirred the fire to flame;
   I could feel its scorching breath,
As behind him with the axe I came,
   And struck the stroke of death.

"Dead at a blow, without a groan,
   The sapling still in his hands,
The man fell forward like a stone
   Amid the burning brands.

"The stark limbs lay without, but those
   I thrust in the fiery tomb——'
With shuddering groan the Sergeant rose,
   And paced the narrow room;

And cried aloud, "Oh, task of hell,
   That *I* should his captor be!
My God! if it be possible,
   Let this cup pass from me!"

The spent light flickered and died; and, lo,
   The dawn about them lay;
And each face a ghastlier shade of woe
   Took on in the dismal gray.

Around the hut the changeful gale
   Seemed now to sob and moan,
And mingled with the doleful tale
   A dreary undertone.

"I piled dry wood in the hollow trunk,
  The unsparing shrift went on;
And watched till the tedious corse had shrunk
  To ashes, and was gone.

"That night I knew my soul was dead;
  For neither joy nor grief
The numbness stirred of heart and head,
  Nor tears came for relief.

"And when morning dawned, with no surprise
  I awoke to my solitude,
Nor blood-clouds flared before mine eyes,
  As men had writ they should;

"Nor fancy feigned dumb things would prate
  Of what no man could prove—
Only a heavy, heavy weight,
  That would not, would not move.

"Only a burden ever the same
  Asleep or awake I bore,
A dead soul in a living frame
  That would quicken never more.

"Three nights had passed since the deed was done,
  And all was calm and still
(You'll say 'tis a lie; I say 'tis none;
  I'll swear to it, if you will)—

"Three nights—and, mark me, that very day
  I had stood by the ashy cave,
And the toppling shell had snapped, and lay
  Like a lid on my comrade's grave.

" And yet, I tell you, the man lived on !
  Though the ashes o'er and o'er
I had sifted till every trace was gone
  Of what he was, or wore.

" Three nights had passed ; in a quiet unstirred
  By wind or living thing,
As I lay upon my bed, I heard
  His axe in the timber ring !

" He hewed ; he paused ; he hewed again,
  Each stroke was like a knell !
And I heard the fibres wrench, and then
  The crash of a tree as it fell.

" And I fled ; a hundred leagues I fled—
  In the crowded haunts of town
I would hide me from the irksome dead,
  And would crush remembrance down.

" But in all that life and ceaseless stir,
  Nor part nor lot I found ;
For men to me as shadows were,
  And their speech had a far-off sound.

" For I had lost the touch of souls,—
  Men's lives and mine betwixt,
Wide as the space that parts the poles,
  There was a great gulf fixed.

" Sorrow and joy to me but seemed
  As one from an alien sphere,
I lived and saw, or as one who dreamed,—
  I was lonelier there than here.

"To the sense of all life's daily round
   I had lost the living key,
And I grew to long for the only sound
   That had meaning on earth for me.

"Again o'er the weary forest-tracks
   My burden hither I bore;
And I heard the measured ring of the axe
   In the midnight as before.

"And as ever he hewed the long nights through,
   Nor harmed me in my bed,
A feeble sense within me grew
   Of friendship with the dead.

"And, believe me, I could have lived, lived long,
   With this poor stay of mine,
But the faithless dead has done me wrong!
   Three nights and never a sign,

"Though I've thrice out-watched the stars!—Last night
   Seeing he came no more.
Despair anew was whispering flight,
   When I sank as dead on the floor.

"Take me away from this cursed abode!
   Not a jot for my life I care;
He has left me alone, and my weary load
   Is greater than I can bear.

"But I say, if my mate still walked about
   I had never told you the tale!"
As he spoke the sound of an axe rang out,
   In a lull of the fitful gale.

He sprang to his feet; a cunning smile
  O'er all his visage spread;
"Why, man, I lied to you all the while!
  It was all a lie!" he said.

"Leave go!"—for the trooper dragged him out
  Under the angry sky.
"The man's alive!—you can hear him shout:—
  Would you hang me for a lie? . . .

"Not that way! No, not that!" he hissed,
  And shook in all his frame;
But the Sergeant drew him by the wrist
  To whence the sounds yet came,

Moaning ever, "What have I done,
  That I should his captor be?
Oh, God! to think that my sister's son
  Should be led to his death by me!"

The tempest swelled; and, caught by the blast,
  In wanton revel of wrath,
Tumultuous boughs flew whirling past,
  Or thundered across their path.

Yet ever above the roar of the storm,
  Louder and louder yet
The axe-strokes rang, but no human form
  Their 'wildered vision met.

When they reached a spot where a charred stump prone
  On an ashy hollow lay,
The doomed man writhed with piteous moan,
  And well-nigh swooned away.

When they came to a tree on whose gaping trunk
  Some woodman's axe had plied,
The struggling captive backward shrunk,
  And broke from the trooper's side.

"To left! For your life! To left, I say!"
  Was the Sergeant's warning call;
For he saw the tree in the tempest sway,
  He marked the threatening fall.

But the vengeful wreck its victim found;
  It seized him as he fled;
Between one giant limb and the ground,
  The man lay crushed and dead.

The Sergeant gazed on the corse aghast,
  Yet he cried as he bent the knee,
"Father, I thank Thee that Thou hast
  Let this cup pass from me!"
                              J. BRUNTON STEPHENS.

TO A BLACK GIN.

DAUGHTER of Eve, draw near—I would behold thee.
Good Heavens! Could ever arm of man enfold thee?
Did the same Nature that made Phryne mould thee?

Come thou to leeward; for thy balmy presence
Savoureth not a whit of *mille-fleurescence* ;—
My nose is no insentient excrescence.

Thou art not beautiful, I tell thee plainly,
Oh! thou ungainliest of things ungainly;
Who thinks thee less than hideous doats insanely.

TO A BLACK GIN.

Most unæsthetical of things terrestrial,
Hadst thou indeed an origin celestial?
Thy lineaments are positively bestial!

Yet thou my sister art, the clergy tell me;
Though, truth to state, thy brutish looks compel me
To hope these parsons merely want to *sell* me.

A hundred times and more I've heard and read it;
But if Saint Paul himself came down and said it,
Upon my soul I would not give it credit.

"God's image cut in ebony," says some one;
'Tis to be hoped some day thou may'st become one;
Thy present image is a very rum one.

Thy "face the human face divine!" . . . O, Moses
Whatever trait divine thy face discloses,
Some vile Olympian cross-play pre-supposes.

Thy nose appeareth but a transverse section;
Thy mouth hath no particular direction,—
A flabby-rimmed abyss of imperfection.

Thy skull development mine eye displeases;
Thou wilt not suffer much from brain diseases;
Thy facial angle forty-five degrees is.

The coarseness of thy tresses is distressing,
With grease and raddle firmly coalescing,
I cannot laud thy system of "top-dressing."

Thy dress is somewhat scant for proper feeling;
As is thy flesh too,—scarce thy bones concealing;
Thy calves unquestionably want *revealing*.

TO A BLACK GIN.

Thy rugged skin is hideous with tattooing,
And legible with hieroglyphic wooing—
Sweet things in art of some fierce lover's doing.

For thou some lover hast, I bet a guinea,—
Some partner in thy fetid ignominy,
The *raison d'être* of this piccaninny.

What must *he* be whose eye thou hast delighted?
His sense of beauty hopelessly benighted!
The canons of his taste how badly sighted!

What must his gauge be, if thy features pleased him?
If lordship of such limbs as thine appeased him,
It was not "*calf* love" certainly that seized him.

And is he amorously sympathetic?
And doth he kiss thee? . . . Oh my soul prophetic!
The very notion is a strong emetic!

And doth he smooth thine hours with oily talking?
And take thee conjugally out-a-walking?
And crown thy transports with a tom-a-hawking?

I guess his love and anger are combined so;
His passions on thy shoulders are defined so;
"His passages of love" are *underlined* so;

Tell me thy name. What? Helen? (Oh, Œnone
That name bequeathed to one so foul and bony,
Avengeth well thy ruptured matrimony!)

Eve's daughter! with that skull and that complexion?
What principle of "natural selection"
Gave thee with Eve the most remote connection?

TO A BLACK GIN.

Sister of L. E. L——, of Mrs Stowe, too!
Of E. B. Browning! Harriet Martineau, too
Do theologians know where fibers go to?

Of dear George Eliot, whom I worship daily!
Of Charlotte Brontë! and Joanna Baillie!—
Methinks that theory is rather "scaly."

Thy primal parents came a period later—
The handiwork of some vile imitator;
I fear they had the devil's *imprimatur*.

This in the retrospect.—Now, what's before thee?
The white man's heaven, I fear, would simply bore thee;
Ten minutes of doxology would floor thee.

Thy Paradise should be some land of Goshen,
Where appetite should be thy sole devotion,
And surfeit be the climax of emotion;—

A land of Bunya-bunyas towering splendid,—
Of honey-bags on every tree suspended,—
A Paradise of sleep and riot blended;—

Of tons of 'baccy, and tons more to follow,—
Of wallaby as much as thou couldst swallow,—
Of hollow trees, with 'possums in the hollow;—

There, undismayed by frost or flood, or thunder,
As joyous as the skies thou roamest under,
There should'st thou . . . Cooey . . Stop! she's off.
 . . . No wonder.

J. BRUNTON STEPHENS.

MY OTHER CHINEE COOK.

Yes, I got another Johnny; but he was to Number One
As a Satyr to Hyperion, as a rushlight to the sun;
He was lazy, he was cheeky, he was dirty, he was sly,
But he had a single virtue, and its name was "rabbit-
pie."

Now those who say the bush is dull are not so far astray,
For the neutral tints of station life are anything but
gay;
But, with all its uneventfulness, I solemnly deny
That the bush is unendurable along with rabbit-pie.

We had fixed one day to sack him, and agreed to moot
the point,
When my lad should bring our usual regale of cindered
joint,
But instead of cindered joint we saw and smelt, my
wife and I,
Such a lovely, such a beautiful, oh! such a rabbit-pie!

There was quite a new expression on his lemon-coloured
face
And the unexpected odour won him temporary grace,
For we tacitly postponed the sacking point till by-and-
bye,
And we tacitly said nothing save the one word, "rabbit-
pie."

I had learned that pleasant mystery should simply be
endured,
And forebore to ask of Johnny where the rabbits were
procured!

I had learned from Number One to stand aloof from
   how and why,
And I threw myself upon the simple fact of rabbit-pie.

And when the pie was opened, what a picture did we
   we see!
"They lay in beauty side by side, they filled our
   home with glee!"
How excellent, how succulent, back, neck, and leg and
   thigh;
What a noble gift is manhood! what a trust is rabbit-
   pie!

For a week the thing continued, rabbit-pie from day
   to day;
Though where he got the rabbits John would ne'er
   vouchsafe to say;
But we never seemed to tire of them, and daily could
   descry
Subtle shades of new delight in each successive rabbit-
   pie.

Sunday came; by rabbit reckoning, the seventh day
   of the week;
We had dined; we sat in silence, both our hearts (?)
   too full to speak;
When in walks Cousin George, and, with a sniff, says
   he, "Oh my!
What a savoury suggestion! what a smell of rabbit-
   pie!"

"Oh, why so late, George?" says my wife, "the rabbit-pie is gone;
But you *must* have one for tea, though. Ring the
   bell, my dear, for John.

MY OTHER CHINEE COOK.

So I rang the bell for John, to whom my wife did signify,
"Let us have an early tea, John, and another rabbit-pie."

But John seemed taken quite aback, and shook his funny head,
And uttered words I comprehended no more than the dead;
"Go, do as you are bid," I cried, "we wait for no reply;
Go! let us have tea early, and another rabbit-pie!"

Oh, that I had stopped his answer! But it came out with a run:
"Last-a week-a plenty puppy; this-a week-a puppy done!"
Just then my wife, my love, my life, the apple of mine eye,
Was seized with what seemed "mal-de-mer,"—"sick transit" rabbit-pie!

And George! By George, he laughed, and then he howled like any bear!
The while my wife contorted like a mad convulsionnaire;
And I—I rushed on Johnny, and I smote him hip and thigh,
And I never saw him more, nor tasted more of rabbit-pie.

And the childless mothers met me, as I kicked him from the door,
With loud maternal wailings, and anathemas galore;

I must part with pretty Tiny, I must part with little Fly,
For I'm sure they know the story of the so-called "rabbit-pie."

J. BRUNTON STEPHENS.

DROUGHT AND DOCTRINE.

COME, take the tenner, doctor. . . . Yes, I know the bill says "five,"
But it ain't as if you'd merely kep' our little un alive;
Man, you saved the mother's reason when you saved that baby's life,
An' it's thanks to you I hav'n't a ravin' idiot for a wife.
Let me tell you all the story, an' if then you think it strange
That I'd like to fee you extry—why, I'll take the bloomin' change.
If yer bill had said a hundred. . . . I'm a poor man, doc., an' yet
I'd 'a slaved till I had squared it; ay, still been in yer debt.
Well, you see, the wife's got notions on a heap o' things that ain't
To be handled by a man as don't pretend to be a saint;
So I minds "the cultivation," smokes my pipe, an' makes no stir,
An' religion, and such p'ints, I lays entirely on to her.
Now she got it fixed within her that, if children die afore
They've been sprinkled by the parson, they've no show for evermore;
An' though they're spared the pitchforks, an' the brimstun an' the smoke,

They ain't allowed to mix up there with other little folk.
So, when our last began to pine, an' lost his pretty smile,
An' not a parson to be had within a hunder mile—
(For though there is a chapel down at Bluegrass Creek, you know,
The clergy's there on dooty only thrice a year or so)—
Well, when our yet unchristened mite grew limp an' thin an' pale,
It would 'a cut you to the heart to hear the mother wail
About her "unregenerate babe," an' how, if it should go,
'Twould have no chance with them as had their registers to show.
Then awful quiet she grew an' hadn't spoken for a week,
When in came brother Bill one day with news from Bluegrass Creek.
"I seen," says he, "a notice on the chapel railin' tied.
They'll have service there this evenin'—can the youngster stand the ride?
For we can't have parson here, if it be true as I've heard say
There's a dyin' man as wants him more'n twenty mile away;
So——" he hadn't time to finish ere the child was out of bed
With a shawl about its body, an' a hood upon its head.
"Saddle up," the missus said. I did her biddin' like a bird,
Perhaps I thought it foolish, but I never said a word;
For though I have a vote in what kids eat, drink, or wear,
Their spiritual requirements are entirely her affair.

We started on our two hours' ride beneath a burning sun,
With Aunt Sal and Bill for sureties to renounce the Evil One;
An' a bottle in Sal's basket that was labelled "Fine Old Tom"
Held the water that regeneration was to follow from.
For Bluegrass Creek was dry, as Bill that very day had found,
An' not a sup o' water to be had for miles around;
So, to make salvation sartin for the babby's little soul
We had filled a dead marine, sir, at the family water-hole.
Which every forty rods or so Sal raised it to her head,
An' took a snifter, "Just enough to wet her lips," she said.
Whereby it came to pass that when we reached the chapel door
There was only what would serve the job, an' deuce a dribble more.
The service had begun—we didn't like to carry in
A vessel with so evident a carritur for gin,
So we left it in the porch, an', havin done our level best,
Went an' owned to bein' "miserable offenders" with the rest.
An' nigh upon the finish, when the parson had been told
That a lamb was waiting there to be admitted to the fold,
Rememberin' the needful, I gets up an' quietly slips
To the porch to see a swagsman—with our bottle to his lips.
Such a faintness came all over me, you might have then an' there
Knocked me down, sir, with a feather, or tied me with a hair.

DROUGHT AND DOCTRINE.

Doc., I couldn't speak or move; an' though I caught
    the beggar's eye,
With a wink he turned the bottle bottom up an'
    drank it dry.
An' then he flung it from him, being suddenly aware
That the label on't was merely a deloosion an' a
    snare;
An the crash cut short the people in the middle of
    A-men,
An' all the congregation heard him holler, "Sold
    again"!
So that christ'nin was a failure; every water flask
    was drained,
Even the monkey in the vestry not a blessed drop
    contained;
An' the parson in a hurry cantered off upon his
    mare,
Leavin' baby unregenerate an' missus in despair.
That night the child grew worse, but my care was for
    the wife,
I feared more for her reason than for that wee spark
    of life.

. . . .

But you know the rest—how Providence contrived
    that very night
That a doctor should come cadgin' at our shanty for
    a light.

. . . .

Baby? Oh! he's chirpy, thank ye—been baptized—his
    name is Bill,
It's weeks an' weeks since parson came an' put him
    through the mill;
An' his mother's mighty vain upon the subjeck of his
    weight,
An' a reg'lar cock-a-hoop about his spiritual state.

So now you'll take the tenner; oh, confound the
    bloomin' change!
Lord, had Billy died!—but, doctor, don't you think it
    summut strange
That them as keeps the gate should have refused to let
    him in
Because a fool mistook a drop of Adam's ale for gin?

J. BRUNTON STEPHENS.

TO A WATER WAGTAIL.

MERRY, babbling, restless bird!
All day long thy voice is heard.
Be it wet, or be it fine,
Winter frost, or summer shine,
Autumn brown, or bloomy spring,
Thou art ever chattering.
Let me wander where I will
Still I hear thy noisy bill.

If afar 'tis mine, to stray
Down some creek's meandering way,
Where the graceful wattle showers
O'er the stream her yellow flowers,
And the fair clematis twines
Round the whisp'ring casuarines—
There with thy glad mate art thou,
Gossiping upon a bough.

There in spring thou lovest best
To build thy little cup-like nest,
In the shade, upon a limb,
Just above the water's brim.

TO A WATER WAGTAIL.

Often have I ventured nigh,
Its tiny, spotted eggs to spy ;
Often for that liberty
Hast thou soundly scolded me.

Thou at milking time each day
Dost thy various antics play,
In thy suit of white and black,
On some old, sedate cow's back,
Hopping with a dainty tread
First to tail and then to head ;
Stopping now, as though thou'dst say,
" If I'm heavy, tell me, pray ! "

When the dawn is glimmering red,
And each bonny flow'ret's head
Gently towards the ground is borne,
Weighted with the dews of morn,
As across the hills I roam
To drive the lazy cattle home,
Thy blithe note I'm sure to hear
From some fence or stump anear.

When the hues of sunset die
Slowly from the western sky,
And the gloaming shadows creep
O'er the land, and from the deep
Veil of dark'ning blue aloft
Steals the star of evening soft,
On the breezes calm and cool
Floats thy voice from willowed pool.

Often, too, when twilight's fled,
And decent folk are all abed,
If, perchance, awake I lie,
I can hear thee somewhere nigh,

TO A WATER WAGTAIL.

Paying, doubtless, am'rous vows
'Mongst the moonlit garden boughs—
Till, in sooth, I 'gin to think
Thou dost never sleep a wink.

Prythee, cease—thou babbling elf!
Thou dost like to hear thyself,
Ever here while I do rhyme,
Thou art chatt'ring all the time;
Perched upon the mossy fence,
Like a bird of consequence,
Hast thou with those peering eyes
Come my lines to criticise?

What is all thy talk about?
Something very learned, no doubt,
Since it keeps thee thus for hours
Lecturing the bees and flowers.
Hadst thou more of dignity,
I could well imagine thee
An old professor, wise and staid,
In academic gown arrayed.

Minstrel of the solitudes
Of our boundless Austral woods,
Spirit of each stream and glen,
Lover of the homes of men,
Chatter on in ceaseless joy;
None will harm thee or annoy;
For thy fearless happy ways
Win our hearts and cheer our days.

JAMES THOMAS.

A LITTLE TIN PLATE.

Amidst the massive sideboard's burnished wealth—
Rich flagons, loving cups, and wassail bowls,
Brave trophies of the river and the hunt,
And old-world tankards bossed with pictured tale—
Fair in the centre, as a place of pride,
On special pedestal, there rests a plate,
An old tin plate—a battered, dinted plate,
With alphabet for legend round its marge
Encircling Wellington in bold relief,
His cocked hat glory vying with his nose
To vouch the portrait true past breath of doubt—
A shabby, sorry plate—a dingy plate—
A Pariah of plates, yet still a plate
That has its story, and the story thus :—

That plate there was bought by Jack Hill,
   'Bout the time of the rush to Split Creek,
For to give to his kid, little Bill.
   I remember it, same as last week.
Little Bill was a bright four-year-old,
   Could toddle and talk with the best—
Blue eyes, an' his curly hair gold,
   An' such limbs—you should see him undressed !
Most kids has some ways of their own,
   An' Bill's was the takingest out.
To watch that there infant alone
   Was as good any day as a shout.
Jack Hill—which the name was a blind—
   Was as fond of the child as could be ;
That loving, an' tender, an' kind,
   You'd have thought he was three parts a she.

It was all he had left of his luck
   Since his wife, poor young creatur', had died ;
But though patches was not to be struck,
   He was happy with Bill by his side.
Most days Bill to lessons was sent,
   While his father worked eighty foot down,
But at night the boy slep' in the tent,
   In a crib like the smartest in town ;
An' on Sundays no shaft an' no school,
   But a regular treat for the pair,
With a stroll in the bush, as a rule,
   An' a extra bit lisp of a prayer.
Jack was never a psalm-singing one,
   There wasn't much shuffle in him,
But what the young mother begun
   He wouldn't allow to go dim.
An' he used to tell yarns to that kid,
   Me being his mate—do you take ?—
For to put Bill to sleep, an' they did,
   But they'd keep *me* all night wide awake—
Such twisters of fairies with wings
   As lived in each flower, on each bough,
An' of all sorts of fanciful things,
   Which their names, though, has slipped me just now ;
But never no bogeyfied rot
   That them nurses prefer, as it seems,
And that proved Jack to know what was what,
   For the boy always smiled in his dreams.
Times kep' quisby, for when we were through,
   An' had bottomed clean on to the lead,
The wash-dirt turned out a dead slew ;
   'Twas enough to make any heart bleed—
Not a speck ! not a load for an ant,
   Not as much as would fill a fly's eye,
We hadn't a show for a slant,

It was plain that our luck was sky-high.
Says I, "Let's jack up, man alive,
  An' try further down on the Creek!"
"All right!" says my mate, "but we'll drive
  Right and left to the end of this week.
So we drove for a couple of days,
  An' still we was out in the cold,
When, sudden as straw in a blaze,
  I'm blamed, if we didn't strike gold!
Such gold, too, the nuggety kind;
  Like plums stuck in duff, they was thick,
With a prospect of plenty behind,
  For it bettered each stroke of the pick.
At first we was quite took aback,
  Luck like this! when we thought luck was spent.
Then I touched flesh in silence with Jack,
  An' at it, like tigers, we went.
We'd got it, at last—the right sort!
  But we didn't say one single word,
For, whatever the pair of us thought,
  'Twas our picks, not our tongues, as we stirred.
At night, when snug fixed in our beds,
  There'd be plenty of time to rejoice—
With that, man, right over our heads,
  We was scared by the sound of a voice!—
'Twas the schoolmaster come to report
  As poor little Bill was took bad.
Jack downs with his pick quick as thought,
  And ups to the surface like mad!
When I follows—I waited to get
  A bag of them plums, if you please—
There was Jack, like a statter he sat,
  With Bill, half asleep, on his knees.
Says I, thinking 'twould take off the rough
  (For I see that the kid was real bad),

"Here's a sack full of comfortin' stuff!"—
  "Speak soft," hisses Jack; "are you mad?
Chuck that muck in the corner—an' start
  For the township—an' rouse up old Heard,
An' tell him to come an' look smart!"
  I was off like a redshank, my word!
Old Heard was a doctorin' bloke,
  Knew as much as most "medical men,"
Which ain't lashings—a beggar to soak,
  But sober enough now and then.
He was right, for a wonder, this day,
  An' as wise as a mopoke with that;
So we into his visitin'-shay,
  An' along the back track at a bat!—
Heard hauls out a watch from his kick,
  Feels Bill's pulse, as it seemed, half an hour;
Next he has a long suck at his stick
  (Which, to judge by his look, tasted sour);
Then he shakes his old chump to and fro,
  At a dignified pendylum pace
An' he mutters, half 'loud and half low,
  "Bad case—ah! a very bad case."
Says Jack, "So I thought; now, fair's fair—
  You've to save him, that's *what* you've to do.
For a week or so, Heard, you keep square;
  An' if, by God's grace, he pulls through,
D'ye see that bag there? *half* is mine;
  You shall have it—ah! handle the weight.
Says I, "Come, our forces we'll join,
  For I goes the other half, mate."
Well, old Heard did his best for that fee,
  Kep' as straight as a clear splitting pine,
But no use, for it wasn't to be,
  Not for all the gold south of the line.
When He says that the flower must fade,

The gardeners may watch and may tend,
But His is the will that's obeyed—
　I suppose it's all right in the end.
" Water—water!"—that hoarse little cry
　Grew weaker and weaker, until
For hours that there darlin' would lie
　Like a pretty wax figure—so still.
Don't you snuff? no, quite right—as you say,
　It's a habit that's best left alone;
It makes one's eyes water, too—hey!
　But it comforts me sometimes, I own.
Well, an hour before little Bill died,
　He picked up that 'dentical plate
Which had been his partickilar pride,
　An' he holds it out straight to my mate
(It caught one big tear as it fell).
Says he, " Pa, dear, you gave this to Bill
For learning his letters so well.
　Will you keep it, an' think of me still?
Mamma will be glad that I've come,
　And for you we will both of us wait
Up there in that beautiful home,
　An' mind, pa! you bring me my plate!"
'Twas a mere childish fancy at best,
　More like to cause laughter than tears,
But it shows how that innocent blest
　Of the death we so dread had no fears—
Then he turns to a blubb'ring old fool,
　An', says he, " Stupid Bob, don't you cry;
Little Bill isn't going to school,
　He's going to heaven—good-bye!"
He laid his sweet head on Jack's arm,
　With the other hand tight in his own,
An' he passed away smilin' an' calm,
　An' Jack, poor old Jack, was alone!

At first he was stunned-like was Jack,
  But none the less ready for work.
My word! he did more than his whack;
  He was never a cove as would shirk—
An' as if to make up for our loss
  That there claim kep' on, plum after plum;
Every day we were droppin' across
  Half-a-dozen as big as your thumb.
But Jack—and I think I'd a share
  In them feelin's—thought more of one curled
Golden lock of his dead darlin's hair
  Than of all the blamed gold in the world.

It spread round the camp like a shot
  That Jack Hill an' Bob Smith were in luck,
But none of our neighbours had got
  A slice of the plum-duff *we'd* struck—
Just tucker was all they could raise,
  An' some of 'em not even that;
Such is Fortune's cantankerous ways,
  All purr, or all claw, the old cat.
Well, one night—you're not tired? no—all right;
  There isn't much more to be told.
One dark, bitter cold August night
  We've turned in dead beat, an' the gold
Is under Jack's head—both asleep—
  When two beggars crawl into the tent;
They had watched right enough—an' they creep,
  Like a couple of hounds on the scent,
One towards me—an' the other, by Jack,
  Slips a hand where the shammy is stowed;
T'other fist, for safe, silent attack,
  Grips a sharp butcher's knife—well, I'm blowed,
Jack wakes—but too late; through the air,

Quick as lightning, sir, down comes the knife
Dead straight for his heart—an'—well, there,
  That little tin plate saves his life.

  .   .   .   .

We'd a tussle, of course—twig this scar?
  But we nobbled 'em both—one I shot,
And the other's in Pentridge, Black Parr;
  I think it was ten years he got.
Jack settled in Melbourne long since,
  No cause for to fossick or roam,
An' them cups an' things, fit for a prince,
  Come out with a fortune from Home;
Which his name isn't Jack—no—nor Hill,
  I told you, you'll mind, at the start—
Oh, yes, he's a widower still,
  Though South Yarra tries hard for his heart.
I fancy that plate is the charm
  As drives Cupid's arrows back bent,
An' who knows but it shields him from harm
  As it did that dark night in the tent?
But though Jack is well bred, an' I ain't,
  Though he's reckoned a " man of much weight,"
He's neither a prig nor a saint,
  An' he never goes back on his mate.
He'd relations afloat on the Flood—
  He's the boss of this elegant place—
Here he comes!—it's my nevvy, my lud,
  Charles Smith—hem! Sir Bayard Fitz-Sayce.

                        GARNET WALCH.

WOOL IS UP.

Earth o'erflows with nectared gladness,
    All creation teems with joy;
Banished be each thought of sadness,
    Life for me has no alloy.
Fill a bumper, drain a measure,
    Pewter, goblet, tankard, cup,
Testifying thus our pleasure
    At the news that "wool is up."

'Thwart the empires, 'neath the oceans,
    Subtly speeds the living fire;
Who shall tell what wild emotions
    Spring from out that thridden wire;
"Jute is lower, copper weaker,"
    This will break poor neighbour Jupp;
But for me, I shout "Eureka!"
    Wealth is mine—for wool is up.

What care I for jute or cotton,
    Sugar, copper, hemp, or flax,
Reeds like these are often rotten,
    Turn to rods for owners' backs.
Fortune, ha! I have thee holden
    In what Scotia calls a "grup,"
All my fleeces now are golden,
    Full troy weight—for wool is up.

I will dance the gay fandango,
    Though to me its steps be strange,
Doubts and fears you all can hang go,
    I will cut a dash on 'Change.

WOOL IS UP.

Atra Cura, you will please me
  By dismounting from my crup,
Per, you no more shall tease me,
  Pray, get down—for wool is up.

Jane shall have that stylish bonnet,
  Which my scanty purse denied;
Long she set her heart upon it,
  She shall wear it now with pride.
I will buy old Dumper's station,
  Reign as king at Gerringhup,
For my crest a bust of Jason,
  With this motto, "wool is up."

I will keep a stud extensive;
  Bolter, here, I'll have those greys,
Those Sir George deemed too expensive,
  You can send them—with the bays.
Coursing! I should rather think so;
  Yes, I'll take that "Lightning" pup:
Jones, my boy, you needn't wink so,
  I can stand it—wool is up.

Wifey, love, you're looking charming,
  Years with you are but as days;
We must have a grand house-warming
  When these painters wend their ways.
Let the ball-room be got ready,
  Bid our friends to dance and sup;
Bother, how can I go steady?
  I'm worth thousands—wool is up!

GARNET WALCH.

WOOL IS DOWN.

BLACKER than e'er the inky waters roll
   Upon the gloomy shores of sluggish Styx,
A surge of sorrow laps my leaden soul,
   For that which was at "two" is now "one—six."
"Come disappointment, come," as has been said
   By someone else who quailed 'neath Fortune's frown,
Stab to the core the heart that once has bled,
   For "heart" read "pocket"—wool, ah wool is down.

"And in the lowest deep a lower deep,"
   Thou sightless seer, indeed it may be so,
The road too well we know is somewhat steep,
   And who shall stay us when that road we go?
Thrice cursèd wire; whose lightning strikes to blast,
   Whose babbling tongue proclaims throughout the town
The news, which, being ill, has travelled fast,
   The dire intelligence—that wool is down.

A rise in copper and a rise in jute,
   A fall alone in wool—but what a fall!
Jupp must have made a pile this trip, the brute,
   He don't deserve such splendid luck at all.
The smiles for him—for me the scalding tears;
   He's worth ten thousand if he's worth a crown,
While I—untimely shorn by Fate's harsh shears—
   Feel that my game is up when wool is down.

Bolter, take back these prancing greys of thine,
   Remove as well the vanquished warrior's bays,
My fortunes are not stable, they decline;
   Aye, even horses taunt me with their neighs.

And thou, sweet puppy of the "Lightning" breed,
  Through whose fleet limbs I pictured me renown,
Hie howling to thy former home with speed,
  Thy course with me is up—for wool is down.

Why, Jane, what's this?—this pile of letters here?
  Such waste of stamps is really very sad.
Your birthday ball, oh, come not twice a year,
  Good gracious me! the woman must be mad.
You'd better save expense at once, that's clear,
  And send a bellman to invite the town!
There—there—don't cry; forgive my temper, dear,
  But put these letters up—for wool is down.

My station "Gerringhup," yes, that must go,
  Its sheep, its oxen, and its kangaroos,
First 'twas the home of blacks, then whites, we know,
  Now is it but a dwelling for "the blues,"
With it I leave the brotherhood of Cash
  Who form Australian Fashion's tinsel crown;
I tread along the devious path of Smash,
  I go where wool has gone—down, ever down.

Thus ends my dream of greatness; not for me
  The silken couch, the banquet, and the rout,
They're flown—the base residuum will be
  A mutton chop and half-a-pint of stout—
Yet will I hold a corner in my soul
  Where Hope may nestle safe from Fortune's frown.
Thou hoodwinked jade! my heart remaineth whole—
  I'll keep my spirits up—though wool be down.

GARNET WALCH.

AUSTRALASIA.

ILLUSTRIOUS COOK, Columbus of our shore,
To whom was left this unknown world t' explore,
Its untraced bounds on faithful chart to mark,
And leave a light where all before was dark :—
And thou the foremost in fair learning's ranks,
Patron of every art, departed Banks,
Who, wealth disdaining, and inglorious ease,
The rocks and quicksands dared of unknown seas;
Immortal pair, when in yon spacious bay
Ye moored awhile its wonders to survey,
How little thought ye that the name from you
Its graceful shrubs and beauteous wild-flowers drew
Would serve, in after times, with lasting brand,
To stamp the soil, and designate the land,
And to ungenial climes reluctant scare
Full many a hive that else had settled there.
  Ah, why, Britannia's pride, Britannia's boast,
Searcher of every sea, and every coast,
Lamented Cook, thou bravest, gentlest heart,
Why didst thou fall beneath a savage dart?
Why were thy mangled relics doomed to grace
The midnight orgies of a barbarous race?
Why could'st thou not, thy weary wandering past,
At home in honour'd ease recline at last?
And like the happier partner of thy way
In cloudless glory close life's setting day.
And thou, famed Gallic captain, La Perouse,
When from this bay thou led'st thy fated crews,
Did thy twin vessels sink beneath the shock
Of furious hurricane, or hidden rock?
Fell ye, o'erpowered on some barbarian strand,
As fell before, De Langle's butchered band?

Lingered the remnants of thy shipwrecked host
On some parched coral isle, some torrid coast,—
Where no green tree, no cooling brook is seen,
Nought living is, or e'er before has been,
Save some lone mew, blown from the rocky nest,
Had lit, perchance, her homeward wing to rest;
Till gnawed by want, with joy a comrade dead
They saw, and ravenous on his body fed,
And soon, his bones picked bare, with famished eye
Each glared around, then drew who first should die.
Till of thy ghastly band the most unblest
Survived,—sad sepulchre of all the rest.
And now, his last meal gorged, with frenzy fired,
And raging thirst, the last lorn wretch expired.
Whate'er thy fate, thou saw'st the floating arks
That peopled this new world, the teeming barks
That ardent Philip led to this far shore,
And, seeing them, alas! wert seen no more.
Ah! could'st thou now behold what man has done,
Though seven revolving lustres scarce have run,
How would'st thou joy to see the savage earth
The smiling parent of so fair a birth!
Lo! thickly planted o'er the glassy bay,
Where Sydney loves her beauties to survey,
And every morn delighted sees the beam
Of some fresh pennant dancing in her stream,
A masty forest, stranger vessels moor,
Charged with the fruits of every foreign shore;
While, landward,—the thronged quay, the creaking crane,
The noisy workman and the loaded wain,
The lengthened street, wide square, and column'd front
Of stately mansions, and the gushing font,
The solemn church, and busy market throng,

And idle loungers saunt'ring slow among—
The lofty windmills that with outspread sail
Thick line the hills, and court the rising gale,
Show that the mournful genius of the plain,
Driv'n from his primal solitary reign,
Has backward fled and fix'd his drowsy throne
In untrod wilds to muse and brood alone.
And thou, fair Port, whose triad sister coves
Peninsulate these walls; whose ancient groves
High low'ring Southward, rear their giant form,
And break the fury of the polar storm.
Fairest of Ocean's daughters! who dost bend
Thy mournful steps to seek thy absent friend,
Whence she,—coy wild-rose, on her virgin couch
Fled loath from Parramatta's am'rous touch.
Skirting thy wat'ry path, lo! frequent stand
The cheerful villas 'midst their well-cropp'd land;
Here lowing kine, there bounding coursers graze,
Here waves the corn, and there the woody maize,
Here the tall peach puts forth its pinky bloom,
And there the orange scatters its perfume,
While, as the merry boatmen row along,
The woods are quicken'd with their lusty song.
Nor here alone hath labour's victor band
Subdued the glebe, and fertilized the land;
For lo, from where at rocky Portland's head
Reluctant Hawkesbury quits his sluggard bed,
Merging in ocean,—to young Windsor's tow'rs,
And Richmond's high green hills, and native bow'rs,
Thence far along Nepean's pebbled way
To those rich pastures where the wild herds stray,
The crowded farm-house lines the winding stream
On either side, and many a plodding team
With shining ploughshare turns the neighb'ring soil,
Which crowns with double crop the lab'rer's toil.

Hail, mighty ridge! that from thy azure brow
Survey'st these fertile plains, that stretch below,
And look'st with careless unobservant eye,
As round thy waist the forked lightnings ply,
And the loud thunders spring with hoarse rebound
From peak to peak, and fill the welkin round
With deaf'ning voice, till with their boist'rous play
Fatigued in mutt'ring peals they stalk away;—
Parent of this deep stream, this awful flood,
That at thy feet its tributary mud,
Like the fam'd Indian, or Egyptian tide,
Doth pay, but direful scatters woe beside:—
Vast Austral Giant of these rugged steeps,
Within those secret cells, rich glittering heaps
Thick piled are doomed to sleep till some one spy
The hidden key that opes thy treasury;
Now mute, how desolate thy stunted woods,
How dread thy chasms, where many an eagle broods,
How dark thy caves, how lone thy torrents' roar,
As down thy cliffs precipitous they pour,
Broke on our hearts, when first with venturous tread
We dared to rouse thee from thy mountain bed.
Till, gained with toilsome steps thy rocky heath,
We spied the cheering smokes ascend beneath,
And, as a meteor shoots athwart the night,
In boundless champaign burst upon our sight,
Till, nearer seen, the beauteous landscape grew
Op'ning like Canaan on rapt Israel's view.

WILLIAM CHARLES WENTWORTH.

ADDENDA.

TOO LATE FOR THEIR PROPER PLACE.

DROUGHT.

Written in 1877, when the Drought was at its worst.

The days are hot, the nights are warm,
  The grass is parch'd and dry,
And when the clouds portend a storm,
  They pass unfruitful by;
They threateningly obscure the sky
  Before the sun has set,
But ere the night has well begun,
  The stars in heaven are met.

All calm and bright in azure fields,
  No sign of moisture there,
Each passing day successive yields
  A tribute to despair;
The earth is shrunken by the heat,
  Great cracks run through the plain
Like open mouths agape with thirst,
  The thirst which calls for rain.

Dense clouds of smoke come sweeping by
  From tracts by fire laid bare,
And the great sun's red fiery eye
  Sends forth a sickly glare;
Day follows day with heat intense
  And when a storm sweeps o'er,
'Tis but a rush of smoke and dust,
  Some rain spits, nothing more.

DROUGHT.

In the great stream beds, muddy holes,
  Where once was water deep,
Are filled with rotting carcasses
  Of cattle and of sheep ;
Along the banks in ghastly groups
  (Full half their number gone)
The starving stock all feebly crawl,
  Poor wrecks of skin and bone.

Their ribs are bare, their hips project,
  Their eyes are sunk and glazed ;
Their bones will shortly whiten on
  The meadow where they grazed.
And down the dusty, grassless roads,
  Come travelling thousands more,
To help to swell the dismal wreck—
  'Twas bad enough before.

Poor helpless muttons—jaded beeves,
  That faintly tottering pass ;
Your luckless fellows, like the leaves,
  Are gone, but not to grass.

Where the grass is not there they lie,
  Too thin to cause much smell ;
Their sun-dried hides where they did die
  Have marked their route full well.

Oh ! many men who, but last year,
  Counted their stock with pride,
With pockets bare, through empty runs,
  Will now be doomed to ride.

Oh ! Demon Drought ! that sweeps away
  The hard-earned wealth of years.
Too late ! too late ! the rain has come ;
  It now seems nought but tears

O'er blighted hopes, o'er herds destroyed,
  O'er vacant hill and glen,
O'er ruined hearths and households void,
  And grey and broken men.
      (OLD SALTBUSH) WALTER SMITH.

WHEN I AM DEAD.

When I am dead lay me down to rest
In some shady dell where the wild flowers spring;
Where the golden beams shall come from the west,
And smile through the trees where the wild birds sing.
And leave me there in my lonely grave
With nought but the green turf o'er my head,
For the flowers shall bloom and the blossoms wave
To show where I sleep when I am dead.

For these are the scenes I have loved in life,
And when death comes I would lay me here,
The busy town with its noise and strife
Would break my rest if you laid me near,
And the want and woe would make me sad;
But away in the woods I have no dread—
For there in my heart I was ever glad,
And shall sleep in peace when I am dead.

And shed no tears when you lay me there,
But weep for those who are left behind,
For they shall wake to trouble and care
Whilst I shall sleep with a tranquil mind.
For who will speak of the evil I've done,
When you lay me down in my narrow bed?
May the friends who have loved me, many a one,
Think of me kindly when I am dead.

Then let me rest; I have wandered long,
And fought in the world's unequal fight,
Where the weak must ever give way to the strong,
And he who has wealth is always right.
Where the poor must stand up in the house of God,
Where the rich can sit without fear or dread.
Then lay me not 'neath the churchyard sod
But away in the woods, when I am dead.

For why should I sleep in a pauper's grave,
When here is a tomb that is fit for a King,
Then lay me down where the blossoms wave
'Neath the shady trees where the wild birds sing,
For it seems to me as if God were near,
Nearer, here, where the wild woods spread.
In life I have felt His presence here,
And He will guard me when I am dead.

JOHN BRIGHT.

ENVOI.

FROM THE "AUSTRALIAN PRINTER'S KEEPSAKE."

When building up the Gothic type
  In the Abbey's Almonrie,
Such labour must have seemed in sooth
  A trivial one to see--
To print the first book in the land
  Of Saxon speech and flow;
Yet pregnant seeds were planted then,
  Four Hundred Years ago.

Oh, great Reformer of that age!
  Thy task had then begun,
And when it ended time avowed
  'Twas well and wisely done;
For knowledge and fair liberty
  Alike to thee we owe,
Thy efforts ushered in the twain
  Four Hundred Years ago.

Tho' far removed by ocean wastes
  From that dear Mother Land,
We cherish her historic past,
  We share her triumphs grand,
Exulting in her mighty sons;—
  And in the foremost row
Is seen the Father of our craft
  Four Hundred Years ago.

Immortal Caxton!   Rolling years
  But add unto thy fame;
Where'er our English tongue is heard,
  All venerate thy name.
Even here, beneath the Austral Pole
  Our hearts are all aglow
To honour thee and thy emprise
  Four Hundred Years ago.

THOS. L. WORK.

NOTES.

A Voice from the Bush (page 1). This poem has hitherto been printed among the works of Adam Lindsey Gordon, but its real authorship is well-known among the students of Australian literature, and though the author wishes his name not to appear, he has revised the proofs of it for us, so that the world now for the first time has the correct version of the poem.

Austral (page 5). A *nom-de-plume* of Mrs J. G. Wilson of Wellington, N.Z., née Miss Adams of St Enoch's, Victoria, who has contributed a number of beautiful poems to *The Australasian*, including the two quoted, which have been selected, apart from their intrinsic excellence, for their vivid touches of New Zealand scenery.

Australie (page 8). A *nom-de-plume* of Mrs Hubert Heron, a daughter of Sir Wm. Manning, a Judge in the Supreme Court of N.S. Wales, and Chancellor of the University of Sydney. Australie is one of her Christian names. Her poem "Braidwood" has been given as being as faithful as a photograph of N.S.W. mountain scenery. Both poems appeared in her volume, "The Balance of Pain" (Geo. Bell & Sons of London, 1877.)

Alexander W. Bathgate (page 20) is a Solicitor at Dunedin, N.Z.; a writer of mature excellence, whose best pieces are excluded by this volume's limitation of subject.

H. H. Blackham (page 19) lives at Trevilla, One Tree Hill, S. Australia. His poem has been selected as picturing what one frequently sees even in so new a country as Australia—for instance, along the Old Bathurst Road, superseded by the railway over the Blue Mountains of N.S.W.

John Bright (page 263), an early friend of Adam Lindsey Gordon in South Australia, is constantly on the move; when last heard of was on his way to Carpentaria. We have quoted "When I am dead" as exactly what one would have expected from Gordon himself in sentiment. It is from a little pamphlet entitled "Wattle blossoms and Wild flowers gathered by the Way," published by Crabb & Brotherton, St Kilda, Melbourne.

NOTES.

Jennings Carmichael (page 24), lives at St Kilda, Victoria. "Tomboy Madge" appeared in the *Weekly Times*, Melbourne, and in addition to its merits is quoted for the vivid picture it gives of Australian picknicking.

Alfred T. Chandler (page 28), born at Geelong, Victoria, 1852, is a journalist, on the *South Australian Advertiser*, and on the Hansard staff, Adelaide. His volume, from which our quotations have been made, "A Bush Idyll, and Other Poems" (E. S. Wigg, Adelaide; S. Mullen, Melbourne), has established him as the first living poet of South Australia, and gives promise of a lasting reputation.

Marcus Clarke (page 26), after A. L. Gordon, the most distinguished writer in Australia, though less famous as a poet than as a novelist and journalist. The author of the celebrated novel, "His Natural Life." Born at Kensington 1847. Educated at St Paul's. Emigrated to Victoria in his seventeenth year. Patchett Martin wrote of him: "Whether in verse or prose, it was impossible for him to be other than bright, witty and forcible. As a literary critic, within the limit of his artistic sympathies, he was admirable." The poem quoted was written for the album of Mrs H. G. Turner, of Melbourne, and has been selected as characteristic of the man whose ability and literary influence in Australia were alike conspicuous.

J. F. Daniell (page 38), well known in Melbourne as the author of "Rhymes for the Times," a poetical commentary on current events appearing in the columns of the *Herald*, one of which was the fine poem quoted.

Alfred Domett, C.M.G. (page 40). The most eminent New Zealander. Poet and statesman. Born in Surrey. Educated at St John's College, Cambridge. In 1842 went, among the earliest settlers, to Wellington, New Zealand. Held many public offices in New Zealand, of which he was Premier in 1862, 1863. In 1871 returned to England, where he died 2nd November 1887. Soon after his return to England he published "Ranolf and Amohia," of which Longfellow wrote:—

Cambridge, August 26, 1878.

MY DEAR SIR,—You have sent me a splendid poem. There is ample space in it to move and breathe. It reminds me of the great pictures of the old masters. . . . . Your descriptions of scenery are very powerful and beautiful. And just at present, while I am busy with poems of "Poems and Places," you can readily imagine how much they delight me.

I have taken the liberty of making many extracts for the volume entitled "Oceanica." . . . .—With great regard, yours faithfully,

HENRY W. LONGFELLOW

NOTES. 267

In 1883 he had a second edition of "Ranolf and Amohia" published by Messrs Kegan Paul, Trench & Co., having previously, in 1877, published "Flotsam and Jetsam," a volume of fugitive poems (Smith, Elder & Co.), containing his famous Christmas hymn ("In the Solemn Centuries Long Ago"). So far back as 1832 he published a small volume of poems.

Lindsay Duncan (Mrs **T. C. Cloud,** of *Wallaroo Bay, S. Australia*) (page 55), has written many beautiful pieces in the *Adelaide Observer*, including the following, which has been chosen, not as by any means her best, but because it comes most within the scope of this collection. The unsuccessful emigrant dying in want, far from what he holds dearest, and all to whom he is dearest, is, unfortunately, an occasional feature of Australia.

Wm. Forster, Premier of, and afterwards Agent-General for, New South Wales (page 58). One of the most distinguished politicians and men of letters that Australia has produced. Poet and journalist. His "Devil and the Governor" made a great mark. He published three volumes of poems—"The Weir-wolf," "The Brothers," and "Midas," the last being posthumous. He wrote nothing that really comes within the scope of this selection, but no volume from the Australian poets would be complete without his being represented, so a typical passage from the "Midas" (published by Kegan Paul, Trench & Co), his finest work, is given. He was born at Madras, and died a few years ago.

Frances Tyrrell Gill (page 62). One of the most gifted poetesses of Australia. Though her works have never been collected in a volume, she has contributed many beautiful poems to *The Australasian* and other leading papers. "The Wind in the She-oak Tree" appeared both in *The Australasian* and *The Leader*.

Keighley Goodchild ("Keighley") (page 67). Son of John Goodchild, librarian of the Mechanics' Institute, Echuca, Victoria. Is a pressman. Has a good deal of Gordon's "home wit." "While the Billy Boils," comes from a little volume entitled, "Who Are You?" published at *The Advertiser* office, Echuca, and has been selected as a fair specimen of the school of Gordon.

Adam Lindsey Gordon (page 69). Born at Fayal, in the Azores, 1833. Educated at Cheltenham College, Woolwich, and Oxford. Emigrated to S. Australia about 1851. Became the best amateur steeple-chase-rider in the Colonies. Published three volumes of poems—"Sea Spray and Smoke Drift," "Bush Ballads and Galloping Rhymes," and "Ashtaroth: a Dramatic Lyric," which have since been collected into one volume, published by Messrs Massina & Co., of Melbourne, and S. Mullen & Sons, of Ludgate Hill, E.C., which has gone through several editions. He published his last volume of poems in 1868. *The Cheltenham Examiner* says: "That monetary difficulties beset him to the end is well known to his friends, and his inability to raise even £50 on his works when printed and complete was the last feather that broke the camel's back." He died by his own rifle, June 24th, 1870.

Gordon is the national poet—the Burns of Victoria. His sayings are proverbs, and his name a household word. For his poems selected *vide* Introduction. His name has hitherto been given as Lindsay, but in the form filled up by his father at his entry into Cheltenham College it is Lindsey.

Henry Halloran. *Vide* Introduction.

Charles Harpur (page 75). The grey forefather of Australian poets, the first born in Australia, was born at Windsor, N.S.W., in 1817, and educated at the Government School, of which his father was master. With this exception, a self-taught man. From 1843 onwards was engaged in squatting and farming, and from 1858 to 1866 held also the gold commissionership at Araluen. Died 10th June 1868. His favourite poets were Shakespeare, Milton, Wordsworth, and Shelley. Owing to financial difficulties, no full edition of his works was ever published in his lifetime, but he brought out a collection of sonnets in 1840, and his shorter poems have appeared in newspapers from time to time. In 1883 his widow brought out a complete edition of his works (Geo. Robertson & Co., of London and Australia), from which the poems quoted are taken. His great poem, "The Witch of Hebron," was ineligible from its subject, but one of those quoted, "The Cloud," is, to our mind, as noble in its simplicity as any poem in Australian literature, and worthy of a place in any general selection of English poetry. Kendall wrote of him:—

> The burden of a perished faith
>   Went sighing through his speech of sweetness,
> With human hints of Time and Death,
>   And subtle notes of incompleteness.
>
> But when the fiery power of youth
>   Had passed away and left him nameless,
> Serene as Light, and strong as Truth,
>   He lived his life untried and fameless.
>
> And, far and free, this man of men
>   With wintry hair and wasted feature,
> Had fellowship with gorge and glen,
>   And learned the loves and runes of Nature.

> Strange words of wind, and rhymes of rain,
>   And whispers from the inland fountains,
> Are mingled in his various strain
>   With leafy breaths of piny **mountains.**
>
> But, as the under-currents **sigh**
>   Beneath the surface of **a river,**
> The music of Humanity
>   Dwells in his **forest psalms for ever.**
>
> No soul was he to sit on heights,
>   And live with **rocks apart and scornful;**
> Delights of men **were his delights,**
>   And common **troubles made him mournful.**
>
> The flying forms of **unknown powers**
>   With lofty wonder **caught and filled him;**
> But there were **days of gracious hours,**
>   When sights and sounds familiar thrilled him.
>
> The pathos worn **by wayside things,**
>   The passion found **in simple faces**
> Struck deeper than **the life of springs,**
>   Of strength, of storms, and sea-swept places.
>
> But now he sleeps, the tired bard,
>   The deepest sleep, and lo, I proffer
> These tender leaves of my regard
>   With hands that falter as they offer.

Ebenezer Storry Hay (Fleta) (page 93), was a Solicitor at Dunedin, N.Z., born at Kilsyth, Scotland. Died ætat 37. Had he lived might have been a New Zealand Shelley. No more delicate writer has appeared in the antipodes.

Thomas Heney (page 94), wrote the only Australian Whitmanesque poem of any importance, "The Hut on the Flat," in a capital volume entitled "Fortunate Days" (Sydney, Turner & Henderson). There is no more graphic picture of bush life than this poem, a veritable photograph in fidelity.

Philip J. Holdsworth (page 104), a cashier in the Colonial Treasury, Sydney, and editor of the *Illustrated Sydney News*. His "Station Hunting on the Warrego" has been quoted as the most terrible picture of exploration in Australian poetry. He has written many beautiful and powerful poems, and is emphatically Kendall's successor in New South Wales. In 1880 he published " Station-hunting on the

Warrego" and other poems. (Sydney, Wm. Maddock, 381 George Street). Kendall wrote of him, "You are an authentic singer. The immaculate fire is in you, and it will glorify you in time."

R. H. Horne. Vide introduction.

John Rowell (page 120), Governor of the Adelaide gaol, in 1882 published a volume entitled "Rose Leaves from an Australian Garden" (Adelaide, Carey & Page). A poet of great facility and wealth of expression. A *magnum opus* may be justly expected from him.

John Liddell Kelly (page 121). Born in Lanarkshire, Scotland, 19th Feb. 1850. From compositor rose to reporter; emigrated to New Zealand on account of falling health. Author of Prize Jubilee Poem in competition open to New Zealand. Now engaged as sub-editor, *Auckland Star*. Visited South Sea Islands two years ago to get material for poems on Tahitian, Samoan, and Tongan life and scenery. Author of libretto of comic opera, "Pomare, or Love in Topsy Turveydown;" also "Tarawera; or the Curse of Tuhotu," —descriptive of the volcanic eruption last year. Mentioned and poems quoted in volume entitled "A Hundred Scottish Poets." Brother of James Kelly, author of the volume "The Printer's Carnival and other Poems," who died some years ago. His father also was poetical.

Henry Kendall. Vide special introduction.

Frances Sescadorowna Lewin (page 122), of "Egerton," St Mary's, South Australia, has published a charming little volume of poems entitled "Songs of the South" (Adelaide, Scryingour & Sons). "The Story of Abel Tasman" has been selected for its graceful handling of one of the most picturesque bits in the story of Australia, though condemned by accurate Mr E. A. Petherick as unauthentic.

George Gordon M'Crae (page 125). One of the chief poets of Australia. Author of two aboriginal lays "Mamba (the Bright-eyed)" (Melbourne, H. T. Dwight, 1867), and "Balladeãdro" (H. T. Dwight, 1867), written after the manner of Scott, but with a knowledge of native customs and traditions, reminding one of Hiawatha. Contributed a "Rosebud from the Garden of Taj" to the *Melbourne Review*, and is the author of other works, which the editor, unfortunately, cannot recall, as he has not seen them since he left Australia. The quotation given in the text is explained by the note appended here:—

"The story of Balladeãdro is founded on a tradition once current among the aborigines of our western tribes, the MS. notes of which, as taken down by the wife of a former protector of aborigines, came into my hands many years ago.

"It is evident to me, after repeated and careful perusal of the lady's papers, that the story (which is very gracefully told) has received little if any colouring at the hands of the transcriber. As regards the "black" or magic art, practised by the doctors of the tribes, her information agrees fully with my own personal experience.

"I have been present on two occasions when the wizard was engaged in charming, or rather in attempting to charm away the lives of certain persons of other and distant tribes. The ceremony observed was precisely similar to that which I have described in 'Balladeãdro.'

"An outline sketch of the intended victim was engraved on the shuttle-shaped body of a spear rest, or throwing stick, a lock of the doomed one's hair was suspended from the upper extremity, and the lower or handle end was wrapped in twisted grass, in order to prevent any injury to the fingers of the wizard from the poisonous unguents with which the picture was smeared.

"These preparations being complete, the spear-rest was stuck upright in the ground, and very close to the wizard's fire. As the heat caused the poisonous ointment to sink into the ground he was at hand to renew it, singing the while, and as the poison dried and the image grew hot, he told me that the intended victim at a distance was suffering the most terrible agonies. Sometimes wearied out with watching and incantation the wizard leaves the stick to fate and goes to sleep. If on awaking he finds it has toppled over into the fire he takes it for granted that the object of his hate is no more. I remember, in one of these instances which I have quoted, this accident happened, but the victim singled out (a young woman some forty miles distant at the time) was none the worse in consequence.

"The wizard said that there must have been something wrong with the picture or the poison, or perhaps something deficient in the incantation itself, but nothing could shake his first principles of 'obeism.'

"Balladeãdro (I would wish to add) besides exhibiting the superstitions and ceremonies of a rapidly disappearing race makes us aware of a patriotism or love of country, obtaining largely among a people hitherto supposed to be incapable of such a sentiment, and added to this, the possession of natural affection, and the finer feelings which most writers deny them. G. S. M'C."

Arthur Patchett Martin (page 142), born at Woolwich, 1850, brought out to Australia in 1852. Educated at C.E. School, St Mark's, Fitzroy, and Melbourne University; entered civil service of Victoria; founded with H. S. Turner, A. M. Topp, and others the *Melbourne Review*; the first number of which appeared Jan. 1876, and which has proved the most successful as well as the most ambitious of Australian periodicals; was editor of it for six years. Has published " Sweet

Girl Graduate" and "An Easter Omelette," both containing original poems; in 1878, "Lays of To-day, or verses in jest and earnest' (George Robertson); and in 1881 "Fernshawe"—Sketches in prose and verse (Geo. Robertson), republished in London in 1885 by Griffith, Farran & Co., and most favourably received by the London and provincial press. In 1882 he returned to England, and in an article in *Temple Bar* (Feb. 1884) entitled "An Australian Poet," introduced Adam Lindsey Gordon to the London public. One of the very best Australian writers, but unfortunately too busy with journalism to be able to devote the proper leisure to literature. We have called him elsewhere "the Australian R. L. Stevenson" for his qualities, as a critic and essayist. The poems quoted are all from Fernshawe the most handsomely got up volume of *Belles lettres* ever printed in Australia.

E. G. Millard (of Yarrabee Park, Narrandera, New South Wales) (page 154). The poem is a picture of a rally in which the author took part, after a well-known Warrigal horse. It came out in the *Australasian* and went the round of the Colonial papers.

Agnes Neale (Mrs Aheane), (page 157). A South Australian poetess, may be called the Australian Adelaide Proctor, a writer of much sweetness and grace, with a pure vein of piety running through her work; she has contributed many strikingly beautiful poems to the Australian press, but has published no volume.

Sir Henry Parkes (page 163). The Gladstone of Australia, a man of such towering ability that he has made the premiership of N.S.W. almost his perquisite. Entirely a self-made man, and yet has had the formation of more cabinets than any man in Australia, has a fine taste for art, has developed at his seat, Falconbridge, the most exquisite wild-flower-garden in existence, and has published three volumes of poems, "Murmurs of the Stream," "Stolen Moments" (James Tegg, Sydney), and "The Beauteous Terrorist and other Poems" by a Wanderer (Geo. Robertson & Co., London and Australia). The poem quoted, "Solitude," is from this volume, as is "Inez," which will appear in the larger anthology in course of preparation by the editor of this volume for Griffith, Farran & Co. A special interest attaches to these two poems apart from their own merits, for they were the favourites of the late Alfred Domett, himself an Australian premier and author of the greatest antipodean poem, who just before his death copied them out and sent them to the editor in his own handwriting as specially worthy of a place. Sir Henry's "Solitude," a fragment from William Wentworth's "Australasia," and Marcus Clarke's celebrated "Album Verses," are the only instances in which the editor has broken through the rule laid down of inserting nothing that was not offered by the authors. He felt that three such men must be represented.

Robert Richardson, B.A. (page 164), an Australian native, an old Sydney Grammar School captain, and a graduate of Sydney University, is the "Roving Australian" familiar to all readers of the *Sydney Morning Herald*. Author of "Beneath the Southern Cross," &c. Has been for some years at "Home." The poem quoted is chosen as giving a dainty picture of the delightful boating round Sydney.

J. Steele Robertson (page 167), of the Melbourne University, usually writes under the *nom-de-plume* of "Jayessar." The exquisite little landscape-poem quoted is taken from the *Melbourne University Review.*

J Howlett Ross (Victoria) (page 168), is a promising young poet, elocutionist, and journalist, born in Australia, and educated at the Scotch College, Melbourne; now doing literary work in London. The following poem has been chosen as bemoaning in music worthy of its subject himself, the death of Henry Kendall, the best known Australian-born poet.

Percy Russell (page 170). Now doing literary work in London. Author of "King Alfred," a most successful writer, editor of *Food*, poet, critic, and journalist. The poem below came out in the *European Mail*, and was republished in various Australian papers. It has been selected as emphasising the fact set forth in the last line of the sonnet. The public, rightly or wrongly, identifies him with the Anglo-Australian in the *European Mail.*

J. Sadler (page 172), of the Savings Bank of South Australia, Adelaide, South Australia. His spirited poem quoted, worthy of Bret Harte, describing the great event of South Australia, appeared in the *Adelaide Observer*, under the *nom-de-plume* of "Ab. Original." Mr Sadler's bright and racy poems have appeared in many colonial papers.

William Sharp (page 173). Not an Australian, but on a visit which he paid to the colonies in 1877, wrote some admirable poems of bush life, unexcelled for photographic observation. As we wrote in the Introduction, Mr Sharp's reputation as poet, editor, and critic is too established to need recitation here.

Charles Allan Sherard (page 183), a solicitor at Charlton, Victoria, in our opinion without doubt the best Australian poet, whose works have not yet appeared in book form. He has written some really exquisite pieces in what we have ventured to call the Victorian School —poems on Swinburnian models, but with subject and colouring so racy of the soil as to be almost original. His subjects are interesting, and he can write with dramatic power as well as with beautiful and poetical expression.

Douglas Brooke Wheelton **Sladen, B.A., LL.B.** (page 193), the editor of this book, and therefore can give nothing about himself beyond a bare summary. Educated at Temple Grove, East Sheen, Cheltenham College, Trinity College, Oxford, and Melbourne University; took open classical scholarships at Cheltenham and Trinity, and graduated B.A. at Oxford, with a first class in modern history. Then emigrated to Melbourne, where he graduated B.A. and LL.B. at the University, and in 1882 was appointed to the newly-founded chair of history in the University of Sydney, which he resigned in 1884, to pursue his historical studies at "Home." He has published the following volumes: "Frithjof and Ingebjorg" (sent home to be published by Kegan Paul, 1881), "Australian Lyrics," 1st edition (Geo. Robertson, Melbourne. 1882), "A Poetry of Exiles," 1st edition (C. E. Fuller, Sydney, 1883), "A Summer Christmas" (Griffith, Farran & Co., 1884), "In Cornwall and Across the Sea" (Griffith, Farran & Co., 1885), "Australian Lyrics," 2nd edition (Griffith, Farran & Co., 1885), "A Poetry of Exiles," 2nd edition (Griffith, Farran & Co., 1886), "Edward the Black Prince" (Griffith, Farran & Co., 1887), and two novels under assumed names, "Dick Stalwart, an Oxonian," by O. C. (in the *Queenslander*), and "Seized by a Shadow," by Rose Mullion (Griffith, Farran & Co., 1885). He is at present doing the Australian part of a slang dictionary for a large firm of London publishers, and editing the larger anthology of Australian poetry which Messrs Griffith, Farran & Co. will bring out shortly.

A. C. Smith (page 216) was a presbyterian minister in Victoria, but went up to Queensland, where he is a pretty constant contributor to the press under the initials A. C. S. He is a writer of the school of Gordon, and has published some very fine poems.

Walter Smith (page 201), well known to all colonial readers as "Old Saltbush." His poem quoted, "Drought," is of great value, as giving a vivid picture of the curse of Australia (from the Dubbo District itself, where sheep have died by millions from it), written by a practical man living on the spot.

J. Brunton Stephens (page 218) enjoys the highest reputation of any poet living in Australia, and deservedly, for as a humorous poet he has written pieces as delicious as C. S. Calverley's (to whose school of humour he belongs), and as a serious poet, not to mention other poems, he has written the magnificent "Convict Once," after "Ranolf and Amohia," the most important poem on an Antipodean subject. He rivals Kendall in beauty of writing, and has a prodigious command of rhyme and quaint allusion. The essential quality of his work is subtlety—subtlety of humour, subtlety of metre, and subtly beautiful expression and feeling. His poems are more in the mouths of the Australian public than any colonial poets', except Gordon's. He has been long before the public, but unfortunately the only one of his volumes which we have before us is "Convict Once, and Other Poems" (Geo. Robertson & Co., 1885), from which we take all the poems quoted, except the typically Australian one, "The Midnight Axe," which has only recently been published in the *Queenslander*, and which the reader will naturally compare with Kendall's weird poems and the "Hut on the Flat." The author thought he would be best represented by "The Midnight Axe," "Drought and Doctrine," "The Black Gin," and "Universally Respected." Space would not allow us to give the last named as well as the first, so we substituted a popular favourite, "My Other Chinee Cook." "Universally Respected" will be given in the larger anthology.

James Thomas (page 242), a native of New South Wales, educated at the premier school of Australia, the Old King's School, Parramatta, founded fifty years ago. As he was only born in 1861, the highest expectations may be formed of his future as a poet. He has a decidedly original mind, for he has forsaken the ordinary Australian models and given us delicate and faithful pictures of Australian bush and bird life that might have been written by Emerson or Bryant. He has published no volume as yet. He will be represented again in the larger anthology.

Garnet Walch (page 245), son of Major Walch, 54th regiment, one of the most brilliant writers of Australia; born in Tasmania, 1843; educated partly in England, partly at Heidelberg, Baden. Returning to Tasmania, joined his brothers in the firm of Walch Brothers, publishers and booksellers, then went to N.S.W. and edited the local paper at Parramatta, began independent literary life in Sydney, then went to Melbourne, and for six years was secretary of the Athenæum. He has published a succession of Christmas annuals, a volume of poems entitled "The Little Tin Plate," and an important and interesting work entitled "Victoria in 1880." He has almost regularly supplied the theatres with an extravaganza at Christmas. His poems and plays are distinguished by a most contagious and exuberant wit and great facility

William Charles Wentworth (page 256), "The Australian Patriot," born at Norfolk Island, 1791. In 1813, with Blaxland and Lawson, discovered the first pass over the Blue Mountains; in 1816 went to Cambridge, where he wrote his prize poem, "Australasia," from which we have quoted. The prize, however, was won by the celebrated W. M. Praed. He went back to Sydney in 1824, became the first great statesman and journalist of Australia; in 1849 took in hand the foundation of Sydney's splendid University, in whose great hall his statue stands as founder. He was also the father of Responsible Government, for it was owing to him that in 1854 the Constitution Bill was passed, which resulted in the first constitution being granted to Australia in 1856. In 1862, he established himself in England, and spent the last ten years of his life there. Until the rise of Gordon, his "Australasia" was quoted more than any other Australian poem.

The Envoi (page 261) is from the Australasian "Printers' Keepsake," an admirable little garland of prose and verse, by working compositors in Victoria. The writer of the Poem quoted, Thos. L. Work, and R. H. Skeeles, have some especially clever pieces, but the whole volume is good, though unfortunately nothing else came exactly within our limitations.

A STUDY

OF

HENRY KENDALL AS A BUSH POET.

I.

I PURPOSED once to take my pen and write
   Not songs like some, tormented and awry
   With passion, but a cunning harmony
Of words and music caught from glen and height,
And lucid colours born of woodland light,
   And shining places where the sea-streams lie;
But this was when the heat of youth glowed white,
   And since I've put the faded purpose by
I have no faultless fruits to offer you
   Who read this book; but certain syllables
   Herein are borrowed from unfooted dells,
And secret hollows dear to noontide dew;
And these at least, though far between and few,
   May catch the sense like subtle forest spells.

II.

So take these kindly, even though there be
   Some notes that unto other lyres belong:
   Stray echoes from the elder sons of Song;
And think how from its neighbouring, native sea
The pensive shell doth borrow melody.
   I would not do the lordly masters wrong,
   By filching fair words from the shining throng
Whose music haunts me, as the wind a tree!
   Lo! when a stranger, in soft Syrian glooms
     Shot through with sunset, treads the cedar dells,
     And hears the breezy ring of elfin bells
   Far down by where the white-haired cataract booms,
     He, faint with sweetness caught from forest smells,
   Bears thence, unwitting, plunder of perfumes.

These sonnets are the introduction to Kendall's "Leaves from Australian Forests," and set forth his purpose, and, it must be conceded, his achievements. Their speech is as accurate as it is musical. For Kendall is essentially a Bush poet—an Australian Bush poet—not as Gordon was, but (excluding from our consideration the white intruder into the primæval forests) more essentially than Gordon was. For he was a much closer and more reverent observer of animal and vegetable life. He was the friend of nature—with man he was less intimate. In depicting the robust, muscular, dare-devil bushman—stockman or trooper—Kendall cannot be compared with Gordon, who only had to reflect his own life, as the great Italian painters painted their own portraits from mirrors. Gordon wrote, as he lived, like a man who would " put his horse " at anything or " square up " to anybody. But as a Bush-landscape-painter Kendall has no equal in Australia.

In his admirable " Poets and Prosewriters of New South Wales," published one and twenty years ago, Mr G. P. Barton, reviewing Kendall's first book (published when he was twenty years of age) made some remarks which have received a substantial endorsement from the Poet's later writings. He says:—

" One striking merit in Mr Kendall's poetry is, that its colouring is strictly local, and that he has endeavoured to give voice to the majestic scenery of his native land. Whatever opinion may be formed of his poetry, it cannot be denied that it is distinctly Australian poetry. This is a hopeful sign, inasmuch as it speaks of a mind naturally original and averse to imitation. He has not commenced the study of his art by studying Tennyson, but by studying the wild and splendid scenery that surrounded him at his birth.

His capacity in descriptive poetry is very great ; in fact, it appears to be the distinctive mark of his genius. He has an artist's eye for landscape, and if his shading is rather too dark, his outlines are none the less true. No local writer has reproduced the scenes familiar to us with so much effect ; and again he has sought inspiration in the characters and events of this country—endeavouring to paint the wild society of the interior as well as its peculiar scenery. He has chaunted the savage melodies of the aboriginals—painted the sufferings of the explorers—and given a poetic interest even to the life of the stockmen. These are facts which mark him out as an Australian poet and an original poet ; for there is no writer in this field whom he could imitate. This portion at least of his writings may be pronounced perfect."

Mr Barton's remarks have in the main been borne out, but he claims too much. Kendall could paint loneliness admirably well. No one has drawn finer pictures of that aspect of Bush life which is peace or dreariness according as one pines for solitude or pines for society. He has written the most beautiful and the most terrible scenes we have of existence in the depths of the Bush—of the utter forsakenness of the explorer's fate. But for poems of what Mr Barton calls the "wild society of the interior," we should not go to Kendall. He could put himself on the standpoint of the lonely bushman, as we have said, admirably well ; but he had little sympathy with the roistering side of the bushman's nature. His own nature was too delicate, too poetic, too beautiful. This side of Bush life was reserved for men of rougher fibre, more robust and dashing in their genius. In Gordon the man overshadowed the poet, in Kendall the poet the man. Gordon was a thorough bushman, though, like Kendall, by nature sad. He could appreciate the bushman's idea of "having out a spree," utterly reckless of costs or consequences. Consequently, Gordon, in writing on such themes, used the "Bret Harte" method of looking at the debauch, the escapade, the "row" from the point of view of the actors, while Kendall, like Calverley, wrote from the standpoint of the amused looker-on, laughing in his sleeve. This makes his "Jim the Splitter," "Billy Vickers," and the like, unsatisfactory. Even in his own particular line of "Australianised Calverley," he is distinctly inferior to Brunton Stephens, a humorous poet of a very high order. But to catch the zest of the wild life of the Bush, one may read through all that Kendall ever wrote, and never find a page that is worthy to be mentioned beside the glorious "Sick Stockrider" or "Wolf and Hound." If one wants to see the difference between the two writers in this line, one should read the ride "From the Wreck" in conjunction with "The Song of the Cattle-Hunters" and "After the Hunt." Kendall wrote them because he was able, as well as he was able; Gordon wrote his as one bushman giving an account of the ride to another bushman, and with all the embellishment of his ringing, glowing poetry. It is the same in their racing pieces. Kendall wrote like a poet who had been to the races; Gordon like a poet who had raced. But we have no wish to decry Kendall because he could not rival Gordon in bushman's ballads and never wrote an Australian Hiawatha like George Gordon M'Crae. This volume does not wish to dwell on what he could not do, but on what he could do more than ordinarily well. Take, for instance, his description of the death of the two explorers immortalised in Melbourne—Burke and Wills—it was published when the poet was only twenty :—

Set your face toward the darkness—tell of deserts weird and wide,
Where unshaken woods are huddled, and low languid waters glide;
Turn and tell of deserts lonely; lying pathless, deep, and vast,
Where in utter silence ever Time seems slowly breathing past;
Silence only broken when the sun is flecked with cloudy bars,
Or when tropic squalls come hurtling underneath the sultry stars!
Deserts thorny, hot, and thirsty, where the feet of men are strange,
And Eternal Nature sleeps in solitudes which know no change.
Weakened with their lengthened labours, past long plains of stone and sand,
Down those trackless wilds they wandered, travellers from a far-off land;
Seeking now to join their brothers, struggling on with faltering feet,
For a glorious work was finished, and a noble task complete!
And they dreamt of welcome faces—dreamt that soon unto their ears
Friendly greetings would be thronging with a nation's well-earned cheers;
Since their courage never failed them, but with high unflinching soul,
Each was pressing forward, hoping, trusting all should reach the goal.

. . . .

Though he rallied in the morning, long before the close of day
He had sunk, the worn-out hero, fainting, dying, by the way!
But with Death he wrestled hardly: three times rising from the sod,
Yet a little further onward o'er the weary waste he trod;
Facing fate with heart undaunted, still the chief would totter on,
Till the evening closed about him—till the strength to move was gone.

Then he penned his latest writing, and, before the life was spent,
Gave the records to his comrade; gave the watch he said was lent;
Gave them with his last commandments, charging him that night to stay,
And to let him lie unburied when the soul had passed away.

Through that night he uttered little, rambling were the words he spoke;
And he turned and died in silence, when the tardy morning broke.
Many memories come together, whilst in sight of death we dwell,
Much of sweet and sad reflection through the weary mind must well;
As those long hours glided past him, till the east with light was fraught,
Who may know the mournful secret—who can tell us what he thought?

Very lone and very wretched was the brave man left behind,
Wandering over leagues of waste land, seeking, hoping help to find;
Sleeping in deserted wurleys; fearful, many nightfalls through,
Lest unfriendly hands should rob him of his hoard of wild nardoo.

Ere he reached their old encampment—ere the well-known spot he gained,
Something nerved him—something whispered, that his other chief remained:
So he searched for food to give him, trusting they might both survive
Till the aid so long expected from the cities should arrive;
So he searched for food, and took it to the gunyah, where he found
Silence broken by his footfalls—death and darkness on the ground.

Weak and wearied with his journey, there the lone survivor stooped;
And the disappointment bowed him, and his heart with sadness drooped.
But he rose and raked a hollow with his wasted feeble hands,
Where he took and hid the hero, in the rushes and the sands;
But he like a brother laid him out of reach of wind and rain,
And for many days he sojourned near him, on that wild-faced plain.
Whilst he stayed beside the ruin—whilst he lingered with the dead,
Oh! he must have sat in shadow, gloomy as the tears he shed.

Where our noble Burke was lying—where his sad companion stood,
Came the natives of the forest—came the wild men of the wood:
Down they looked and saw the stranger—he who there in quiet slept—
Down they knelt, and o'er the chieftain bitterly they moaned and wept;
Bitterly they mourned to see him all uncovered to the blast—
All uncovered to the tempest as it wailed and whistled past.
And they shrouded him with bushes, so in death that he might lie,
Like a warrior of their nation, sheltered from the stormy sky.

This is not given as by any means a specimen of Kendall's best work, but as his most typical exploration-poem. In "At Euroma" and "Leichhardt," on a kindred subject, published in a later book, we find more of his distinctive beauties.

> The songs austere of the forests drear,
>   And the echoes of clift and cave,
> When the dark is keen where the storm hath been,
>   Fleet over the far-away grave.

And through the days when the torrid rays
  Strike down in a coppery gloom,
Some spirit grieves in the perished leaves
  Whose theme is that desolate tomb.

No human foot, or paw of brute,
  Halts now where the stranger sleeps;
But cloud and star his fellows are,
  And the rain that sobs and weeps.
The dingo yells by the far iron fells,
  The plover is loud in the range,
But they never come near to the slumberer here,
  Whose rest is a rest without change.

Ah! in his life had he mother or wife
  To wait for his step on the floor?
Did beauty wax dim while watching for him
  Who passed through the threshold no more?
Doth it trouble his head? He is one with the dead;
  He lies by the alien streams;
And sweeter than sleep is death that is deep,
  And unvexed by the lordship of dreams.

LEICHHARDT.

Born by hills of hard grey weather, far beyond the northern seas,
German mountains were his "sponsors," and his mates were German trees.
Grandeur of the old-world forests passed into his radiant soul,
With the song of stormy crescents, where the mighty waters roll.
Thus he came to be a brother of the river and the wood—
Thus the leaf, the bird, the blossom, grew a gracious sisterhood!
Nature led him to her children in a space of light divine—
Kneeling down, he said—" My mother, let me be as one of thine!"
So she took him—thence she loved him—lodged him in her home of dreams:
Taught him what the trees were saying, schooled him in the speech of streams.

For her sake he crossed the waters—loving her, he left the place
Hallowed by his father's ashes, and his human mother's face,
Passed the seas and entered temples, domed by skies of deathless beam—
Walled about by hills majestic—stately spires and peaks supreme!
Here he found a larger beauty—here the lovely lights were new,
On the slopes of many flowers, down the gold green dells of dew,

In the great august cathedral of his holy Lady, he
Daily worshipped at her altars, nightly bent the reverent knee—
Heard the hymns of night and morning, learned the psalm of solitudes,
Knew that God was very near him—felt His Presence in the woods!

But the starry angel, Science, from the home of glittering wings,
Came one day and talked to Nature, by melodious mountain springs—
"Let thy son be mine," she pleaded, "lend him for a space," she said,
"So that he may earn the laurels I have woven for his head!"
And the Lady, Nature, listened; and she took her loyal son
From the banks of moss and myrtle—led him to the Shining One!
Filled his lordly soul with gladness—told him of a spacious zone
Eye of man had never looked at—human foot had never known;
Then the angel, Science, beckoned, and he knelt and whispered low—
"I will follow when you lead me"—two-and-thirty years ago.

On the tracts of thirst and furnace—on the dumb, blind, burning plain,
Where the red earth gapes for moisture, and the wan leaves hiss for rain,
In a land of dry fierce thunder, did he ever pause and dream,
Of the cool green German valley, and the singing German stream?
When the sun was as a menace glaring from a sky of brass,
Did he ever rest in visions, on a lap of German grass?
Past the waste of thorny terrors, did he reach a sphere of rills,
In a region yet untravelled, ringed by fair untrodden hills?
Was the spot where last he rested, pleasant as an old world lea?
Did the sweet winds come and lull him with the music of the sea?

Let us dream so—let us hope so! Haply, in a cool green glade,
Far beyond the zone of furnace, Leichhardt's sacred shell was laid!
Haply in some leafy valley, underneath blue gracious skies,
In the sound of mountain water, the heroic traveller lies!
Down a dell of dewy myrtle, where the light is soft and green,
And a month, like English April, sits—an immemorial queen,
Let us think that he is resting—think that by a radiant grave,
Ever come the songs of forest and the voices of the wave!
Thus we want our sons to find him—find him under floral bowers,
Sleeping by the trees he loved so—covered with his darling flowers!

So far we have not been quite in accord with Mr Barton. We know now, though he did not, that while he was writing in New South Wales to laud Kendall as the first Station-life poet, poems that have now a world-wide celebrity were being written on the same subject in Victoria, and no one would claim that Kendall had competed with Longfellow by producing an aboriginal poem to compare with Hiawatha. Nor do we think that in his poems on exploration he throws up the stern realities like Gordon, whose poem on Burke and Wills our promise to his publishers precludes us from quoting, or P. J. Holdsworth and others. In Leichhardt especially it will be seen that his poetical soul loved to dwell more on the so-called poetical aspects than on the grim practical ones. For few poets have had such a delicate, tender poetical soul as this native-born New South Welshman—who might justly be called the Australian Shelley. Indeed, in his brilliant appreciation of colour, his swift recognition of that Proteus, the spirit of Nature in all her changes of form, in the delicate music of his verse, his marvellous ease, his felicity and fecundity of expression, and his courageous assertion of opinions which men are generally unwilling to proclaim, he had much to make him comparable to the immortal author of "Queen Mab."

Kendall was as bold in bringing into prominence his adherence to Romanism in a secular, or at best an undenominational, community, as Shelley was in letting his peculiar views be known in a community which persecuted the unorthodox. But though he had so much in common with Shelley, the influence of Swinburne is much more apparent in this Australian poet's writings, than the influence of Swinburne's master. But the genius of the man is shown most, perhaps, by his handling of the language and the metres which the polished rapier-thrusting buffoonery of Mr Gilbert's opera-libretti has overwhelmed with ridicule, except when they are handled by true poets. Kendall can write long poems with the ante-penultimate rhyme, put an utterly bald expression like "two-and-thirty years ago" into a position of emphasis and solemnity, and yet not fall from the sublime. Some of his most serious "In Memoriam" poems would be quite comic, if one did not feel the restraining power of the man's genius. He could solemnify. There is such a true breath of religiousness about his poems, though they never preach, that scoffs are disarmed ; and his genius is further demonstrated by the fact that he has written one of the two or three prize poems that are worth reading after the event with which they are connected has passed. His poem for the opening of the Sydney Exhibition is magnificent—we should say, perhaps the finest prize poem written in the English language. The rest of Mr Barton's claims we most cordially endorse, for as a Bush landscape painter, Kendall has never had an equal, especially in the gloomier tints.

What a power of word painting he had will be seen from the poems, "The Hut by the Black Swamp," "Cooranbean," and "The Curse of Mother Flood," here in part appended.

From "The Hut by the Black Swamp."

> The moss that like a tender grief
> About an English ruin clings—
> What time the wan autumnal leaf
> Faints after many wanderings
> On windy wings—
>
> That gracious growth whose quiet green
> Is as a love in days austere,
> Was never seen—hath never been
> On slab or roof, deserted here
> For many a year.
>
> Nor comes the bird whose speech is song—
> Whose songs are silvery syllables
> That unto glimmering woods belong,
> And deep meandering mountain-dells
> By yellow wells.

But rather here the wild dog halts,
   And lifts the paw, and looks, and howls;
And here, in ruined forest-vaults,
   Abide dim, dark, death-featured owls,
     Like monks in cowls.

Across this Hut the nettle runs,
   And livid adders make their lair
In corners dank from lack of sun;
   And out of fetid furrows stare
     The growths that scare.

Here Summer's grasp of fire is laid
   On bark and slabs that rot and breed
Squat ugly things of deadly shade—
   The scorpion, and the spiteful seed
     Of Centipede.

Unhallowed thunders harsh and dry,
   And flaming noontides mute with heat,
Beneath the breathless, brazen sky,
   Upon these rifted rafters beat
     With torrid feet.

And night by night, the fitful gale
   Doth carry past the bittern's boom,
The dingo's yell, the plover's wail,
   While lumbering shadows start, and loom,
     And hiss through gloom.

No sign of grace—no hope of green,
   Cool-blossomed seasons mark the spot;
But, chained to iron doom, I ween,
   'Tis left, like skeleton, to rot
     Where ruth is not.

For on this Hut, hath Murder writ
   With bloody fingers hellish things;
And God will never visit it
   With flower or leaf of sweet-faced Springs,
     Or gentle wings.

This little poem is a very good one to quote, because it shows in contrast the quiet beauty of Kendall's landscape painting, and the intenseness of his lurid compositions.

From "Cooranbean."

Whenever an elder is asked—a white-headed man of the woods—
Of the terrible mystery masked where the dark everlastingly broods,
Be sure he will turn to the bay with his back to the glen in the range,
And glide like a phantom away, with a countenance pallid with change.
From the line of dead timber that lies supine at the foot of the glade
The fierce-featured eagle-hawk flies—afraid as a dove is afraid;
But back in that wilderness dread are a fall and the forks of a ford—
Ah! pray and uncover your head, and lean like a child on the Lord.

A sinister fog at the wave—at the change of the moon cometh forth
Like an ominous ghost in the train of a bitter black storm of the North!
At the head of the gully unknown, it hangs like a spirit of bale;
And the noise of a shriek and a groan strikes up in the gusts of the gale.
In the throat of a feculent pit is the beard of a bloody-red sedge;
And the foam like the foam of a fit sweats out of the lips of the ledge;
But down in the water of death, in the livid dead pool at the base—
Bow low with inaudible breath: beseech with the hands to the face!

A furlong of fetid black fen, with gelid green patches of pond
Lies dumb by the horns of the Glen—at the gates of the Horror beyond;
And those who have looked on it, tell of the terrible growths that are there—
The flowerage fostered by Hell—the blossoms that startle and scare;
If ever a wandering bird should light on Gehennas like this,
Be sure that a cry will be heard, and the sound of the flat adder's hiss.
But, hard by the jaws of the bend is a ghastly Thing matted with moss—
Ah, Lord! be a father, a friend for the sake of the Christ on the Cross.

Black Tom with the sinews of five—that never a hangman could hang—
In the days of the shackle and gyve, broke loose from the guards of the gang.

Thereafter, for seasons a score, this devil prowled under the ban:
A mate of red talon and paw—a wolf in the shape of a man.
But, ringed by ineffable fire, in a thunder and wind of the North,
The sword of Omnipotent ire—the bolt of high heaven went forth!
But, wan as the sorrowful foam, a gray mother waits by the sea
For the boys that have never come home these fifty-four winters and three.

From the folds of the forested hills there are ravelled and roundabout tracks
Because of the terror that fills the strong-handed men of the axe!
Of the workers away in the range, there is none that will wait for the night
When the storm-stricken moon is in change, and the sinister fog is in sight.
And later and deep in the dark, when the bitter wind whistles about,
There is never a howl or a bark from the dog in the kennel without.
But the white fathers fasten the door, and often and often they start
At a sound like a foot on the floor, and a touch like a hand on the heart.

This is to our mind the weirdest and most bloodcurdling, at the same time as it is the most beautiful and powerful of Kendall's lurid pieces. In fierceness of curses it is surpassed by "The Curse of Mother Flood" (quoted next), but that poem always strikes us as less natural and more of a rhetorical exercise.

> Wizend the wood is, and wan is the way through it;
>   White as a corpse is the face in the fen;
> Only blue adders abide in and stray through it—
>   Adders and venom and horrors to men.
> Here is the "ghost of a garden" whose minister
>   Fosters strange blossoms that startle and scare.
> Red as man's blood is the sun that, with sinister
>   Flame, is a menace of hell in the air.
> Wrinkled and haggard the hills are—the jags of them
>   Gape like to living and ominous things
> Storm and dry thunder cry out in the crags of them—
>   Fire, and the wind with a woe in its wings.
>
> Never a noon without clammy-cold shroud on it
>   Hitherward comes, or a flower-like star!
> Only the hiss of the tempest is loud on it—
>   Hiss and the moan of a bitter sea bar.

Here on this waste, and to left and to right of it
    Never is lisp or the ripple of rain :
Fierce is the daytime and wild is the night of it—
    Flame without limit and frost without wave!
Trees half alive, with the sense of a curse on them,
    Shudder and shrink from the black heavy gale;
Ghastly, with boughs like the plumes of a hearse on them ;
    Barren of blossom and blasted with bale.

Under the cliff that stares down to the south of it—
    Back by the horns of a hazardous hill,
Dumb is the gorge with a grave in the mouth of it,
    Still, as a corpse in a coffin is still.
Never there hovers a hope of the Spring by it—
    Never a glimmer of yellow and green :
Only the bat with a whisper of wing by it
    Flits like a life out of flesh and unseen.
Here are the growths that are livid and glutinous,
    Speckled, and bloated with poisonous blood ;
This is the haunt of the viper-breed mutinous ;
    Cursed with the curse of weird Catherine Flood.

.   .   .   .

Here, in a pit with indefinite doom on it,
    Here, in the fumes of a feculent moat,
Under the alp with inscrutable gloom on it
    Squats the wild witch with a ghoul at her throat
Black execration that cannot be spoken of—
    Speech of red hell that would suffocate Song,
Starts from this terror with never a token of
    Day and its loveliness all the year long.
Sin without name to it—man never heard of it—
    Crime that would startle a fiend from his lair,
Blasted this glen, and the leaf and the bird of it—
    Where is there hope for it, Father, O where?

Far in the days of our fathers, the life in it
    Blossomed and beamed in the sight of the sun ;
Yellow and green and the purple were rife on it,
    Singers of morning and waters that run.
Storm of the equinox shed no distress on it,
    Thunder spoke softly, and summer-time left
Sunset's forsaken bright beautiful dress on it—
    Blessing that shone half the night in the cleft.

> Hymns of the highlands—hosannas from hills by it,
> Psalms of great forests made holy the spot;
> Cool were the mosses and clear were the rills by it—
> Far in the days when the Horror was not.

. . . .

But Kendall is seen at his very best, not in these lurid colours, but in the delicate tints of light and shadow, the lovely contrasts of moss and stream, the languorous shade, the sleepy perfumed air, the luxuriance, and the untroddenness of his native forests. In fact, he is essentially a forest-poet: his genius did not exult upon the mountain-top, it luxuriated in dells. Here are some instances—

Bell Birds.

> The silver-voiced bell-birds, the darlings of day-time!
> They sing in September their songs of the May-time;
> When shadows wax strong, and the thunderbolts hurtle,
> They hide with their fear in the leaves of the myrtle;
> When rain and the sunbeams shine mingled together,
> They start up like fairies that follow fair weather;
> And straightway, the hues of their feathers, unfolden
> Are the green and the purple, the blue and the golden.
>
> October, the maiden of bright yellow tresses,
> Loiters for love in these cool wildernesses;
> Loiters, knee-deep in the grasses, to listen
> Where dripping rocks gleam and the leafy pools glisten:
> Then is the time when the water-moons splendid
> Break with their gold, and are scattered or blended
> Over the creeks, till the woodlands have warning
> Of the songs of the bell-bird and wings of the Morning.
>
> Welcome as waters unkissed by the summers
> Are the voices of bell-birds to thirsty far-comers.
> When fiery December sets foot in the forest,
> And the need of the wayfarer presses the sorest,
> Pent in the ridges for ever and ever,
> The bell-birds direct him to spring and to river,
> With ring and with ripple, like runnels whose torrents
> Are toned by the pebbles and leaves in the currents.

Often I sit looking back to a childhood,
Mixt with the sights and the sounds of the wildwood,
Longing for power and the sweetness to fashion
Lyrics with beats like the heart-beats of Passion;—
Songs interwoven of lights and of laughters
Borrowed from bell-birds in far forest-rafters;
So I might keep in the city and alleys
The beauty and strength of the deep mountain-valleys:
Charming to slumber the pain of my losses
With glimpses of creeks and a vision of mosses.

From "Mooni."

He that is by Mooni now,
Sees the water-sapphires gleaming
Where the River Spirit dreaming
Sleeps by fall and fountain streaming
   Under lute of leaf and bough!—
Hears where stamp of Storm with stress is,
Psalms from unseen wildernesses
Deep amongst far hill-recesses—
   He that is by Mooni now.

Yea, for him by Mooni's marge
Sings the yellow-haired September,
With the face the gods remember
When the ridge is burnt to ember,
   And the dumb sea chains the barge!
Where the mount like molten brass is,
Down beneath fern-feathered passes
Noonday dew in cool green grasses
   Gleams on him by Mooni's marge.

Who that dwells by Mooni yet,
Feels in flowerful forest arches,
Smiting wings and breath that parches
Where strong Summer's path of march is,
   And the suns in thunder set!
Housed beneath the gracious kirtle
Of the shadowy water-myrtle—
Winds may kiss with heat and hurtle,
   He is safe by Mooni yet!

> Days there were when he who sings
> (Dumb so long through passion's losses)
> Stood where Mooni's water crosses
> Shining tracks of green-haired mosses,
>   Like a soul with radiant wings;
> Then the psalm the wind rehearses—
> Then the song the stream disperses,
> Lent a beauty to his verses—
>   Who to-night of Mooni **sings**.
>
> Ah, the theme—the sad, gray theme!
> Certain days are not above me,
> Certain hearts have ceased **to love me**,
> Certain fancies fail to move **me**,
>   Like the effluent morning dream.
> Head whereon the white is stealing,
> Heart whose hurts are past all healing,
> Where is now the first pure feeling?—
>   Ah, the theme—the sad, **gray** theme!
>
> . . . . .
>
> Still to be by **Mooni cool**—
> Where the water-blossoms glister,
> And by gleaming vale **and** vista,
> Sits the English April's sister,
>   Soft and sweet and wonderful!
> **Just** to rest beyond the burning
> **Outer** world—its sneers and **spurning**—
> Ah, my heart—my heart is yearning
>   Still to be by Mooni cool.
>
> . . . . .

His "Orara," is full of beautiful thoughts and expressions.

> . . . . .
>
> The soft white feet of afternoon
>   Are on the shining meads,
> The breeze is as a pleasant tune
>   Amongst the happy reeds.
>
> . . . . .
>
> The air is full of mellow sounds
>   The wet hill heads are bright
> And, down the fall of fragrant grounds,
>   The deep ways flame with light.

A rose-red space of stream I see
  Past banks of tender fern:
A radiant brook, unknown to me
  Beyond its upper turn.

The singing silver life I hear,
  Whose home is in the green
Far-folded woods of fountains clear,
  Where I have never been.

Ah, brook above the upper bend,
  I often long to stand,
Where you in soft cool shades descend
  From the untrodden land!

Ah, folded woods that hide the grace
  Of moss and torrents strong,
I often wish to know the face
  Of that which sings your song!

But I may linger, long, and look
  Till night is over all:
My eyes will never see the brook
  Or sweet strange waterfall!

The world is round me with its heat
  And toil, and cares that tire;
I cannot with my feeble feet
  Climb after my desire.

But on the lap of lands unseen,
  Within a secret zone,
There shine diviner gold and green
  Than man has ever known.

And where the silver waters sing,
  Down hushed and holy dells,
The flower of a celestial spring—
  A tenfold splendour dwells.

Yea, in my dream of fall and brook,
  By far sweet forests furled,
I see that light for which I look
  In vain through all the world.

> The glory of a larger sky
>   On slopes of hills sublime,
> That speak with God and Morning, high
>   Above the waves of Time!
>
> Ah! haply in this sphere of change,
>   Where shadows spoil the beam,
> It would not do to climb that range,
>   And test my radiant Dream.
>
> The slightest glimpse of yonder place,
>   Untrodden and alone,
> Might wholly kill that nameless grace
>   The charm of the Unknown.
>
> And therefore though I look and **long**,
>   Perhaps the lot is right
> Which keeps the river of **the song**
>   A beauty out of sight.

Hitherto, Gordon has had very much the start of Kendall in England, and, so far as the semi-cultivated portion of poetry-readers are concerned, we doubt not will continue to have. But with that cultivated class of intellect that delights to be made the confidante of Nature, as Gilbert White, Richard Jefferies, and John Burroughes have made it, and revels in all that is genuinely redolent of a forest life that is fresh to it, we venture to prophesy that Kendall will become a supreme favourite, as soon as he is recognised. He was a child of the Australian forest, and continued such all his life. No one who did not love the forest as a mother could have written this exquisite "September in Australia."

SEPTEMBER IN AUSTRALIA.

> Grey Winter hath gone, like a wearisome guest,
>   And, behold, for repayment,
> September comes in with the wind of the West,
>   And the Spring in her raiment!

The ways of the frost have been filled of the flowers,
  While the forest discovers
Wild wings with the halo of hyaline hours,
  And a music of lovers.

September, the maid with the **swift, silver feet!**
  She glides, and she graces
The valleys of coolness, the slopes of the heat,
  With her blossomy traces.
Sweet month with a mouth that **is made of a rose,**
  She lightens and lingers
In spots where the harp of **the evening** glows,
  Attuned by her fingers.

The stream from its home in the hollow hill slips
  In a darling old fashion;
And the day goeth down with **a song on its lips,**
  Whose key-note is passion.
Far out in the fierce, bitter front **of the sea**
  I stand, and remember
Dead things that were brothers and sisters of thee,
  Resplendent September.

The West, when it blows at the fall of the noon,
  And beats on the beaches,
Is filled with a tender and **tremulous tune**
  That touches and teaches:
The stories of Youth, of the burden of Time,
  And the death of Devotion,
Come back **with** the wind, and **are** themes of the rhyme,
  In the **waves** of the Ocean.

We, having a secret to others unknown,
  In the cool mountain-mosses,
May whisper together, September, alone
  Of our loves and our losses.
One word for her beauty, and one for the grace
  She gave to the hours;
And then we may kiss her, and **suffer her face**
  To sleep with the flowers.

High places that knew of the gold and the white
  On the forehead of Morning,
Now darken and quake, and the steps of the Night
  Are heavy **with** warning!

Her voice in the distance is lofty and loud,
  Through the echoing gorges;
She hath hidden her eyes in a mantle of cloud,
  And her feet in the surges!

On the tops of the hills; on the turreted cones—
  Chief temples of thunder—
The gale, like a ghost, in the middle watch moans,
  Gliding over and under.
The sea flying white through the rack and the rain,
  Leapeth wild at the forelands;
And the plover, whose cry is like passion with pain,
  Complains in the moorlands.

O, season of changes—of shadow and shine—
  September the splendid!
My song hath no music to mingle with thine,
  And its burden is ended:
But thou, being born of the winds and the Sun,
  By mountain, by river,
May lighten and listen, and loiter and run,
  With thy voices for Ever.

And the following little poem, entitled "The Warrigal" (Wild Dog), will prove that he observed animal life as faithfully as still life and landscape:—

Through forest boles the storm-wind rolls,
  Vext of the sea-driven rain,
And up in the clift through many a rift
  The voices of torrents complain.
The sad marsh-fowl and the lonely owl
  Are heard in the fog-wreaths grey,
When the Warrigal wakes and listens, and takes
  To the woods that shelter the prey.

In the gully-deeps, the blind creek sleeps;
  And the silvery, showery moon
Glides over the hills and floats and fills,
  And dreams in the dark lagoon;
While halting hard by the station-yard,
  Aghast at the hut-flame nigh,
The Warrigal yells, and the flats and fells
  Are loud with his dismal cry.

On the topmost peak of mountains bleak,
    The South wind sobs, and strays
Through moaning pine, and turpentine
    And the rippling runnel ways;
And strong streams flow and great mists go,
    Where the Warrigal starts to hear
The watchdog's bark break sharp in the dark,
    And flees like a phantom of Fear!

The swift rains beat, and the thunders fleet
    On the wings of the fiery gale,
And down in the glen of pool and fen
    The wild gums whistle and wail,
As over the plains, and past the chains
    Of waterholes glimmering deep,
The Warrigal flies from the shepherd's cries
    And the clamour of dogs and sheep.

The Warrigal's lair is pent in bare
    Black rocks at the gorge's mouth;
It is set in ways where Summer strays,
    With the sprites of flame and drouth,
But when the heights are touched with lights
    Of hoarfrost, sleet, and shine,
His bed is made of the dead grass-blade
    And the leaves of the windy pine.

He roves through the lands of sultry sands,
    He hunts in the iron range,
Untamed as surge of the far sea verge,
    And fierce, and fickle, and strange.
The white man's track and the haunts of the black
    He shuns, and shudders to see;
For his joy he tastes in lonely wastes,
    Where his mates are torrent and tree.

We venture to think that there is nothing more Landseer-like in the whole range of Australian poetry than this brilliant lyric. There are others of Kendall's poems which ought to be included in any selection, such as "Coogee." But we have already, in our anxiety to do justice to Kendall, transgressed our limits, so we must conclude; and no article on Kendall could conclude more fitly than with his own sad verses written

"AFTER MANY YEARS."

The song that once I dreamed about,
  The tender, touching thing,
As radiant as the rose without—
  The love of wind and wing—
The perfect verses to the tune
  Of woodland music set,
As beautiful as afternoon,
  Remain unwritten yet.

It is too late to write them now,
  The ancient fire is cold;
No ardent lights illume the brow
  As in the days of old.
I cannot dream the dream again
  But, when the happy birds
Are singing in the sunny rain,
  I think I hear its words.

I think I hear the echo still
  Of long forgotten tones,
When evening winds are on the hill,
  And sunset fires the cones.
But only in the hours supreme
  With songs of land and sea,
The lyrics of the leaf and stream,
  This echo comes to me.

No longer doth the earth reveal
  Her gracious green and gold;
I sit where youth was once, and feel
  That I am growing old.
The lustre from the face of things
  Is wearing all away;
Like one who halts with tired wings,
  I rest and muse to-day.

There is a river in the range
  I love to think about:
Perhaps the searching feet of change
  Have never found it out.
Ah! oftentimes I used to look
  Upon its banks, and long
To steal the beauty of that brook
  And put it in a song.

I wonder if the slopes of moss
  In dreams so dear to me—
The falls of flower and flower-like floss—
  Are as they used to be!
I wonder if the waterfalls,
  The singers far and fair
That gleamed between the wet green walls
  Are still the marvels there!

Ah! let me hope that in that place
  The old familiar things,
To which I turn a wistful face,
  Have never taken wings.
Let me retain the fancy still
  That, past the lordly range,
There always shines, in folds of hill,
  One spot secure from change!

I trust that yet the tender screen
  That shades a certain nook
Remains, with all its gold and green,
  The glory of the brook!
It hides a secret, to the birds
  And waters only known—
The letters of two lovely words,—
  A poem on a stone.

Perhaps the lady of the past
  Upon these lines may light,
The purest verses and the last
  That I may ever write.
She need not fear a word of blame;
  Her tale the flowers keep;
The wind that heard me breathe her name
  Has been for years asleep.

But, in the night and when the rain
  The troubled torrents fills,
I often think I see again
  The river in the hills.
And when the day is very near,
  And birds are on the wing,
My spirit fancies it can hear
  The song I cannot sing.

Other works by
DOUGLAS B. W. SLADEN.

FRITHJOF AND INGEBJORG and other Poems, by an Australian Colonist. In green cloth boards. Price 5s. Published by Kegan Paul, Trench & Co., 1 Paternoster Square, London, E.C.

And published by GRIFFITH, FARRAN & CO., of London and Sydney.

AUSTRALIAN LYRICS,
A POETRY OF EXILES, } 2nd Editions, in white parchment covers scarlet-printed, on thick rough-edged hand-made paper, square 20mo. Price 1s. each.

EDWARD THE BLACK PRINCE. Uniform with the two last named, but thrice as thick. Price 4s.

A SUMMER CHRISTMAS. A Story of Station Life in Australia. In green cloth boards. Price 6s.

IN CORNWALL AND ACROSS THE SEA. A thick Octavo Volume in scarlet and white binding. Printed on thick rough-edged hand-made paper. Price 6s.

SEIZED BY A SHADOW. A Novel with a Ghost Story. Written under the pseudonym of Rose Mullion. In fancy paper covers. Price 1s.

Mr Sladen is also preparing to the order of Messrs Griffith, Farran & Co., to be issued shortly, a selection from Australasian Poets without limitation of subject, which will form a Handsome Octavo Volume of 500 pages.

THE CANTERBURY POETS.

EDITED BY WILLIAM SHARP. 1/- VOLS., SQUARE 8VO.

Cloth, Red Edges . 1s. | Red Roan, Gilt Edges, 2s. 6d.
Cloth, Uncut Edges . 1s. | Pad. Morocco, Gilt Edges - 5s.

Christian Year.
Coleridge.
Longfellow.
Campbell.
Shelley.
Wordsworth.
Blake.
Whittier.
Poe.
Chatterton.
Burns. Poems.
Burns. Songs.
Marlowe.
Keats.
Herbert.
Victor Hugo.
Cowper.
Shakespeare: Songs, etc.
Emerson.
Sonnets of this Century.
Whitman.
Scott. Marmion, etc.
Scott. Lady of the Lake, etc.
Praed.
Hogg.
Goldsmith.
Mackay's Love Letters.
Spenser.
Children of the Poets.
Ben Jonson.
Byron (2 Vols.).
Sonnets of Europe.
Allan Ramsay.
Sydney Dobell.
Pope.
Heine.
Beaumont and Fletcher.
Bowles, Lamb, etc.
Sea Music.
Early English Poetry.
Herrick.

Ballades and Rondeaus.
Irish Minstrelsy.
Milton's Paradise Lost.
Jacobite Ballads.
Australian Ballads.
Moore's Poems.
Border Ballads.
Song-Tide.
Odes of Horace.
Ossian.
Fairy Music.
Southey.
Chaucer.
Golden Treasury.
Poems of Wild Life.
Paradise Regained.
Crabbe.
Dora Greenwell.
Goethe's Faust.
American Sonnets.
Landor's Poems.
Greek Anthology.
Hunt and Hood.
Humorous Poems.
Lytton's Plays.
Great Odes.
Owen Meredith's Poems.
Imitation of Christ.
Toby's Birthday Book.
Painter-Poets.
Women-Poets.
Love Lyrics.
American Humor. Verse.
Scottish Minor Poets.
Cavalier Lyrists.
German Ballads.
Songs of Beranger.
Poems by Roden Noel.
Songs of Freedom.
Canadian Poems.
Modern Scottish Poets.

London: WALTER SCOTT, LIMITED, 24 Warwick Lane.

THE SCOTT LIBRARY.

Cloth, uncut edges, gilt top.   Price 1/6 per volume.

ALREADY ISSUED.

- Romance of King Arthur.
- Thoreau's Walden.
- Thoreau's Week.
- Thoreau's Essays.
- Confessions of an English Opium-Eater.
- Landor's Conversations.
- Plutarch's Lives.
- Browne's Religio Medici.
- Essays and Letters of P. B. Shelley.
- Prose Writings of Swift.
- My Study Windows.
- Lowell's Essays on the English Poets.
- The Biglow Papers.
- Great English Painters.
- Lord Byron's Letters.
- Essays by Leigh Hunt.
- Longfellow's Prose.
- Great Musical Composers
- Marcus Aurelius.
- Epictetus.
- Seneca's Morals.
- Whitman's Specimen Days in America.
- Whitman's Democratic Vistas.
- White's Natural History.
- Captain Singleton.
- Essays by Mazzini.
- Prose Writings of Heine.
- Reynolds' Discourses.
- The Lover: Papers of Steele and Addison.
- Burns's Letters.
- Volsunga Saga.
- Sartor Resartus.
- Writings of Emerson.
- Life of Lord Herbert.

THE SCOTT LIBRARY—continued.

English Prose.
The Pillars of Society.
Fairy and Folk Tales.
Essays of Dr. Johnson.
Essays of Wm. Hazlitt.
Landor's Pentameron, &c.
Poe's Tales and Essays.
Vicar of Wakefield.
Political Orations.
Holmes's Autocrat.
Holmes's Poet.
Holmes's Professor.
Chesterfield's Letters.
Stories from Carleton.
Jane Eyre.
Elizabethan England.
Davis's Writings.
Spence's Anecdotes.
More's Utopia.
Sadi's Gulistan.
English Folk Tales.
Northern Studies.
Famous Reviews.
Aristotle's Ethics.
Landor's Aspasia.

Tacitus.
Essays of Elia.
Balzac.
De Musset's Comedies.
Darwin's Coral-Reefs.
Sheridan's Plays.
Our Village.
Humphrey's Clock, &c.
Tales from Wonderland.
Douglas Jerrold.
Rights of Woman.
Athenian Oracle.
Essays of Sainte-Beuve.
Selections from Plato.
Heine's Travel Sketches.
Maid of Orleans.
Sydney Smith.
The New Spirit.
Marvellous Adventures
 (From the Morte d'Arthur.)
Helps's Essays.
Montaigne's Essays.
Luck of Barry Lyndon.
William Tell.
Carlyle's German Essays

London: WALTER SCOTT, LIMITED, 24 Warwick Lane.

New Series of Critical Biographies.

Edited by ERIC ROBERTSON and FRANK T. MARZIALS.

GREAT WRITERS.

Cloth, Gilt Top, Price 1s. 6d.

ALREADY ISSUED—

LIFE OF LONGFELLOW. By Prof. E. S. ROBERTSON.
LIFE OF COLERIDGE. By HALL CAINE.
LIFE OF DICKENS. By FRANK T. MARZIALS.
LIFE OF D. G. ROSSETTI. By JOSEPH KNIGHT.
LIFE OF SAMUEL JOHNSON. By Col. F. GRANT.
LIFE OF DARWIN. By G. T. BETTANY.
CHARLOTTE BRONTE. By AUGUSTINE BIRRELL.
LIFE OF CARLYLE. By RICHARD GARNETT, LLD.
LIFE OF ADAM SMITH. By R. B. HALDANE, M.P.
LIFE OF KEATS. By W. M. ROSSETTI.
LIFE OF SHELLEY. By WILLIAM SHARP.
LIFE OF GOLDSMITH. By AUSTIN DOBSON.
LIFE OF SCOTT. By Professor YONGE.
LIFE OF BURNS. By Professor BLACKIE.
LIFE OF VICTOR HUGO. By FRANK T. MARZIALS.
LIFE OF EMERSON. By RICHARD GARNETT, LL.D.
LIFE OF GOETHE. By JAMES SIME.
LIFE OF CONGREVE. By EDMUND GOSSE.
LIFE OF BUNYAN. By Canon VENABLES.

GREAT WRITERS—continued.

LIFE OF CRABBE. By T. E. KEBBEL, M.A.
LIFE OF HEINE. By WILLIAM SHARP.
LIFE OF MILL. By W. L. COURTNEY.
LIFE OF SCHILLER. By H. W. NEVINSON.
LIFE OF CAPTAIN MARRYAT. By DAVID HANNAY.
LIFE OF LESSING. By T. W. ROLLESTON.
LIFE OF MILTON. By RICHARD GARNETT.
LIFE OF GEORGE ELIOT. By OSCAR BROWNING.
LIFE OF BALZAC. By FREDERICK WEDMORE.
LIFE OF JANE AUSTEN. By GOLDWIN SMITH.
LIFE OF BROWNING. By WILLIAM SHARP.
LIFE OF BYRON. By Hon. RODEN NOEL.
LIFE OF HAWTHORNE. By MONCURE CONWAY.
LIFE OF SCHOPENHAUER. By Professor WALLACE.
LIFE OF SHERIDAN. By LLOYD SANDERS.
LIFE OF THACKERAY. By HERMAN MERIVALE and FRANK T. MARZIALS.
LIFE OF CERVANTES. By H. E. WATTS.
LIFE OF VOLTAIRE. By FRANCIS ESPINASSE.
LIFE OF LEIGH HUNT. By COSMO MONKHOUSE.
LIFE OF WHITTIER. By W. J. LINTON.

Bibliography to each, by J. P. ANDERSON, British Museum.

LIBRARY EDITION OF "GREAT WRITERS."

Printed on large paper of extra quality, in handsome binding, Demy 8vo, price 2s. 6d. per volume.

London: WALTER SCOTT, LIMITED, 24 Warwick Lane.

NEW BOOKLETS.

Crown 8vo, Gilt Lettering, One Shilling each.

By COUNT LEO TOLSTOÏ.

WHERE LOVE IS, THERE GOD IS ALSO.

THE TWO PILGRIMS.

WHAT MEN LIVE BY.

THE GODSON.

IF YOU NEGLECT THE FIRE, YOU DON'T PUT IT OUT.

WHAT SHALL IT PROFIT A MAN?

Published originally in Russia, as tracts for the people, these little stories possess all the grace, naïveté, and power which characterise the work of Count Tolstoï, and while inculcating in the most penetrating way the Christian ideas of love, humility, and charity, are perfect in their art form as stories pure and simple.

London: WALTER SCOTT, 24 Warwick Lane, Paternoster Row.

COMPACT AND PRACTICAL.

In Limp Cloth; for the Pocket. Price One Shilling.

THE EUROPEAN
CONVERSATION BOOKS.

FRENCH.   **ITALIAN.**
SPANISH. **GERMAN.**
NORWEGIAN.

CONTENTS.

Hints to Travellers—Everyday Expressions—Arriving at and Leaving a Railway Station—Custom House Enquiries—In a Train—At a Buffet and Restaurant—At an Hotel—Paying an Hotel Bill—Enquiries in a Town—On Board Ship—Embarking and Disembarking—Excursion by Carriage—Enquiries as to Diligences—Enquiries as to Boats—Engaging Apartments—Washing List and Days of Week—Restaurant Vocabulary—Telegrams and Letters, etc., etc.

The contents of these little handbooks are so arranged as to permit direct and immediate reference. All dialogues or enquiries not considered absolutely essential have been purposely excluded, nothing being introduced which might confuse the traveller rather than assist him. A few hints are given in the introduction which will be found valuable to those unaccustomed to foreign travel.

London: WALTER SCOTT, LIMITED, 24 Warwick Lane.

NEW EDITION IN NEW BINDING.

In the new edition there are added about forty reproductions in fac-simile of autographs of distinguished singers and instrumentalists, including Sarasate, Joachim, Sir Charles Hallé, Paderewsky, Stavenhagen, Henschel, Trebelli, Miss Macintyre, Jean Gérardy, etc.

Quarto, cloth elegant, gilt edges, emblematic design on cover, 6s. May also be had in a variety of Fancy Bindings.

THE MUSIC OF THE POETS:
A MUSICIANS' BIRTHDAY BOOK.

EDITED BY ELEONORE D'ESTERRE KEELING.

THIS is a unique Birthday Book. Against each date are given the names of musicians whose birthday it is, together with a verse-quotation appropriate to the character of their different compositions or performances. A special feature of the book consists in the reproduction in fac-simile of autographs, and autographic music, of living composers. Three sonnets by Mr. Theodore Watts, on the "Fausts" of Berlioz, Schumann, and Gounod, have been written specially for this volume. It is illustrated with designs of various musical instruments, etc.; autographs of Rubenstein, Dvorák, Greig, Mackenzie, Villiers Stanford, etc., etc.

London: WALTER SCOTT, LTD., 24 Warwick Lane.

www.ingramcontent.com/pod-product-compliance
Lightning Source LLC
Chambersburg PA
CBHW031850220426
43663CB00006B/568